Highlights

A Year of Puzzles, Fun Facts, Jokes, Crafts, Games, and More!

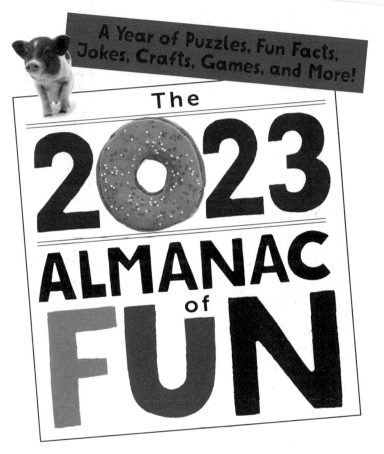

The
2023
ALMANAC of FUN

HIGHLIGHTS PRESS
Honesdale, Pennsylvania

SUNDAY	MONDAY	TUESDAY	WEDNESDAY
NEW YEAR'S DAY 1	**World Introvert Day** Studies show that introverts make up 30 to 50 percent of the U.S. population. **2**	**Festival of Sleep Day** Get some shut-eye after staying up until midnight to ring in 2023! **3**	**WORLD BRAILLE DAY** 4
National Bubble Bath Day Grab your rubber ducky and scrub-a-dub-dub! **8**	**NATIONAL APRICOT DAY** 85 percent of our nation's apricots are grown in California. **9**	**COMMON SENSE** On this day in 1776, Thomas Paine published his pamphlet *Common Sense*, which argued for American independence from England. **10**	**Step in a Puddle and Splash Your Friends Day** Don't forget your rain boots! **1**
National Bagel Day Why does a seagull fly over the sea? *Because if it flew over the bay, it would be a bagel!* **15**	**MARTIN LUTHER KING JR. DAY** **16**	**KID INVENTORS' DAY** What will you create? **17**	**NATIONAL MICHIGAN DAY** Dive into celebrating this state, which is home to more than 11,000 inland lakes! **18**
LUNAR NEW YEAR Happy Year of the Rabbit! **22**	**MEASURE YOUR FEET DAY** **23**	**GLOBAL BELLY LAUGH DAY** Why did the student eat his homework? *Because his teacher told him it was a piece of cake!* **24**	*Catch!* In 1957, the toy company Wham-O produced first Frisbees. **25**
Care for a drink? The Coca-Cola Company began in Atlanta, Georgia, in 1892. **29**	**NATIONAL CROISSANT DAY** **30**	**NATIONAL GORILLA SUIT DAY** **31**	**BIRTHSTONE** GARNET

JANUARY

THURSDAY	FRIDAY	SATURDAY
arbin International Ice and Snow Sculpture Festival (China) starts is annual event he largest e and snow tival in e world! **5**	**Feast of the Epiphany** Around the world, this day is also known as Three Kings' Day, Theophany, Dehna, and Little Christmas. **6**	**Jupiter's Moons** In 1610, the astronomer Galileo discovered the first three of Jupiter's moons, now called Io, Europa, and Ganymede. **7**
engers, assemble! mely Comics (later alled Marvel) was unded on this day in 1939. **12**	**MAKE YOUR DREAMS COME TRUE DAY** **13**	**National Dress Up Your Pet Day** Take pictures and share them with your friends! **14**
On your mark, get set, go! In 1903, the now opular bicycle race Tour de France was announced. **19**	**Penguin Awareness Day** **20**	**National Squirrel Appreciation Day** Get nutty! **21**
NATIONAL PPOSITE DAY initely forget this day nd *don't* celebrate. **26**	**INTERNATIONAL HOLOCAUST REMEMBRANCE DAY** **27**	**National Kazoo Day** No kazoo? No problem! Make your own with a comb and waxed paper. **28**

ZODIAC SIGNS

APRICORN:
DECEMBER 22–
ANUARY 19

AQUARIUS:
JANUARY 20–
FEBRUARY 18

FLOWERS
CARNATION
AND SNOWDROP

GET ORGANIZED MONTH

5 QUICK WAYS TO GET ORGANIZED

1. Keep a daily planner. Write down all the tasks you need to finish each day. Don't forget to check off each item as you complete it!

2. Clean out your backpack every Friday after school.

3. Keep all of your important papers in one place.

4. Each school night, get your backpack ready and lay out your clothes for the next day.

5. Use shoeboxes to store small knickknacks.

The first Get Organized Month was held **January 2005**.

A book never written: **How to Be Neat** by Mac K. Mess

PENCIL MEMO BOARD

For a fun way to store important messages, make this craft!

1. Cut a large rectangle from **corrugated cardboard**. Cut a point at one end. Trace around the shape twice onto corrugated cardboard and cut out the pieces. Stack all three and glue them together.

2. For the pencil's tip, wood, body, metal band, and eraser, cut out **felt** pieces wide enough to wrap over the sides. Glue them on. Add details with a **marker**.

3. **Tape** some **yarn** to the back for a hanger.

Use thumbtacks to post important memos on your board!

Meet at library 4:00 pm

NATIONAL OATMEAL MONTH

To celebrate, ask an adult to help you make a bowl of plain oatmeal, then choose a recipe for the toppings. See how many variations you can try this month!

BANANA SUNDAE

Top with banana slices, a spoonful of yogurt, and a sprinkle of sunflower seeds.

MAPLE NUT

Stir in a handful of cashews or almonds, then decorate with raisins and a drizzle of maple syrup.

PEACHY KEEN

Stir in a drop of almond extract and a drizzle of honey, then top with peach slices and another drizzle of honey.

RING AROUND THE MOON

Put a small scoop of frozen yogurt on top and surround it with a circle of blueberries.

CINNAMON APPLE

Peel and core an apple, then grate it over the oatmeal. Add a sprinkle of cinnamon and a drizzle of honey.

GREAT GRANOLA

Sprinkle granola over the top, then add milk.

NATIONAL HOBBY MONTH

Use this month to enjoy old hobbies or begin new ones.

At the end of the month, get together with friends and share your hobbies with each other in a talent show!

Backstage at this talent show has gotten a little out of control. While the performers figure out what to do next, see how many kittens you can find in this scene.

Depending on a dog's breed, a pooch needs thirty minutes to two hours of exercise each day. A walk is a great way to get a dog moving—and you, too!

WALK YOUR DOG MONTH

These three friends took their dogs on a walk to the park. But their leashes got all mixed up! Follow the tangled leashes to figure out which dog belongs to which kid.

WHAT'S YOUR DOG IQ?

Are you a friend of Fido? A bestie of Barkly? Circle your answers and see how many you can fetch in this canine quiz.

1. **What is a schnoodle?**
   a. A mix between a schnauzer and a poodle
   b. A mix between a poodle and a sheepdog
   c. A long, buttery noodle

2. **At birth, dalmatians are:**
   a. Completely white
   b. Completely black
   c. Red-and-green striped

3. **The greyhound is the fastest type of dog on the planet. How fast can they run?**
   a. 30 miles per hour
   b. 45 miles per hour
   c. Faster than the speed of light

4. **Dogs can see best in what type of light?**
   a. Bright light
   b. Low light
   c. Strobe lights

5. **The Newfoundland has this unique characteristic:**
   a. Webbed feet
   b. No tail
   c. Ability to Hula-Hoop

135 YEARS AGO, MARVIN STONE PATENTED THE FIRST PAPER STRAW.

Stone had the idea to create a manila paper straw to replace straws made of grass that people had been using. Unlike grass straws, which left a grassy taste in drinks, paper straws had the huge selling point of not tasting like anything. **Over time, the material used for most straws changed from paper to plastic. Now many countries ban plastic straws because they are bad for the environment. If you need to use a straw, try using paper or a reusable straw made of glass or bamboo.**

TIC-TAC-TOE

Make a tic-tac-toe board using paper straws.

You Need
- Scissors
- Egg carton
- Paint
- Paintbrush
- Tape
- Paper straws

1. Cut the **egg carton** into ten individual cups.

2. Paint five cups and let dry.

3. Paint an *X* on each of the five painted cups and an *O* on the five other cups. Let dry.

4. Tape **paper straws** together to make the game board.

DRINKING-STRAW AIRPLANE

Using straws helps this unique plane fly far.

1. Cut a 1-inch-by-11-inch strip of **colored paper**. Tape the ends together to make a circle. Make another circle using a 1-inch-by-9-inch strip.

2. Tape three **paper straws** evenly apart inside the larger circle and outside the smaller circle.

3. Throw the airplane with the smaller end in front.

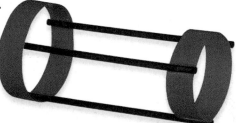

210 YEARS AGO, PINEAPPLES BEGAN TO BE GROWN IN HAWAII FOR COMMERCIAL USE.

Although pineapples aren't originally from Hawaii, the fruit has become a hallmark of the state. We don't know exactly when pineapples came to the island, but Spanish sailor Don Francisco de Paula Marin was reportedly the first to grow the fruit there as a business. Today, about 400 million pineapples are grown in Hawaii.

Pineapples take two to three years to grow.

Pineapple leaves can be used to make cloth, rope, and paper.

Pineapples grow from a plant, not a tree.

PINEAPPLE-COCONUT POPS

1. In a large bowl, stir together 1 (14-ounce) can **sweetened condensed milk**, 1 cup **unsweetened coconut milk**, 1½ cups **whipped topping**, and 1½ cups **crushed pineapple**, drained.

2. Fill twelve 4-ounce **paper cups** two-thirds full. Put a **craft stick** in each cup. Set the cups on a **baking sheet**. Freeze them for at least 6 hours.

3. Gently peel off the cups.

GROW YOUR OWN PINEAPPLE

1. Cut off the top two inches of a fresh pineapple before you cut into the rest. Keep the leaves attached. Scoop away the soft fruit around the hard core, and then let your pineapple top dry for a day or two.

2. Cut off some of the lowest leaves. When the inside of the pineapple is dry, plant it in a pot filled with sandy soil. Cover the pineapple with soil so that only the leaves show. Keep it wet until the new leaves grow. Pineapples grow best in a sunny spot.

ASK AN ADULT FOR HELP WITH CUTTING THE PINEAPPLE.

January 7
HARLEM GLOBETROTTERS DAY

On January 7, 1927, the Harlem Globetrotters played their first game. Although they played regular basketball at first, the exhibition basketball team has since become famous for entertaining crowds with their amazing basketball skills and tricks. **Can you find 18 hidden objects in this picture?**

bell

ruler

fish

artist's brush

fishhook

sailboat

nail

crescent moon

magnet

snake

envelope

flashlight

scarf

canoe

saw

sock

heart

pennant

The Globetrotters have played in front of **148 million fans** in more than 123 countries.

The team did not actually play in Harlem until 1968!

WINTER X GAMES

Held every year in Aspen, Colorado, the Winter X Games are a competition in extreme winter sports, like snowboarding, skiing, and snowmobiling.

Can you find the 15 differences between these two snowboarding photos?

The first **Winter X Games** were held at Big Bear Lake, California, in **1997**. Now the games are held in Aspen, Colorado, each year.

There are also **Summer X Games**, which are held in Los Angeles, California. The sports you'll see there include skateboarding, BMX biking, and surfing.

The "X" in X Games has a few meanings:

1 **Extreme** (as in *extreme sports*)

2 The **unknown**, as **X** is the mathematical symbol for the unknown

3 **Generation X** (those born between early 1960s and early 1980s), since this generation was the first to participate in the **X Games**

January 2

NATIONAL SCIENCE FICTION DAY

Read the letters in green to find out what term Isaac Asimov coined in his 1941 short story "Liar!"

Many science-fiction fans celebrate this unofficial holiday on the birthdate of famous science-fiction author Isaac Asimov. Use one of these story starters or your own idea to write a science-fiction story.

As Dad twisted knobs on the panel, the rocket started to shake and . . .

_____

_____

_____

_____

Knock, knock, knock. The door burst open, and . . .

_____

_____

_____

_____

We looked at the strange metallic substance, which suddenly started to . . .

_____

_____

_____

_____

NATIONAL THESAURUS DAY

Celebrate by spotting eight synonyms hidden in this scene. Can you find the words SMART, BRAINY, INTELLIGENT, BRILLIANT, WISE, GENIUS, BRIGHT, and CLEVER?

What do you call a dinosaur with an extensive vocabulary?

A thesaurus

January 24 is **National Compliment Day.** What synonyms could you use to compliment someone who is kind?

A thesaurus is a reference book that lists synonyms for words.

The author of Roget's Thesaurus, Peter Mark Roget, was born on January 18, 1779.

NATIONAL SPAGHETTI DAY

Wash your hands before and after handling food.

Make these bite-sized spaghetti nests to celebrate!

1. Mix together 4 ounces cooked **spaghetti**, ¼ cup shredded **Parmesan cheese**, ¼ cup shredded **mozzarella cheese**, and ⅔ cup **marinara sauce** in a large bowl.

2. Grease a nonstick 6-cup **muffin tin** with vegetable-oil spray.

3. Use tongs to evenly fill the muffin cups with the spaghetti mixture. Make a dent in the center of each cup to create the nest.

4. Sprinkle ¼ cup cooked **bacon bits** or **vegan-sausage crumbles** on top of the nests.

5. Add ¼ cup shredded **Parmesan cheese** over the nests.

6. Bake at 375°F for 13–15 minutes or until set. Serve with extra sauce, if you wish.

Ask an adult to help with anything sharp or hot.

The word **spaghetti** comes from the Italian word *spaghetto*, meaning "thin string" or "twine."

NATIONAL SOUP MONTH

Celebrate all month long with these soup jokes!

What is a duck's favorite meal?

Soup and quackers

If you leave alphabet soup on the stove and go out, it could spell disaster.

January 19
NATIONAL POPCORN DAY

This popcorn is hiding 20 dog bones.
Can you find them all?

Popcorn kernels can pop up to **3 feet** in the air!

Americans eat **17 billion** quarts of popcorn in a year, more than people in any other country.

Popcorn was a popular breakfast food during the **early 19th** and **late 20th** centuries.

What do you like to put on your popcorn?
Pair it with one of January's other food holidays:

BITTERSWEET CHOCOLATE DAY
JANUARY 10

BUTTERCRUNCH DAY
JANUARY 20

HOT SAUCE DAY
JANUARY 22

Why are you eating alphabet soup?

Because if I were eating number soup, I'd be a cow-culator.

**Knock, knock.
Who's there?
Jupiter.
Jupiter who?
Jupiter fly in my soup?**

Sonnet for a King

This January day was set aside
to celebrate the birthday of a man,
a gentle man, who bravely lived and died
too soon, but left a challenge and a plan.
He was a man of strength and grace and will
who stood for honor, character, and grit,
a man who sought and fought for freedom till
he gave his life, in faith, defending it.
He had a dream of hope, a dream that we,
though different in creed, belief, and race,
could live, as friends, in peace and harmony
and make the world a better place.
"Hold fast to dreams": together we must strive
to understand, and keep the dream alive.

Read the poem, then write your own poem to honor Dr. King.

The line *Hold fast to dreams* is from the poem "Dreams" by Langston Hughes.

The Martin Luther King Jr. Memorial opened in Washington, D.C., in 2011. It features a granite statue of the civil rights leader called the *Stone of Hope*.

Martin Luther King Jr. Day was first celebrated as a federal holiday in 1986.

MLK DAY
OF SERVICE
Corporation for
NATIONAL &
COMMUNITY
SERVICE

The MLK Day of Service was created to inspire Americans to turn Martin Luther King Jr. Day into a day of citizen action volunteer service in King's honor.

Talk with your parents about ways you can volunteer.
Here are some ideas:

- Walk a neighbor's dog or wash their car.
- Help do yardwork for people who can't.
- Make welcome kits for new kids at school.
- Read books to others during your library's story hour.

LUNAR NEW YEAR

Happy 4721—the Year of the Rabbit! This holiday, known as the Spring Festival in China, celebrates the beginning of a new year on the Chinese calendar and lasts for 15 days. People celebrate by visiting their families, decorating their houses, and setting off fireworks and firecrackers. Kids often receive a gift of money in a red envelope.

Join the dragon-dance parade and find the 12 hidden objects in this Hidden Pictures puzzle.

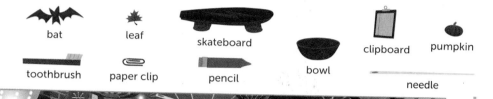

bat   leaf   skateboard   clipboard   pumpkin

toothbrush   paper clip   pencil   bowl   needle

tweezers

carrot

. . . .

What Is Your Zodiac Animal?

Below is a list of the 12 Chinese zodiac animals. Every year is assigned an animal. Look for the year you were born and see which is your zodiac animal. The cycle repeats itself every 12 years.

RAT
1996, 2008, 2020

OX
1997, 2009, 2021

TIGER
1998, 2010, 2022

RABBIT
1999, 2011, 2023

DRAGON
2000, 2012, 2024

SNAKE
2001, 2013, 2025

HORSE
2002, 2014, 2026

GOAT/RAM
2003, 2015, 2027

MONKEY
2004, 2016, 2028

ROOSTER
2005, 2017, 2029

DOG
2006, 2018, 2030

PIG
2007, 2019, 2031

NEW YEAR'S DAY

MAKE A NOISEMAKER
TO RING IN THE NEW YEAR.

Place large **buttons** into a small **jewelry box**.

Tape the box tightly closed.

Tape a **craft stick** to the back of the box.

Decorate your box with **stickers** or **markers**.

PASS THE LUCK, PLEASE!

Many countries around the world have foods that they consider to bring good luck when eaten at the start of the new year. Can you match each food with the country it belongs to?

1

Black-eyed peas and collard greens: The peas represent coins, while the greens stand for "folding money."

Saint Basil's Day cake: The cook sprinkles coins and other trinkets into the cake before baking. Whoever finds the treasure in their slice of cake gets good luck!

2

Pork sausages and lentils: The fat, rich sausage is a symbol of plenty, while the green, coin-shaped lentils represent money.

3

4

Grapes: As the clock strikes midnight, 12 grapes are eaten for each chime of the clock, in hopes of 12 months of prosperity.

Soba noodles: To ensure a long life, noodles must be sucked up and swallowed without breaking or chewing them.

5

Italy

Japan

United States

Spain

Greece

STATIC ELECTRICITY DAY

KIDS' SCIENCE QUESTIONS

Why do we sometimes feel shocks when we touch things?

zap!

That ZAP happens when static electricity gets moving! As you scuff across a rug, your socks may pick up a charge. That's from electrons, negatively charged bits that are part of all atoms. Usually they stay with their atoms, nicely balanced by positive charges. But if they rub onto an object, it gets extra negativity!

Negative charges push away from each other. So the extra electrons move away from that charged sock. Destination: Earth's big surface, where they can spread out (or *ground*). To get there, they need *conductors*—things that a charge can easily move across. Unlike your socks and rug, YOU are a conductor. A charge can flow across you, but it's *static*; it can't keep going until you are almost touching another conductor. Then, ZAP! Electrons leap through the air as a spark. Shocking, huh?

Robert Van de Graaff, an American physicist, invented the Van de Graaff generator in 1931. A Van de Graaff generator is an electrostatic generator that can create static electricity for experiments.

January 10
NATIONAL HOUSEPLANT APPRECIATION DAY

Houseplants do more than just brighten up a room.
They help reduce stress and increase focus.
Some plants may improve the air in your home.

AWESOME BLOSSOM

Pick out your favorite plant at this nursery,
then look for the nine objects hidden in the picture.

book   toothbrush   crayon   lollipop   heart   rolling pin   envelope   pizza   basketball

FUNNY FLORA

Use this plant emoji code to fill in the
missing letters and finish the jokes.
You won't be-leaf how funny they are!

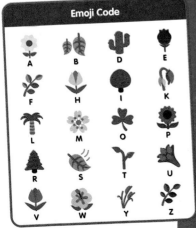

Emoji Code

A	B	D	E
F	H	I	K
L	M	O	P
R	S	T	U
V	W	Y	Z

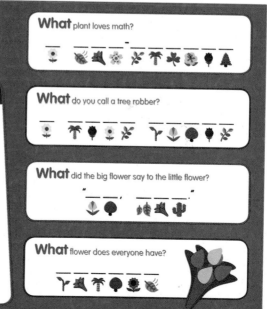

What plant loves math?

What do you call a tree robber?

What did the big flower say to the little flower?

What flower does everyone have?

January 4

NATIONAL TRIVIA DAY

Celebrate by testing out your world knowledge.

1. The average thickness of Antarctica's continental ice sheet is _____.
   a. About four Empire State Buildings deep (more than a mile)
   b. About two Empire State Buildings deep (less than a half mile)

2. During what season in Norway does the sun stay up past midnight?
   a. Summer
   b. Winter

3. Ocean covers more of the planet than land, but we still have what percent of the sea to explore?
   a. 50 percent
   b. 95 percent

4. Most of this island country's plant and animal species, including the lemur, are native nowhere else.
   a. Madagascar
   b. Greenland

January 15

NATIONAL HAT DAY

A brisk breeze just blew everyone's hats off. Put on your thinking cap and help match each hat with its owner!

January 29

NATIONAL PUZZLE DAY

Can you find these hidden jigsaw pieces in this photo of building blocks?

Jigsaw puzzles were invented in the **1760s** by mapmaker John Spilsbury. He glued maps onto wood and cut them into pieces.

January 28 is National Lego Day!

Puzzles became a popular hobby during the Great Depression as an affordable, reusable activity. In **1933**, over **10 million** puzzles were sold per week!

Take a spin around the globe to see how

January 13
📍 SAINT KNUT'S DAY

In Sweden, Saint Knut's Day is the day to get rid of Christmas trees. Swedes eat any edible ornaments, smash gingerbread houses, and put away decorations. In Swedish, this is called *julgransplundring*, which translates to "Christmas tree plundering."

Can you match these other Swedish words with their English translation? *God jul!* (Merry Christmas!)

SWEDISH	ENGLISH
julstjärna	Christmas stocking
julklappsstrumpa	Christmas star
julgranskula	Christmas tree lights
julgransbelysning	Christmas ornament

January 15–16, 2023
📍 PONGALO PONGAL!

In Sri Lanka, Tamil Thai Pongal Day is a two-day harvest festival dedicated to the Sun God. On the first day of the festival, Sri Lankans make rice in large clay pots, outside under the sun. They boil the rice in milk and spices. As the milk boils over, people shout, "Pongalo pongal!" An overflowing pot brings good luck.

The second day of the festival honors the oxen who provide milk, transportation, and help with harvesting rice and other crops. The oxen are bathed and given special food to eat. Then they have their horns painted beautiful colors and are given garlands to wear.

This ox is ready for Tamil Thai Pongal Day!

THE WORLD

people around the world celebrate in January.

HAPPY BIRTHDAY, LIMA!

On January 18, 1535, the conquistador Francisco Pizarro founded Lima, Peru, as "Ciudad de los Reyes" (City of the Kings). Major celebrations and civic events take place across Lima to mark the capital's foundation, including parades, food, dancing, and fireworks!

January 27, 2023

SAINT DEVOTA'S DAY

In Catholicism, Saint Devota is the patron saint of Monaco. The Catholic Church has many patron saints who they believe work to protect different things. **The following are some patron saints. Can you match them with what they protect?**

SAINTS

1. Francis of Assisi
2. John the Baptist
3. Joseph
4. Florian
5. Patrick
6. Anthony
7. Joan of Arc
8. Sebastian

WHAT THEY PROTECT

A. firefighters
B. France
C. animals
D. lost items
E. soldiers
F. carpenters and laborers
G. Ireland
H. baptism

SUNDAY	MONDAY	TUESDAY	WEDNESDAY

BIRTHSTONE
AMETHYST

ZODIAC SIGNS
AQUARIUS:
JANUARY 20–
FEBRUARY 18

PISCES:
FEBRUARY 19–
MARCH 20

Robinson Crusoe D
Imagine what you'd d
you found yourself alc
on a deserted island
with no Wi-Fi.

1

WESTERN MONARCH DAY
Here ye, here ye!
All hail the western
monarch butterfly on
this day.
5

FORE!
On this day in 1971,
Alan Shepard
became the first
(and so far only)
person to hit a
golf ball on
the moon.
6

Wave All Your Fingers at Your Neighbors Day
Hi! Howdy! Hey there!
Give your neighbors
a friendly
hello.
7

Checkmate!
In 1958, 15-year-old Bob
Fischer won the match
that made him the
then-youngest
international chess
grandmaster.
8

Blades of glory! In 1879,
skaters glided on North
America's first artificial
ice rink, set up
in New York City's
Madison Square.
12

NATIONAL TORTELLINI DAY
Pour on some sauce and
enjoy a plate of this belly-
button-shaped pasta.
13

Valentine's Day
Wear your heart on
your sleeve—or
anywhere else.
14

Susan B. Anthony
Susan B. Anthony foug
for women's rights,
including the right to
vote, her whole life.
Because of activists lik
her, women
won the
right to vote
in 1920.
15

International Tug-of-War Day
Grab a rope and some
friends, then dig in
your heels!
19

National Muffin Day
Two muffins are in an
oven. **Muffin 1:** It sure
is warm in here.
Muffin 2: Eek!
A talking
muffin!
20

WASHINGTON'S BIRTHDAY
George often shares
his birthday celebration
with Abe and others.
21

ASH WEDNESD
First day of Lent
22

Tell a Fairy Tale Day
Make up your own!
(Add an ogre or two.)
26

INTERNATIONAL POLAR BEAR DAY
27

Dord is the word. In 1939,
a *Webster's Dictionary*
editor discovered the
book's second edition
included *dord*—a word
that doesn't exist!*
*It was
mistakenly
defined as a
scientific term
for density.
28

THURSDAY	FRIDAY	SATURDAY

GROUNDHOG DAY

Will Punxsutawney Phil and Staten Island Chuck see their shadows?

2

Is it cold, or is it me? In 1947, Snag, Yukon, snagged the record for the coldest temperature ever recorded in North America: 81˚F below 0!

3

Thank a Mail Carrier Day

Whether sun, rain, or snow, they'll still deliver your mail!

4

Get served! Mintonette, better known today as volleyball, was created by William G. Morgan on this day in 1895.

9

Take a message, then take a bow! In 1933, the singing telegram was introduced.

10

Don't Cry Over Spilled Milk Day

Instead, think positive and mop up that milk with some cookies!

11

Tim Tam Day (Australia)

A chocolate-cookie sandwich dipped in chocolate—what's not to love?

16

RANDOM ACTS OF KINDNESS DAY

Nice!

17

PLUTO DAY

In 1930, Clyde Tombaugh discovered the tiny, distant dwarf planet using a cool tool called a blink microscope.

18

Chew on this! In 1896, Leo Hirschfield gave us the Tootsie Roll, named after his five-year-old daughter Clara, whose nickname was "Tootsie."

23

National Tortilla Chip Day

What's this chip's favorite type of dance? Salsa, of course!

24

Celebrate Revels! On this day in 1820, Hiram Revels from Mississippi was the first African American to be sworn into Congress.

25

FEBRUARY

FLOWERS

PRIMROSE
AND VIOLET

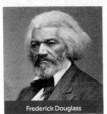
Frederick Douglass

Judge Thurgood Marshall

BLACK HISTORY MONTH

Travel through this timeline of influential African Americans.

Harriet Tubman

Oprah Winfrey

1847 Abolitionist, author, and orator **Frederick Douglass** publishes the antislavery newspaper the *North Star*.

1849 **Harriet Tubman** escapes from slavery and leads others to freedom through the Underground Railroad.

Madam C.J. Walker

Mae Jemison

1905 **Madam C.J. Walker** launches a business creating hair-care products, eventually becoming the first Black woman millionaire.

1909 **W.E.B. Du Bois** co-founds the NAACP (National Association for the Advancement of Colored People).

W.E.B. Du Bois

Toni Morrison

1921 Inventor **George Washington Carver** addresses Congress about the hundreds of uses he discovered for peanuts, including flour, milk, dyes, and cheeses.

1947 **Jackie Robinson** joins the Brooklyn Dodgers, a Major League Baseball team.

1955 **Rosa Parks** takes a stand against segregation and is arrested for refusing to give up her bus seat.

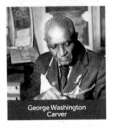
George Washington Carver

Colin Powell

1967 **Judge Thurgood Marshall** is appointed to the Supreme Court.

1986 **Oprah Winfrey** first goes on the air with her national TV show.

1992 Astronaut **Mae Jemison** blasts off on the space shuttle Endeavor.

1993 Author **Toni Morrison** wins the Nobel Prize in Literature.

2001 Four-star general **Colin Powell** is appointed U.S. secretary of state.

Jackie Robinson

Barack Obama

2008 **Barack Obama**—a senator from Illinois, born in Hawaii—is elected the 44th president of the United States.

2015 **Misty Copeland** is named a principal dancer with the American Ballet Theatre.

705.3
Rosa Parks

Ame Ai
Misty Copeland

BAKE FOR FAMILY FUN MONTH

Grab an apron and get baking!
How many of your family's favorites can you make this month?

Ask an adult to help with anything sharp or hot.

Tapioca flour gives this gluten-free treat its chewy texture.

BRAZILIAN CHEESE BREAD

You Need

- 24-cup mini-muffin tin
- Non-stick spray
- ½ cup milk
- ⅓ cup vegetable oil
- 1 egg
- ½ teaspoon salt
- 1½ cups tapioca flour
- ½ cup shredded Parmesan cheese

1. Preheat the oven to 350°F. Spray a 24-cup mini-muffin tin with non-stick spray.

2. Whisk together ½ cup milk, ⅓ cup vegetable oil, 1 egg, and ½ teaspoon salt.

3. Whisk in 1½ cups tapioca flour a little at a time until blended. Mix in ½ cup shredded Parmesan cheese.

4. Fill muffin cups with batter until they are two-thirds full.

5. Bake for 20–25 minutes until golden brown and puffy. If using a 12-cup muffin tin, bake for 30–35 minutes.

NATIONAL LIBRARY LOVERS' MONTH

Why did the fish go to the library?

To find some bookworms

Find 12 bookworms hidden in the library.

The Library of Congress, the largest library in the world, has more than **167 million** items on about 838 miles of bookshelves—nearly the distance from Washington, D.C., to Cape Canaveral, Florida.

In 2016, there were **1.4 billion** in-person visits to public libraries across the U.S., the equivalent of about 4 million visits each day. That's 2,664 per minute.

AUTHOR AUTHOR!

Match up "Books Never Written" with their authors.

_____ 1. Face to Face with a Bear

_____ 2. How to Catch Worms

_____ 3. Running the Mile

_____ 4. Strong Bones

_____ 5. Two Kinds of Numbers

_____ 6. What Dogs Do

_____ 7. Tasty Squash

_____ 8. All About Atoms

_____ 9. Sing Out Loud

_____ 10. Summer School

A. Evan N. Odd

B. Heidi Bones

C. Otto Breath

D. Terry Fied

E. Earl E. Byrd

F. Cal C. Uhm

G. Mike Rofone

H. Nova Kayshon

I. Sue Keeney

J. Molly Cule

SPELL CHECK

Uh-oh! Someone misprinted the titles of these classic children's books. Can you fix them?

Where the Mild Things Are

The Phantom Trolltooth

Harold and the Purple Marker

Green Eggs and Him

Goodnight Noon

Harriet the Shy

Winnie-the-Pooch

CHILDREN'S DENTAL HEALTH MONTH

Sink your teeth into this! Can you find the 20 non-beaver teeth hidden in this scene?

RIDDLE SUDOKU

Fill in the squares so that the six letters appear once in each row, column, and 2 x 3 box. Then read the yellow squares to find out the answer to the riddle.

Letters: C N O R S W

				W	
		N		O	
S	W				
				S	O
	S		R		
	N			C	

RIDDLE: Why do kings and queens go to the dentist?

ANSWER: To get ___ ___ ___ ___ ___ ___

What time do you go to the dentist?

Tooth-hurty

The first toothbrushes were tree twigs. Chewing on the tips of the twigs spread out the fibers, which were then used to clean the teeth.

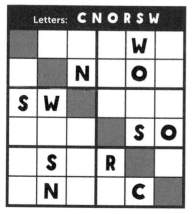

February 12, 1963
60 YEARS AGO, CONSTRUCTION BEGAN ON THE GATEWAY ARCH IN ST. LOUIS, MISSOURI.

The Arch was built in honor of the pioneers who settled in the American West. At 630 feet tall, it is the tallest monument in the United States—and the tallest arch in the world!

Can you find the 14 objects hidden in this picture?

star

paint can

saucepan

mitten

belt

ruler

broccoli

tooth

umbrella

ice-cream cone

nail

spool of thread

teacup

fish

The Gateway Arch isn't just 630 feet tall—it's also 630 feet wide!

There is a four-minute elevator ride that takes you to the top of the Arch.

This is the Mississippi River, the second longest river in North America.

February 5, 1903

120 YEARS AGO, THE FIRST TEDDY BEAR WENT ON SALE.

A few months earlier, President Theodore ("Teddy") Roosevelt was on a hunting trip that became famous after he showed mercy to a bear. This story inspired store owners Morris and Rose Michtom to make a stuffed bear. President Roosevelt granted them permission to use his name, and they called the toy a "teddy bear."

Toy-Store Teaser

The stuffed animals in this toy store are missing their price tags! The total cost of the toys in each row and column is given below. Each of the four kinds of stuffed animals costs a different dollar amount. Can you figure out the price of each type of stuffed animal?

HINT: The lion costs $6.00.

The most well-traveled stuffed bear is Magellan T. Bear. It became the first teddy bear to go to space, fly around the world, and visit the South Pole.

A Beary Cool Jet Pack

1. Wrap two **rubber bands** around the body of your **teddy bear**. Slide an empty **travel-sized shampoo bottle** under the rubber bands.

2. Push some yellow and orange **tissue paper** into the neck of the bottle. **Tape** the paper in place, if needed.

February 1, 2023

NATIONAL GIRLS & WOMEN IN SPORTS DAY

Since 1987, National Girls & Women in Sports Day has spotlighted the history of women's athletics. Held the first Wednesday of February, it also recognizes the progress made since the passing of Title IX of the Education Amendments of 1972, which ensures that students receive educational—and athletic—opportunities free from discrimination based on gender.

Alex, Brooke, and Claire are about to dive into the pool. Circle the correct answers to the questions below about famous female firsts. Then for each answer, shade in a square in the matching swim lane (A, B, or C). The first swimmer to reach the end of her lane wins!

	A	B	C
1. At age 13, Donna de Varona was the youngest to compete on the 1960 U.S. Olympic _____ team.	discus	swimming	boxing
2. Fore! In 2014, 11-year-old Lucy Li was the youngest girl to qualify to compete in the Women's U.S. Open _____ tournament.	snowboard	polo	golf
3. Goal! In 1987 at age 15, Mia Hamm became the youngest member ever of the U.S. women's national ____ team.	soccer	ice hockey	judo
4. Tatyana McFadden was 15 when she won two gold medals at the Paralympics on the U.S. _____ team.	wheelchair racing	wheelchair rugby	wheelchair boccia
5. In 1904, teenager Amanda Clement became baseball's first paid female _____.	cheerleader	quarterback	umpire
6. In 1948, Alice Coachman became the first African American woman to win an Olympic track-and-field gold medal for the _____.	beanbag toss	high jump	bobsled
7. Nadia Comăneci of Romania was the first female to be awarded a perfect score of ____ in an Olympic gymnastics event.	100	10	25
8. Wilma Rudolph, once considered the fastest woman in the world, was the first American woman to win three gold medals in a single Olympics for _____.	running	skiing	curling
9. Janet Guthrie was the first woman racecar driver to earn a starting spot in both the Daytona 500 and the _____ 500.	Cincinnati	Peoria	Indianapolis
10. Tara Lipinski glided into history as the youngest person ever to hold the titles of world and Olympic champion in _____.	ice-skating	basketball	canoeing

February 5, 2023

SUPER BOWL LVII

It's been a windy day in the stadium. With the game tied and just a few seconds left on the clock, Chase Gridiron must get to the end zone to score the winning touchdown. Help him find his way around the other players and also the objects that have blown onto the field.

That's 57 Super Bowls since the first in 1967. Each year, the two winningest teams of the American Football Conference and the National Football Conference face off in a championship game. This year, Super Bowl LVII kicks off at State Farm Stadium in Glendale, Arizona.

SUPER BOWL

SUPER STATS

Tackle this quiz!

1. Which city has hosted the most Super Bowls?

a. Los Angeles

b. New Orleans

c. Miami

2. Which team has competed at the most Super Bowls?

a. New England Patriots

b. Pittsburgh Steelers

c. Dallas Cowboys

3. Which was the most watched Super Bowl of all time?

a. XLV (2011)

b. XLIX (2015)

c. LIII (2019)

4. Who has appeared at the most halftime shows?

a. World Famed Tiger Marching Band

b. Justin Timberlake

c. Beyoncé

BONUS! Unscramble the letters on the 10 foam fingers to answer the riddle: What do football champions put their cereal in?

START

SNACK BOWL

Super Bowl Sunday is second only to Thanksgiving as America's biggest food holiday. Maybe that's why February is also National Snack Food Month! Here's what people have eaten, by the numbers, on recent Super Bowl Sundays:

More than **1.35 billion** wings

More than **12.5 million** takeout pizzas

29 million pounds of chips (with dip)

160 million avocados (Holy guacamole!)

3.8 million pounds of popcorn

OPERA DAY

An opera is like a play, except all the words are sung, not spoken. Opera singers are known for their powerful voices that can be heard at the back of the opera house without a microphone. Some—including Enrico Caruso, Maria Callas, Luciano Pavarotti, Kiri Te Kanawa, and Jessye Norman—have become as famous around the world as rock stars.

Match the famous opera house to its home country.

Bolshoi Theatre	Argentina
La Scala	Australia
Metropolitan Opera House	Austria
Nhà hát lớn Hà Nội	France
Palais Garnier	Italy
Sydney Opera House	Russia
Teatro Colón	United States
Wiener Staatsoper	Vietnam

KIDS' SCIENCE QUESTIONS

Can a voice get loud enough and high enough that glass can break?

Yes! A singing voice can create sound waves that crack glass. When you tap the side of an empty drinking glass, the sides of the glass bend back and forth—very slightly and very quickly—at the same speed each time and make a sound. This is the natural frequency of the glass. A thicker glass will have a slower natural frequency, and a deeper sound, than a thin glass. When a singer's voice matches the natural frequency of the glass, each sound wave gives a little push; each push adds a little more bend to the glass. If each bend becomes bigger and bigger until the glass cannot bend any farther, it breaks. But you can listen to an opera without worrying about your goldfish bowl! This works only on very thin glass.

Do Re Mi...

The opera *Sands of Time* was written to last exactly **3 minutes and 34 seconds**—the time it takes to boil an egg.

On February 24, 1988, after his performance in Berlin, Italian opera singer Luciano Pavarotti received **165 curtain calls,** and was applauded for 1 hour and 7 minutes.

February 11

GET OUT YOUR GUITAR DAY

Study these two jam sessions at the B.B. King Museum in Indianola, Mississippi, the hometown of the master blues guitarist. Can you find at least 20 differences?

NAME THAT GUITAR

Some instruments are nearly as famous as the musician who played them. Which guitarist plucked which guitar?

Willie Nelson   Blackie

B.B. King   Red Special

Eric Clapton   Frankenstrat

Eddie Van Halen   Lucille

Brian May   Trigger

ANATOMY OF A GUITAR

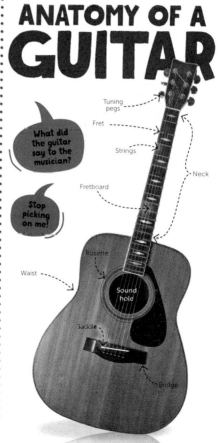

What did the guitar say to the musician?

Stop picking on me!

Tuning pegs

Fret

Strings

Neck

Fretboard

Waist

Rosette

Sound hole

Saddle

Bridge

37

NATIONAL FROZEN YOGURT DAY

Most people may not crave this frozen treat in the middle of winter, but it's still a day to celebrate!

What do the frozen-yogurt cups in each row (horizontally, vertically, and diagonally) have in common?

Yogurt has been around for thousands of years, but it didn't become commercially frozen until the **1970s**. Frozen yogurt picked up in popularity eleven years ago, in **2012**. What are your favorite toppings?

CHILI DAY

Chili peppers have more vitamin C than oranges.

What better way to warm up on a chilly February day than with chili? There are many variations, but all chili recipes include peppers. This word grid is peppered with fifteen different kinds. Each will fit into the grid only one way. Use the number of letters in each word as a clue to where it might fit.

Word List

3 letters
~~AJI~~

4 letters
BELL
PUYA

5 letters
ANCHO
DATIL
HATCH

6 letters
ROCOTO

7 letters
CAYENNE
POBLANO
SERRANO
TABASCO

8 letters
CHIPOTLE
HABANERO
JALAPEÑO
PIRI PIRI

A chili pepper's heat is ranked on a special scale called the Scoville scale. Bell peppers are up to 100 Scoville heat units, while habanero peppers can be up to **350,000 SCOVILLE** heat units.

Chili Cookoff
Try these on the road.

TEXAS: BOWL O' RED
Leave out the beans or tomatoes: this chili is meat and peppers only.

NEW MEXICO: CHILI VERDE Simmer pork in a verde (green) sauce made from tomatillos and jalapeños.

ILLINOIS: SPRINGFIELD CHILLI ← Yes, with two L's
Stir up ground beef, canned tomato sauce, a spice mix that includes chili powder, and a dash of Tabasco.

OHIO: CINCINNATI CHILI It may have a dash of chocolate and cinnamon, but it's almost always on top of spaghetti! Order it "five-way," with spaghetti, chili, onions, beans, and shredded cheddar.

GROUNDHOG DAY

According to German lore, if a hibernating badger sees his shadow on Candlemas Day (a holiday 40 days after Christmas), six more weeks of winter chill are in store. But German immigrants in Pennsylvania soon discovered that badgers are not native to the area, and so groundhogs took over the powers of prognostication.

If Candlemas be fair and bright,

Come, Winter, have another flight;

If Candlemas brings clouds and rain,

Go Winter, and come not again.

—OLD ENGLISH SONG

Punxsutawney Phil is the best-known weathercritter, but he has rivals (and some are more accurate), including Unadilla Bill of Nebraska, Staten Island Chuck of New York, Chuckles of Connecticut, and Pierre C. Shadeaux of Louisiana.

GHD HAT

Since 1887, folks have trekked to Gobbler's Knob to await Phil's prediction. They love to dress up like their favorite forecaster. Now you can, too!

1. Cut out eyes, ears, a nose, and teeth from **felt**. To make the ears and teeth stiffer, glue a second piece of felt to each. Draw a line on the teeth with a **marker**.

2. Attach the felt pieces to a **brown hat** using fabric glue. Use **clothespins** to keep the ears in place until they're dry.

Phil is late for his annual appearance on Gobbler's Knob in Punxsutawney, Pennsylvania. Can you help him find the right path aboveground?

The groundhogs' species name monax comes from a Native American word that means "the digger."

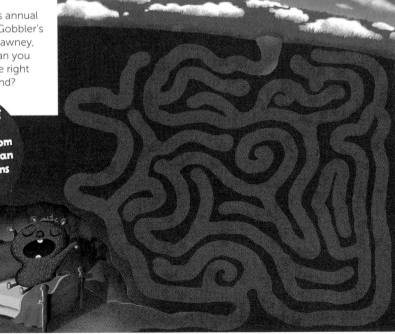

February 14
VALENTINE'S DAY

Amy's class is enjoying their big Valentine's Day party. To add to the fun, someone played matchmaker with the cookies! Each cookie on Amy's tray has one exact match somewhere in the room. Can you find all six matches?

February is also American Heart Month. Eat healthily and exercise to keep yours ticking!

What do you call two birds in love?

Tweet-hearts

VALENTINE'S DAY "FORTUNE" HEARTS

1. Cut out a pair of hearts from **cardstock**. Glue the edges together.

2. Write a Valentine's Day "fortune" on a narrow strip of **paper**.

3. Cut the heart down the center, leaving a small connection at the point.

4. Glue the left side of the fortune into the left half of the heart. Fold the fortune and insert it into the right half of the heart.

5. Write a name on a small strip of paper. Glue it to the heart to hold the left and right sides together.

Natalie

Sam

Ryan

May you always be surrounded by good friends. Valentine!

About 145 million greeting cards are exchanged every Valentine's Day in the U.S. alone.

WASHINGTON'S BIRTHDAY

Since 1885, this federal holiday has honored the February 22 birthday of the first U.S. president. The holiday was later moved to the third Monday of the month to give government workers—and schoolkids—a three-day weekend. Today it is often called Presidents' Day and celebrates Abraham Lincoln (born February 12) and all U.S. presidents, past and present. However, officially, it still is just George Washington's day.

Spell out the last name of each U.S. president below to find something that was named for him or built in his honor. Start each name on a letter in the yellow column, then move in any direction, including diagonally. We've found HOOVER for you.

> **Two other presidents were also born in February: William Henry Harrison (February 9, 1773) and Ronald Reagan (February 6, 1911).**

ROOSEVELT
HOOVER
WASHINGTON
LINCOLN
KENNEDY
JEFFERSON

H	E	V	R	T	Y	L	N
K	O	O	E	D	F	I	S
R	E	S	E	A	J	G	T
E	O	N	N	V	A	L	O
F	I	N	C	W	E	S	N
L	S	H	F	O	R	I	T
J	A	F	H	E	L	G	O
W	E	S	G	I	N	W	N

BONUS!
In what order did these six presidents serve?

February 21, 2023

PANCAKE DAY

What kind of exercises do pancakes do?

I JUMP SPLATZ

Call it Pancake Tuesday, Shrove Tuesday, Fat Tuesday, or Mardi Gras (French for "Fat Tuesday"), this moveable holiday is celebrated 47 days before Easter Sunday. It started as a way to use up rich foods (eggs, sugar, butter) before the Christian season of Lent, which begins the next day, Ash Wednesday.

You'll flip for these jokes, once you unflip and unscramble each answer!

The world's tallest stack of pancakes was a whopping 213 pancakes, measuring 3 feet and 4 inches!

Who flies through the air covered with maple syrup?

PKANOAE PERTE

How is a baseball team like a pancake?

They both need a TARBEL DODO.

What do cowboys put on their pancakes?

SUTIRRP MAEPL

INTERNATIONAL EATS

On the day or week before Lent, other seasonal specialties are served up around the world, including:

Shrove Tuesday, Australia: Pikelets—small buttermilk pancakes, usually topped with jam, whipped cream, or butter

Día de la Tortilla (Day of the Omelet), Spain: Potato omelet

Mardi Gras, New Orleans: King cake, with a tiny baby-shaped charm baked in to represent Jesus

La Chandeleur (Candlemas, February 2), France: Crepes

Pączki Day, Poland: Pączki (pownch-key), sugar-dusted fried dough filled with jam or custard

NATIONAL WEATHERPERSON'S DAY

Try your hand at being a meteorologist—a scientist who studies the weather and uses patterns to predict future weather conditions. Keep track of the weather where you live for a week. **Use this calendar. Draw or write about the weather every day.**

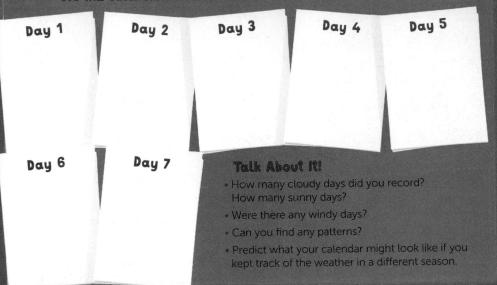

Day 1

Day 2

Day 3

Day 4

Day 5

Day 6

Day 7

Talk About It!

- How many cloudy days did you record? How many sunny days?
- Were there any windy days?
- Can you find any patterns?
- Predict what your calendar might look like if you kept track of the weather in a different season.

WEATHER STUMPER

Every type of weather should only appear once in each row, column, and 2 x 3 box. Fill in the squares by drawing or writing the name of each weather type.

KIDS' SCIENCE QUESTION

Why does the temperature go up a few degrees after it rains?

Air temperature sometimes rises after it rains, but not always. Rain falls when winds mix a mass of cold air with a mass of warm air that's carrying *water vapor*, water in gas form. The cold air makes the water vapor condense into drops, which fall as rain.
If the winds push the warm air into the cold air, then the warm air replaces the cold air. In that case, the temperature goes up. If the winds push the cold air into the warm air, then the temperature goes down.

Why did the woman stand outside with her purse open?

Because she expected some change in the weather.

February 7

NATIONAL PERIODIC TABLE DAY

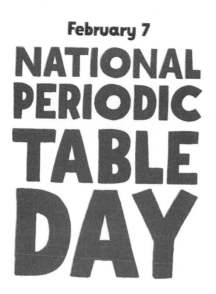

OMg! (That's oxygen and magnesium, to scientists.) Today marks the publication date of chemist John Newlands's first periodic table of elements in 1863. It's also the day before the birthday of Dmltri Mendeleev, a Russian chemist who, in 1869, came up with a way to organize the periodic table by each element's atomic mass (the weight of one atom of the element).

Using the periodic table, combine these elements' symbols to make a word.

barium + cobalt + nitrogen =

_____

barium + sodium + sodium =

_____

calcium + neodymium + yttrium =

_____

molybdenum + uranium + selenium =

_____

americium + erbium + iodine + calcium =

_____

helium + lithium + cobalt + platinum + erbium =

_____

fluorine + uranium + nitrogen =

_____

← hint

Now, make up your own elemental equation!

We would have put a chemistry joke here, but we didn't think we'd get a reaction.

1 H Hydrogen																	2 He Helium
3 Li Lithium	4 Be Beryllium											5 B Boron	6 C Carbon	7 N Nitrogen	8 O Oxygen	9 F Fluorine	10 Ne Neon
11 Na Sodium	12 Mg Magnesium											13 Al Aluminium	14 Si Silicon	15 P Phosphorus	16 S Sulfur	17 Cl Chlorine	18 Ar Argon
19 K Potassium	20 Ca Calcium	21 Sc Scandium	22 Ti Titanium	23 V Vanadium	24 Cr Chromium	25 Mn Manganese	26 Fe Iron	27 Co Cobalt	28 Ni Nickel	29 Cu Copper	30 Zn Zinc	31 Ga Gallium	32 Ge Germanium	33 As Arsenic	34 Se Selenium	35 Br Bromine	36 Kr Krypton
37 Rb Rubidium	38 Sr Strontium	39 Y Yttrium	40 Zr Zirconium	41 Nb Niobium	42 Mo Molybdenum	43 Tc Technetium	44 Ru Ruthenium	45 Rh Rhodium	46 Pd Palladium	47 Ag Silver	48 Cd Cadmium	49 In Indium	50 Sn Tin	51 Sb Antimony	52 Te Tellurium	53 I Iodine	54 Xe Xenon
55 Cs Caesium	56 Ba Barium	57–71 Lanthanides	72 Hf Hafnium	73 Ta Tantalum	74 W Tungsten	75 Re Rhenium	76 Os Osmium	77 Ir Iridium	78 Pt Platinum	79 Au Gold	80 Hg Mercury	81 Tl Thallium	82 Pb Lead	83 Bi Bismuth	84 Po Polonium	85 At Astatine	86 Rn Radon
87 Fr Francium	88 Ra Radium	89–103 Actinides	104 Rf Rutherfordium	105 Db Dubnium	106 Sg Seaborgium	107 Bh Bohrium	108 Hs Hassium	109 Mt Meitnerium	110 Ds Darmstadtium	111 Rg Roentgenium	112 Cn Copernicium	113 Nh Nihonium	114 Fl Flerovium	115 Mc Moscovium	116 Lv Livermorium	117 Ts Tennessine	118 Og Oganesson

57 La Lanthanum	58 Ce Cerium	59 Pr Praseodymium	60 Nd Neodymium	61 Pm Promethium	62 Sm Samarium	63 Eu Europium	64 Gd Gadolinium	65 Tb Terbium	66 Dy Dysprosium	67 Ho Holmium	68 Er Erbium	69 Tm Thulium	70 Yb Ytterbium	71 Lu Lutetium
89 Ac Actinium	90 Th Thorium	91 Pa Protactinium	92 U Uranium	93 Np Neptunium	94 Pu Plutonium	95 Am Americium	96 Cm Curium	97 Bk Berkelium	98 Cf Californium	99 Es Einsteinium	100 Fm Fermium	101 Md Mendelevium	102 No Nobelium	103 Lr Lawrencium

SETSUBUN

Setsubun (節分, or "seasonal division") marks the day before the start of spring according to the Japanese lunar calendar. For many centuries, the people of Japan have been performing these Setsubun rituals to chase away evil spirits, or *oni*, at home and in temples to ensure good luck in the year ahead. Here's how to get into the non-evil spirit:

ONI IT! One family member wears the demon mask.

TOSS IT! In the *mamemaki* (bean-throwing) ceremony, roasted soybeans, gathered in an *asakemasu* (a wooden box), are thrown at the oni.

SHOUT IT! While flinging, chant *"Oni wa soto! Fuku wa uchi!"* ("Demons out! Happiness in!")

CHASE IT! Once the oni is outside, slam the door!

CHEW IT! Afterward, pick up and eat the number of beans equal to your age, plus one.

QUIET! Eat an entire uncut sushi roll, *in silence*, facing toward the year's "lucky direction." (The direction depends on the zodiac sign of the year. For 2023, it's south-southeast!)

February 6
NATIONAL CHOPSTICKS DAY

The earliest chopsticks were likely in use around 5,000 years ago!

Today, try eating all your meals (okay, maybe not a bowl of soup or a sandwich) with chopsticks. Here's how.

1 Tuck the first (lower) chopstick in the nook between your thumb and your index (pointer) finger. Hold it against your thumb and bent ring finger. This chopstick does not move while eating.

Hold the chopsticks near the tops, toward the wider ends, with the tips lined up.

2 Hold the second (upper) chopstick between your index finger and thumb, as you would if holding a pencil—only higher up. Brace this chopstick against your middle finger.

3 Open up the chopsticks by moving just the upper chopstick with your index and middle finger.

4 Moving the upper chopstick down with your index and middle fingers, close the chopsticks over your morsel of food.

February 7, 2023
SEND A CARD TO A FRIEND DAY

A handwritten letter is the perfect way to tell a friend a funny story or just say hello. This outline will give you some ideas of what to write and how to form your letter.

> Put your address at the top right so your friend can write you back.

> Ask what is new with your friend.

> Add the date you wrote the letter.

> Explain why you are writing.

> End your letter with a wish for the future.

> Close a letter to a friend with a short expression like *Your friend* or *Take care.*

> If there's something you forgot to say, add it at the bottom with *P.S.*

75 Willow Street
Flisk, MT 55562
July 1, 2023

Dear Alex,

How are you? My summer is great but I'm super bored today. I could have texted you, but a letter seemed more special. Plus, it takes more time to write!

I miss talking and joking around with you. Remember the skateboards we made for Horatio Hamster? I hope we can see each other soon.

Your friend,
Ava

P.S. Write me back!

February 20
NATIONAL LOVE YOUR PET DAY

Hooray for pets! These critters bring all kinds of joy, even when they're causing mischief. One of the pets in this picture knocked over a houseplant. **Use the clues to figure out which one made the mess.**

> A dog's nose print is unique, much like a human's fingerprint.

> Hamsters' teeth never stop growing.

THE MISCHIEVOUS PET . . .
has white paws.
has brown ears.
doesn't have a pink nose.

Take a spin around the globe to *see how*

February 6
WAITANGI DAY

On this day in 1840, the British government and 540 Māori chiefs signed the Treaty of Waitangi (named after the region where this took place) to create the nation of New Zealand. Māori cultural performances, speeches from Māori and Pakeha (European) dignitaries, and a naval salute are part of the activities.

1. Roll **polymer clay** into a 9-inch-long "snake," wide at one end and thin at the other.

2. On **foil** on a **baking sheet**, arrange the shape into a spiral. With an adult's help, bake the clay according to the instructions. Let the spiral cool.

3. Loop **string** or **cord** to make a lanyard.

Make a Māori koru pendant, inspired by the art of the Māori people of New Zealand.

Often, lanterns will have a riddle written on them. Whoever solves the riddle gets a gift!

February 5, 2023
LANTERN FESTIVAL

While the origin of the Lantern Festival is unknown, one theory says that it began two thousand years ago with Han Mingdi. Han Mingdi was a Chinese emperor who wanted to spread Buddhism throughout China. Buddhist monks would hang lanterns in their temples to honor Buddha on the fifteenth day of the first lunar month. Emperor Han Mingdi said people throughout the country should do the same. Today, the Lantern Festival has become a nationwide tradition where Chinese citizens light and admire lanterns, watch firework shows, eat *tangyuan* (a rice ball with fillings), and enjoy lion dance performances.

Decorate your own lantern for the Lantern Festival!

THE WORLD

To celebrate Fastelavn, Danes eat *fastelavnsboller*, sweet buns filled with cream.

February 19, 2023

📍FASTELAVN

One popular tradition to celebrate this pre-Lenten festival is for Danish children to dress up in fanciful costumes and try to "beat the cat out of the barrel." Don't worry—the wooden barrel only has images of black cats, which represent evil spirits. The person who knocks out the bottom of the barrel is crowned *Kattedronning* ("Cat Queen"), and the person who knocks down the last piece of the barrel is crowned *Kattekonge* ("Cat King").

February 5, 2023

📍NAVAM FULL MOON POYA DAY

This Buddhist holiday usually takes place on the first full moon in February. The tiny country of Sri Lanka, a raindrop-shaped island off the tip of India, celebrates in a big way: Its capital, Colombo, hosts a joyous parade, or *perahera*, featuring thousands of fire dancers, flag bearers, traditional dancers, musicians, and dozens of dazzlingly dressed elephants. Can you find where the three jigsaw pieces fit into this photo of a typical Navam Perahera sight?

49

SUNDAY	MONDAY	TUESDAY	WEDNESDAY

BIRTHSTONES
AQUAMARINE---

BLOODSTONE---

ZODIAC SIGNS

♓ ←---→
PISCES:
FEBRUARY 19–
MARCH 20

♈ ←---→
ARIES:
MARCH 21–
APRIL 19

National Pig Day
What do you call a pig who does karate?

A pork chop!

1

NATIONAL CHEESE DOODLE DAY
This crunchy snack hits the spot!

5

PURIM BEGINS

6

Ring, ring, ring!
On this day in 1876, Alexander Graham Bell received a patent for the telephone.

7

INTERNATIONA WOMEN'S DAY

8

Daylight Saving Begins
Don't be late! "Spring" forward your clocks one hour today.*

*Not you, Arizona and Hawaii.

12

National Napping Day
You snooze, you ~~lose~~ win!

13

National Reuben Sandwich Day
Take a bite out of this unique sandwich: rye bread, Swiss cheese, corned beef, sauerkraut, and Russian dressing.

14

Surf the web!
The first .com domain was created on this day in 1985. The website w symbolics.com. It still exists, but is under new ownership as an online museum of the internet.

15

NATIONAL LET'S LAUGH DAY

19

First Day of Spring
What is the best smell in spring?

20

Harmony Day (Australia)
The message of this day, which celebrates diversity and inclusiveness, is "Everyone belongs."

21

RAMADAN
begins at sunset and continues for 30 day.

2

Make Up Your Own Holiday Day
You know what to do!

26

National Scribble Day
What art can you make with a few scribbles?

27

National Weed Appreciation Day
Not all weeds are bad—take today to appreciate and learn about how helpful they can actually be.

28

Youth Day (Taiwa
This day commemora the victims of the Second Guangzhou uprising in 1911.

29

THURSDAY	FRIDAY	SATURDAY
Read Across America Day Grab your favorite book and start reading! How many books can you read this month? **2**	**"If Pets Had Thumbs" Day** This day gets four thumbs up! **3**	**Marching Band Day** Today's the perfect day to grab an instrument and "march forth!" **4**
Hello, dolly! In 1959, the Barbie doll debuted at the American Toy Fair. **9**	**INTERNATIONAL BAGPIPE DAY** **10**	**Moshoeshoe Day (Lesotho)** This holiday honors King Moshoeshoe I, the founder and national hero of Lesotho. **11**
National Artichoke Hearts Day These veggies may not look like hearts, but they are delicious! **16**	**SAINT PATRICK'S DAY** **17**	*Far out!* In 1965, Alexei Leonov became the first man to walk in space. **18**
National Dip and Day **23**	**National Cheesesteak Day** As they say in Philly, do you want yours "wit" or "witout" (onions)? **24**	*Ciao, Venezia!* In 421—1,601 years ago!—the city of Venice was founded at the stroke of noon. **25**
National Doctors Day Doctors are heroes! They help save and improve lives every day. **30**	**NATIONAL CRAYON DAY** Is it "cran," "cray-ahn," "cray-awn," or "crown"? **31**	**FLOWER** —DAFFODIL

MARCH

Kamala Harris

Marie Curie

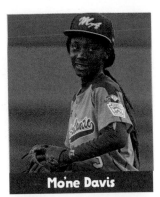

Mo'ne Davis

Amelia Earhart

WOMEN'S HISTORY MONTH

Celebrate by matching each pioneering woman with her historic achievement.

Aretha Franklin

1. Who was the first woman to win a Nobel Prize (1903)?

2. Who was the first woman to make a nonstop solo airplane flight across the Atlantic Ocean (1932)?

3. Who is considered to be America's first prima ballerina (1940s)?

4. Who was the first woman to fly into outer space (1963)?

5. Who was the first woman to reach the summit of Mount Everest (1975)?

6. Who was the first woman to serve on the Supreme Court (1981)?

7. Who was the first woman to be inducted into the Rock & Roll Hall of Fame (1987)?

8. Who was the first girl to pitch a shutout in the Little League World Series (2014)?

9. Who was the first woman elected vice president of the United States (2020)?

INTERNATIONAL WOMEN'S DAY IS MARCH 8. This global day celebrates women's achievements and calls for gender equality.

Sandra Day O'Connor

Maria Tallchief

Junko Tabei

Valentina Tereshkova

NATIONAL UMBRELLA MONTH

> Knock, knock.
> *Who's there?*
> **Butter.**
> *Butter who?*
> **Butter bring an umbrella— it looks like rain.**

Can you tell what's alike in each row of umbrellas, across, down, and diagonally?

Since the invention of the basic umbrella more than four thousand years ago, umbrellas have been made from lots of different materials. Handles and frames have been made from:

**WHALEBONE
ALUMINUM
BAMBOO
FIBERGLASS
STEEL**

Canopies have been made from:

**FEATHERS
SILK
GINGHAM
OILCLOTH
NYLON
PLASTIC**

Read the letters in **blue** from top to bottom to reveal an American slang term for *umbrella*.

NATIONAL MUSIC IN OUR SCHOOLS MONTH

Celebrate by finding these six WORDS (not pictures) hidden in the scene below. Can you find BEAT, CHORUS, CONDUCT, MUSICIAN, NOTE, and PIANO?

> **The most popular instruments to play are:**
> 1. Piano
> 2. Guitar
> 3. Violin
> 4. Drums
> 5. Saxophone

NATIONAL NOODLE MONTH

No one knows for sure where noodles were first invented, but they are believed to have existed in some form in ancient China and Greece. Today, there are noodles of all shapes and sizes, including gluten-free and wheat-free versions, and even noodles made from vegetables.

Use your noodle to take this quiz and figure out which facts are true and which are im-pastas!

T F In Italian, *orecchiette* means "little ears" and *linguine* means "little tongues."

T F Noodles that are cooked *al dente* means they were cooked in a pot without any dents in it.

T F Thomas Jefferson helped popularize macaroni and cheese by serving it to his dinner guests.

T F Although used interchangeably, pasta and noodles are technically two different foods.

T F The name *macaroni* comes from the song "Yankee Doodle."

T F In Japan, somen noodles are hung outside to dry in the sun.

T F It is scientifically impossible to eat spaghetti and meatballs without making a mess.

T F In 1848, the first commercial pasta plant in the U.S. was founded in Brooklyn.

NATIONAL PEANUT MONTH

Make these Peanutty Sesame Noodles to celebrate!

Ask an adult to help with anything hot or sharp.

1. Peel and cut 1 **cucumber** into matchsticks. Wash and chop 2 **green onions**.

2. Toast 4 teaspoons **sesame seeds** in a small pan over medium heat, shaking occasionally, until they darken and become fragrant.

3. Put ½ cup **peanut butter**, 2 tablespoons **brown sugar**, 3 tablespoons **low-sodium soy sauce**, 2 tablespoons **sesame oil**, 2 tablespoons **distilled white vinegar**, and ¼ cup **water** into a blender. Blend until smooth, 20–30 seconds.

4. Put 8 ounces **cooked spaghetti** into a large bowl and add the peanut sauce. Stir.

5. Divide the noodles into four bowls. Top with the cucumber, green onions, and sesame seeds.

Wash your hands before and after handling food.

NATIONAL CRAFT MONTH

**March is a perfect month to plant some flowers.
It's also the perfect month to make some flower crafts!**

Once your flowerpot is completely dry, plant your favorite flower or succulent inside!

DRIP POTS

1. Paint **clear sealer** onto the inside and outside of a **terra-cotta pot**. Let it dry.

2. Paint the outside of the pot with white **acrylic paint**. Let it dry.

3. Mix another color of paint with a few drops of **water** so that it drips like milk.

4. Place the pot upside down on a covered surface. Drip the watery paint onto the pot. Let it dry.

5. Add a coat of clear sealer.

PAPER FLOWERS

If you'd rather fill your pot with flowers that don't need to be watered, try making them instead!

DAFFODIL

1. Flatten three **cupcake liners**. On each, draw a shape with three petals.

2. Stack and arrange them to form a circle. **Glue** them together.

3. Glue a **mini cupcake liner** and a **pompom** on top. **Tape** a **paper straw** to the back.

DAISY

1. Cut out a long strip of **cardstock**. **Glue** the ends together to form a loop. Make three more loops.

2. Stack and arrange the loops to form a circle. Glue them together.

3. Add a small **cardstock** circle. Tape a **paper straw** to the back.

POPPY

1. Cut out six circles from **tissue paper**. Glue them together to form a big circle.

2. Cut out two small **cardstock** circles. Punch a hole in each and in the tissue-paper circle.

3. Push a **fuzzy stick** through one cardstock circle, then the tissue-paper circle, and then the other cardstock circle. Bend the end.

4. Slide a **paper straw** onto the fuzzy stick. Bend the end.

60 YEARS AGO, THE HULA-HOOP WAS PATENTED BY ARTHUR "SPUD" MELIN.

Melin co-founded the toy company Wham-O along with his friend Richard Knerr. They sold about 25 million Hula-Hoops in the first few months after they began producing them. Although decades have passed, kids still play with this toy today. **These friends are having a competition to see who can keep their Hula-Hoop up the longest. Can you find all 15 objects before the last Hula-Hoop falls?**

bowl

hammer

heart

slice of pizza

drinking straw

crescent moon

light bulb

banana

candy corn

boot

snake

flashlight

teacup

sailboat

toothbrush

Wham-O also created other popular toys, including the Frisbee, Slip 'N Slide, and Hacky Sack.

Obstacle Challenge: Hula-Hoops aren't just for spinning. Create your own obstacle course using Hula-Hoops and other objects you have lying around. Then challenge your friends to a race!

March 26, 1953
70 YEARS AGO, DR. JONAS SALK ANNOUNCED THE SUCCESSFUL TEST OF A POLIO VACCINE.

Polio is a contagious virus that attacks the nervous system and can leave its victims paralyzed. Polio epidemics were quite common before the vaccine, and children were affected more than adults. Since Salk's vaccine was distributed to the public, polio cases have dropped drastically. There hasn't been a case of polio that began in the United States since 1979! Without scientists and doctors, we wouldn't have the cutting-edge medicine that keeps us healthy. **Jenny plans to be a doctor when she grows up. While she checks Teddy's vitals, search her room for eight hidden objects.**

slice of cake

cookie

hammer

ladder

seashell

shovel

fried egg

slice of pizza

Find the two doctor kits that look the same.

What Is a Virus?

A virus is a particle so small that we need a special microscope to see it. When a person with the virus sneezes, coughs, or even talks, tiny water droplets carry it into the air.

When virus particles get into another person, they break into some of the trillions of cells that make up that person's body. Then the viruses trick the cells into making copies of them.

A body uses several responses to fight viruses and other germs. Together, these responses are called the immune system. As the immune system kills viruses, it makes antibodies, which help find and fight the virus if it invades again.

Vaccines stop viruses before they make a person sick. The measles, mumps, rubella, and polio are four viruses that scientists have controlled or eliminated.

MARCH MADNESS

Throughout the month of March, 64 women's teams and 68 men's teams will play in a single-elimination **National Collegiate Athletic Association (NCAA) Division I Basketball Tournament**, also known as March Madness. The men's championship game will take place on April 1, 2023, at the NRG Stadium in Houston, Texas. The women's championship game will take place on March 31, 2023, at the American Airlines Center in Dallas, Texas.

TOP CHAMPS

These teams have won the most championships:

Men's NCAA Division I (since 1939)
1. UCLA Bruins (11 wins)
2. Kentucky Wildcats (8)
3. North Carolina Tar Heels (6)

Women's NCAA Division I (since 1982)
1 . UConn Huskies (11 wins)
2. Tennessee Lady Vols (8)
3. Baylor Lady Bears (3)

BASKETBALL OR BASEBALL?

Which sport is each clue about? Take a shot or a swing, and circle the correct answer.

1. Gym-class variations of this sport include "H-O-R-S-E" and "Around the World."

2. Two teams of five players oppose each other in this sport.

3. This sport's championship series was first played in 1903.

4. James Naismith invented this sport in 1891.

5. There's no clock on during this sport.

6. This sport has plays called alley-oop, pick and roll, and V-cut.

7. German teams that play this sport include the Mainz Athletics and the Solingen Alligators.

8 . Chinese teams that play this sport include the Beijing Ducks and the Shanghai Sharks.

What made the chicken good at basketball?

He was great at fowl shots.

March 2023

WORLD BASEBALL CLASSIC

To warm up for the 2023 World Baseball Classic, write each set of colored letters on the corresponding lines to find out the winners of the 2017 series.

UPNNEUJIETRTEAHDPETRSOLTRAAATINECDSONS

1: _____

2: _____

3: _____

4: _____

March 2

READ ACROSS AMERICA DAY

There are 12 objects hidden in this library scene. Can you find them all?

OBJECT LIST

- COFFEEPOT
- ICE-CREAM BAR
- ELEPHANT
- LIGHT BULB
- OIL CAN
- OWL
- PENNANT
- ROLLER SKATE
- SOCK
- BRIEFCASE
- TOP HAT
- UMBRELLA

March 21

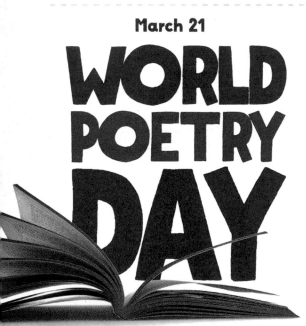

WORLD POETRY DAY

Poetry Superlatives

The **LONGEST** poem ever written—a Sanskrit epic called the *Mahābhārata*—is more than **200,000 lines**. That's **1.8 million words**!

The **OLDEST** poem ever written—*The Epic of Gilgamesh* from ancient Mesopotamia—was written in Sumerian around 2150–1400 BCE. That's **more than 3,000 years ago**!

The **OLDEST** surviving poem written in English is *Beowulf*, which was composed between 700 to 750 AD in Old English.

WORLD THEATER DAY

World Theater Day is celebrated annually on March 27 with theater events around the world. Theater people can be pretty superstitious, so read up on these seven tips to avoid bad luck in the theater.

1. **"Good luck" is bad luck!** Say "break a leg" to wish someone in theater well.

2. **Leave the ghost light on.** A single lit bulb upstage center helps ward off theater ghosts—and helps the crew see in the dark!

3. **Don't say "Macbeth!"** To avoid saying the famous Shakespeare play's title, which supposedly brings bad luck, theater people call it "The Scottish Play."

4. **Mirror, mirror, on the wall—not on stage.** If a mirror breaks on stage, it brings bad luck, so most sets don't include real mirrors.

5. **Don't whistle while you work!** Stagehands once communicated with coded whistles, so whistling backstage could lead to accidents.

6. **What's under your pillow?** Superstitious performers sleep with a script under their pillow to help them memorize lines faster. Just don't try it for your next history exam!

7. **Lucky lefty.** In theater, the left foot is luckier than the right foot, so actors should always walk left foot first into a dressing room.

Have you been to a theater? If so, what did you see?

If you were to write your own play, what would it be about?

Top Act

Here's a list of the top 10 most frequently performed musicals in North American high schools, with a twist—we replaced one word in six of the titles with a synonym in blue. Can you figure out the real names of the six silly musicals?

1. Beauty and the Monstrosity

   _____

2. The Addams Clan

   _____

3. The Miniature Mermaid

   _____

4. Into the Forest

   _____

5. Cinderella

6. Shrek

7. Seussical

8. Little Boutique of Horrors

   _____

9. The Magician of Oz

   _____

10. Annie

What performances did your school do this year?

NATIONAL PI DAY

March 14 (3/14) is celebrated as Pi Day because 3, 1, and 4 are the first three digits of the mathematical symbol π.

Seventeen types of pie are hidden up, down, across, backward, and diagonally. Dig in!

```
        C O C O N U T
      Y I C E C R E A M
    Y P M I N C E M E A T
  U O E P R U N E W H I P R
  T U A Y E L E M O N C E T
  H C R N R E Q B N A P E A R B
  O H T U R T R K E Y L I M E P
  Y E E T E A M Y     N A C E P
  U R E B B L P L         E O
  M R T U Q O U F             S
  Y H T A C M O
  R A T P Q P O T
    H E P H K H B
    R L C I S L
    E A N E X
```

What's the best thing to put in a pie?

WORD LIST

APPLE
BERRY
CHERRY
CHOCOLATE
COCONUT
ICE CREAM
KEY LIME
LEMON
MINCEMEAT
PEACH
PEANUT BUTTER
PEAR
PECAN
PRUNE WHIP
PUMPKIN
RHUBARB
SHOOFLY

A Never-Ending Number

The number pi is infinitely long, but that hasn't stopped people from trying to calculate it. A new record was set in March 2019 when Emma Haruka Iwao calculated pi to 31,415,926,535,897 digits! Why is that number significant? Here are the first 100 digits:

3.14159265358979323846264338327950288419716939937510582097494459230781640628620899862803482534211 7067

More Treats for Your Tongue

Say these tongue twisters three times, fast!

Three slices of pumpkin pie, please!

Pecan pie is perfect for a party.

Crisscrossed crispy piecrust.

March 25

INTERNATIONAL WAFFLE DAY

Here are four meals you can make to celebrate. Rate each recipe you try by filling in the stars.

☆☆☆☆
Cornbread-and-Chili Dinner

Pour **cornbread batter** onto a waffle iron. Cook until lightly browned, about 1½–2 minutes. Top with **chili**, **cheese**, **lettuce**, and **sour cream**.

☆☆☆☆
Waffled-Egg Breakfast

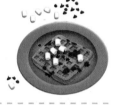

Beat 3 **eggs**. Add **salt** and **pepper**. Pour the eggs onto a waffle iron. Cook through, about 2–3 minutes.

☆☆☆☆
Mini-Pizza Lunch

Add **pizza sauce**, **cheese**, and **mini pepperoni** to the bottom half of a **refrigerated biscuit**. Put on the top half and squeeze the edges together. Cook in a waffle iron for 1–1½ minutes.

☆☆☆☆
S'more Dessert

Mix **chocolate chips** and **mini marshmallows** into **waffle batter**. Cook until the waffles are done.

We hope you're hungry! There are lots of fun food holidays in March. Here are just a few:

March 1
NATIONAL PEANUT BUTTER LOVERS' DAY

There are about 540 peanuts in a 12-ounce jar of peanut butter.

March 7
NATIONAL CEREAL DAY

Most Americans eat around 160 bowls of cereal per year.

March 16
NATIONAL ARTICHOKE HEARTS DAY

Artichokes are flowers. They're part of the daisy family.

March 26
NATIONAL SPINACH DAY

If you see *Florentine* on a menu or in a recipe, there's probably spinach in the dish.

COUNTDOWN TO SPRING

What is your favorite flower?

How do you welcome spring?

6 POPULAR SPRING FLOWERS

crocus

daffodil

tulip

lilac

lily

iris

5 CUTEST RABBIT BREEDS

lionhead rabbit

Netherland dwarf rabbit

mini lop rabbit

rex rabbit

Polish rabbit

4 WAYS TO CELEBRATE SPRINGTIME CRITTERS

Sing back to the robins.

Sketch the creatures that live near your home.

Write a story from a toad's point of view.

Invent dance moves inspired by inchworms.

3 SPRING IDIOMS

"full of the joys of spring"

"spring chicken"

"spring fever"

2 SPRING TONGUE TWISTERS

Parker planted plenty of peas.

Spring makes Spike and Mike want to bike.

1 FIRST DAY OF SPRING

In the Northern Hemisphere, the vernal equinox signals the beginning of spring. On this day, the amount of daylight is almost exactly the same as the amount of darkness. The word *equinox* comes from the Latin for "equal night."

PURIM

This Jewish holiday honors Queen Esther, who persuaded her husband, King Ahasuerus, to save the Jewish people of Persia from the villain Haman. It's a festive day, during which people dress up in costumes, exchange gifts, and give to the poor.

From the Middle Ages onward, actors have performed funny plays called *spiels* that tell the Purim story, known as the Megillah. (*Spiel* means "play" or "skit" in Yiddish, the language Jews spoke in Central and Eastern Europe.) To this day, the name *Haman* is met with boos and the sounds of *groggers* (noisemakers) during these plays—and even during religious services.

MAKE HAMANTASCHEN

Ask an adult for help using the stove, food processor, and oven.

Hamantaschen, which means "Haman's pockets" in Yiddish, are traditional treats eaten at Purim. This three-sided pastry looks like the hat that Haman supposedly wore.

FILLING*

1. Place 1 package (16 ounces) **pitted prunes** in a saucepan and cover with water. Add ½ teaspoon **cinnamon**, 1 tablespoon **sugar**, and 1 tablespoon **lemon juice**. Simmer until fruit is soft and mushy. (Add more water if needed.) Let cool.

2. With an adult's help, chop 1 cup **shelled walnuts or other nuts** in a food processor or blender. Add prune mixture and mix well. Set aside.

   * Prune butter or apple butter can be substituted for prune-nut filling

DOUGH

1. With a mixing bowl, cream together 1 stick **softened butter or margarine** and ¾ cup **sugar.**

2. Beat 3 **egg yolks** in a separate bowl and add to the butter-sugar mixture. Add 1 cup **sour cream**. Mix well.

3. In a large bowl, sift together 3 cups **flour**, 2 teaspoons **baking powder**, and ¼ teaspoon **baking soda**. Add to the butter-sugar mixture. Then add 1 teaspoon **vanilla** and ½ teaspoon **grated orange rind**. Mix well.

4. On a floured board, roll out the dough about ¼-inch thick. If the dough is too sticky, cover and refrigerate for a few hours before rolling out.

5. Cut into 3-inch circles with a cookie cutter or a drinking glass turned upside down.

6. Place a teaspoon of filling in the center of each circle. Fold up two sides of the circle and pinch together. Fold up the third side and pinch together with the other two sides to form a triangle, leaving the center open.

7. Place the hamantaschen on greased baking sheets and into the oven. Bake for about 20 minutes at 350°F, until lightly browned.

SAINT PATRICK'S

LEPRECHAUN SHENANIGANS

A prankster is on the loose on Leprechaun Lane! Someone took an item from one of the shops and hid it. Luckily, he or she left some clues behind. Can you figure out WHO the mischief-maker is, WHAT was taken, and WHERE it was hidden?

CLUES

WHO
I am a prankster, red-haired am I, with golden shoes and bright-green eyes.

WHAT
I'm made of wood and pegs and string. You can play me while you sing.

WHERE
A place with a chimney and mushrooms galore. Look above a spotted door.

BONUS!
Find 5 gold coins, 4 four-leaf clovers, 3 horseshoes, 2 rainbows, and 1 harp.

66

Saint Patrick's Day is celebrated in more countries than any other national festival.

Shamrock Swirl Fudge

1. Line an 8- or 9-inch pan with parchment paper.

2. Put 16 ounces **white chocolate chips** into a microwave-safe bowl.

3. Microwave for 90 seconds at half power. Stir. Add 30 seconds, if necessary.

4. Add 14 ounces **sweetened condensed milk**. Stir until smooth.

5. Put the mixture into the pan. Add a few drops of **food coloring**. Use a metal skewer to swirl it.

6. Top with **cereal bits** and **sprinkles**. Chill for 2 hours.

Ask for an adult's help with anything hot or sharp.

Knock, knock.

Irish.

Irish you would let me in.

KIDS' SCIENCE QUESTIONS

How do you find the end of a rainbow?

A rainbow is sunlight that has been bent and reflected to you by raindrops. As drops fall through the sunlight, they bend light that enters them, separating it into its different colors—red, orange, yellow, green, blue, indigo, and violet. Some of this light is reflected inside the drops and heads toward you.

A rainbow you see is not the same one seen by your friend. Because you're in different positions, the colors reflected to your eyes and to your friend's eyes come from different drops. It appears to you that the rainbow forms an arch that ends, but where you can't see the rainbow anymore and where your friend can't see the rainbow anymore are different places.

A complete rainbow would be a full circle if Earth weren't in the way. You would have to be high above Earth to see more than half a rainbow. Pilots report seeing complete circular rainbows if the conditions are just right, but it's not very common.

WORLD WILDLIFE DAY

Take today to learn about amazing wild animals—like the koala! These marsupials live in Australia. They eat a diet of mainly eucalyptus leaves and sleep about 18 hours a day. The koala cuties pictured here are hanging out in their treetop home. **Look for these 22 hidden objects.**

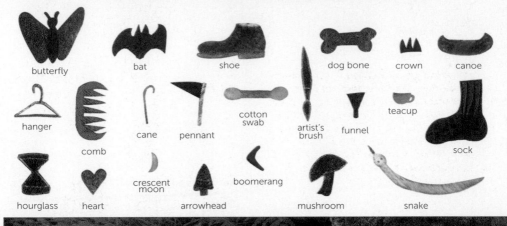

butterfly   bat   shoe   dog bone   crown   canoe

hanger   comb   cane   pennant   cotton swab   artist's brush   funnel   teacup   sock

hourglass   heart   crescent moon   arrowhead   boomerang   mushroom   snake

Why isn't a koala considered a bear?

It doesn't have the right koala-fications.

World Wildlife Day is meant to raise awareness of the importance of living things in our world. How does your local wildlife improve where you live?

March 25, 2023

EARTH HOUR

Earth Hour is a global environmental event that encourages people to turn off their lights for one hour. Earth Hour started in 2007 in Australia and is now celebrated in more than 180 countries and territories around the world. Famous landmarks, including **Big Ben**, the **Statue of Liberty**, the **Eiffel Tower**, and the **Sphinx and Great Pyramids of Giza** have all participated in Earth Hour.

Earth Hour starts at 8:30 p.m. local time on the last Saturday in March.

Big Ben is actually the 13-ton bell at the top of the clock tower.

The Statue of Liberty is modeled after the sculptor's mother.

The Eiffel Tower first opened to the public on March 31, 1889.

The more than 4,500-year-old Sphinx was originally painted in bright colors like red, yellow, and blue.

AM   PM   PM   PM

While getting ready for Earth Hour, Bethany notices that all the country labels have fallen off the world clocks. Using the clues below, help her match each country label with the correct clock.

Mali is 8 hours behind China.

Nepal is 5 hours and 45 minutes ahead of Mali.

Ukraine is 6 hours behind China.

NEPAL

UKRAINE

MALI

CHINA

Which continent has the most time zones?   Asia (11 time zones)

69

March 29
International Mermaid Day

Today is all about mermaids! Andromeda is trying to get to Atlantis.
Help her swim through the maze and to the FINISH.

Where do legends of mermaids come from? Many think they were inspired centuries ago by real-life sea animals called manatees. Sailors who caught sight of these animals may have mistaken them for creatures that were part human, part fish. Tales then spread about the mythical creatures the sailors thought they saw.

The manatee is closely related to another big, gray mammal: the elephant!

Manatees are a type of mammal. Three different species exist, and they all live in warm waters. These creatures feed on sea grass and other plants. An adult manatee—about 10 to 13 feet long and weighing 1,000 to 3,000 pounds (about the weight of an entire defensive line of a pro football team)—can eat 80 pounds of plants each day. Manatees may not be mermaids, but their appetites are the stuff of legends!

March 2023

BLOSSOM KITE FESTIVAL

Kite makers and fliers from around the world come to Washington, D.C., for competitions and demonstrations.

Find what's silly in the picture above. It's up to you!

March 30
TAKE A WALK IN THE PARK DAY

Grab your boots and take a walk in these national parks. Can you match each park to its superlative?

The Great Smoky Mountains National Park is known as the salamander capital of the world.

1. Death Valley
2. Great Smoky Mountains
3. Hot Springs
4. Mount Rainier
5. Wrangell-St. Elias
6. Yellowstone

A. biggest
B. smallest
C. most-visited
D. oldest
E. hottest
F. snowiest

The United States has 62 national parks and 8,565 state parks.

March 6
INDEPENDENCE DAY

In 1957, Ghana gained its independence from the United Kingdom. Although English is Ghana's official language, about 80 languages are spoken in the country. The names of government-sponsored Ghanaian languages are listed here. Use the number of letters in each word as a clue as to where it might fit in the grid.

Take a spin around the globe to see how

AKAN
DAGAARE
DAGBANI
DANGME
EWE
GA
GONJA
KASEM
MFANTSE
NZEMA

Happy 1,402nd! According to the Persian calendar, March 21, 2023, is the first day of the year 1402.

March 21, 2023
HAPPY NEW YEAR!

March 21 is Nowruz, or Iranian New Year. To symbolize rebirth and growth, Iranians prepare *sabzeh* (sab-ZAY), sprouted seeds grown in a dish.

THE WORLD

eople around the world celebrate in March.

Farion (fez) has the Greek coat of arms.

Tsarouchi (clogs) have 60 nails on the sole and weigh more than 3 pounds each!

Fustanella (kilt) has 400 pleats to represent the years of Ottoman occupation.

March 25
GREEK
INDEPENDENCE DAY

The Greek War of Independence started on March 25, 1821. On Greek Independence Day, the national holiday is celebrated with a miltary parade in Athens, the capital city. Children also march in local parades, waving Greek flags and wearing traditional costumes with symbolic significance.

March 7–8, 2023
HOLI

During Holi, people in northern India wear new white clothes. They toss colored powder called *gulal* (goo-LAHL) and colored water on one another. The streets soon fill with children and adults, their new white clothes blooming in wild bouquets of color. Can you find the jigsaw pieces below in this photo of kids holding colored powder during Holi?

Gulal colors hold special meaning. Red is for love, green is for new beginnings, and blue represents Krishna, a Hindu deity.

SUNDAY	MONDAY	TUESDAY	WEDNESDAY

BIRTHSTONE
DIAMOND

ZODIAC SIGNS
ARIES: MARCH 21–APRIL 19

TAURUS: APRIL 20–MAY 20

FLOWERS
SWEET PEA AND DAISY

PALM SUNDAY

2

National Find a Rainbow Day
Rainbows may be caused by light refracting through water droplets, but that doesn't make them less magical. If there's a rain shower today, look to the skies— you just might find a rainbow.

3

INTERNATIONAL CARROT DAY
Calling all carrot lovers. today is your day!

4

PASSOVER
begins at sunset.

5

EASTER

9

National Siblings Day
Let your siblings know how much you love them with a nice note or special treat.

10

National Submarine Day
(The ship, not the sandwich.)

11

GRILLED CHEE SANDWICH DAY

12

A numbers game.
In 1929, the Cleveland Indians became the first baseball team to put numbers on the backs of players' uniforms.

16

National Haiku Poetry Day
Haiku have five beats, then count seven in line two. Finish last with five.

17

Do, re, mi wins!
In 1966, *The Sound of Music* won the Academy Award for Best Picture of the Year.

18

National Garlic
A vampire's least favorite day.

19

23
National Take a Chance Day

National Honesty Day

30

Golden tickets not needed.
In 1907, Hershey Park opened for workers from Hershey's chocolate company.

24

Great move!
In 1950, Chuck Cooper became the first African American hoopster drafted into the NBA.

25

An atomic tragedy
A nuclear reactor disaster took place a Chernobyl atomic po station in the U.S.S in 1986.

20

APRIL

APRIL FOOLS' DAY
Be careful today— things may not be what they seem!

1

NATIONAL CARAMEL POPCORN DAY

6

National Handmade Day
Try your hand at making your own soap, candles, clothes, and more.

7

Now you see it, now you don't. On live TV in 1983, magician David Copperfield made the Statue of Liberty disappear.

8

Teachers' Day (Ecuador)
s day takes place on birthday of Juan ntalvo, a popular adorian er in the 0s.

13

International Moment of Laughter Day
Here's a joke to get you started:

What color is rain?
Watercolor

14

National Laundry Day
Pro tip: One red shirt can make a whole batch of whites pink. Be sure to separate your clothes!

15

National Look-Alike Day
You look familiar!"

20

EID AL-FITR
begins at sunset.

21

EARTH DAY
Reduce, reuse, recycle, repeat.

22

What can you do today to help take care of Earth?

_____

_____

---

lorse Code Day
ning the code is as as

27

Pay It Forward Day
Do something kind today and start a chain reaction of good deeds!

28

National Zipper Day
Three cheers for this invention: zip, zip, hooray!

29

NATIONAL KITE MONTH

As the weather begins to get warmer, celebrate the joy and happiness that come from flying a kite by going out and . . . flying a kite! Invite friends and family to join you as you let your kites soar high into the sky.

Each of these colorful kites has an exact match. Can you find all nine?

Benjamin Franklin's famous experiment in 1752 used a kite and key to demonstrate that lightning is electricity.

The world record for the highest altitude reached by a single kite is **4,879.54 meters** (16,009 feet).

Kites were flown in China more than **2,000 years ago**.

What's the best material for kites?

Flypaper

NATIONAL HUMOR MONTH

What's the funniest thing you've ever seen? For us, it might be this chicken doing stand-up. Think of your favorite jokes while you hunt through this scene for the nine hidden objects. Then perform a stand-up routine of your own!

April 14 is International Moment of Laughter Day!

ruler

button

crescent moon

slice of pizza

domino

kite

golf club

lollipop

magnet

LOOK BOTH WAYS!

The chicken isn't the only one crossing the road. Match up these riddles with their punch lines to find out why.

1. Why did the rabbit cross the road?
2. Why did the farmer cross the road?
3. Why did the gum cross the road?
4. Why did the robot cross the road?
5. Why did the dinosaur cross the road?
6. Why did the lemur cross the road?
7. Why did the cow cross the road?
8. Why did the elephant cross the road?
9. Why did the frog cross the road?
10. Why did the dolphin cross the road?

A. Chickens weren't invented yet.
B. To get to the udder side
C. It was stuck to the chicken's foot.
D. Somebody toad him to.
E. To get to the other tide
F. It was the chicken's day off.
G. To bring back his chicken
H. To prove she could hip-hop
I. To take care of some monkey business
J. He was programmed to.

NATIONAL POETRY MONTH

A poet once described the difference between poetry and prose: prose is walking, poetry is dancing. Here are a few famous lines of poetry. What kind of dance do you think they're doing?

Shall I compare thee to a summer's day? Thou art more lovely and more temperate.
—WILLIAM SHAKESPEARE

'Tis better to have loved and lost Than never to have loved at all.
—ALFRED, LORD TENNYSON

I wandered lonely as a cloud.
—WILLIAM WORDSWORTH

MAKE-A-POEM KIT

Arrange the words on these refrigerator magnets to create your own poetry. Move over, Shakespeare!

SKUNK · OVER · OF · A · FIRE · YOU · EARTH · ME · TREE · TOES · LOVE · HAIR · CLOUDS · UNDER · THE · SEA · FISH · OVER · TO · IS · WATER · US · FLOWER · WE · NEAR · HANDS · SMILE · EYE · SKIES · HEAR · SKY · TRY

Poems can be serious or silly, super long or super short. And guess what? They don't have to rhyme! What are your favorite kinds of poems to read? Maybe you'll enjoy this one—it's one of our favorites!

Singer-songwriter Bob Dylan won the **NOBEL PRIZE** for Literature in 2016.

The first African American book of poems, *Poems on Various Subjects, Religious and Moral,* was written by Phillis Wheatley in 1773.

How do poets say hello?

"Hey, haven't we metaphor?"

ANGLERFISH

The anglerfish
is rather odd.
Its dorsal fin's
a fishing rod.
And dangling
from that line—
a lure—
resembling
a worm for sure.
Imagine
if you think you can:
A fish
both fish
and fisherman.
—EILEEN SPINELLI

NATIONAL
MATHEMATICS AND STATISTICS AWARENESS MONTH

POSTAGE PAW-BLEMS

Which package will cost the most to ship?

STAMPS
- 50¢
- $1
- $2

Does Purrnelope have enough money to send all four packages?

Why was the math book sad?

It had too many problems.

24 TO THE DOOR

Matt Amatics will step only on tiles with equations that equal 24. Can you help him get to his apartment door? He can move up, down, left, or right.

24

FINISH

9 + 12	2 x 11	15 + 9	17 + 7
7 + 15	35 - 11	8 x 3	25 - 2
3 x 4	6 x 4	20 + 3	18 + 7
18 + 6	40 - 16	5 x 7	33 - 10

START

SUM FUN!

Write the correct answer to each question in the blanks.

1. _____ Number of red stripes in the U.S. flag
2. _____ Number of Harry Potter movies
3. _____ Number of days in February during a leap year
4. _____ Number of squares on a chessboard
5. _____ Number of continents
6. _____ Number of seconds in an hour
7. _____ Number of U.S. states that have two words in their name

Add the above answers together to find out how many pounds the world's largest box of chocolates weighed.

April 14, 1828
195 YEARS AGO,
NOAH WEBSTER PUBLISHED THE FIRST EDITION OF THE AMERICAN DICTIONARY OF THE ENGLISH LANGUAGE.

This dictionary took Webster about 22 years to finish. He studied 26 different languages so he could learn the history of each American English word. In the end, he defined over 65,000 words in his book.

After the American Revolution, it was clear that the country was beginning to speak differently than England. Webster felt it was important to have a book that the whole country could use to know how Americans spelled and spoke. Below are some words that Webster changed from their original English spellings.

ORIGINAL ENGLISH SPELLING	WEBSTER'S SPELLING
Colour	Color
Defence	Defense
Centre	Center
Plough	Plow

Some of Webster's spellings didn't make it into his dictionary. He thought *tung* ("tongue") and *wimmen* ("women") matched the words' pronunciations better. But these new spellings didn't catch on.

Words like *skunk*, *hickory*, and *chowder* didn't appear in any British dictionaries because they were distinctively American words.

SEE IT, SAY IT

Have some fun with words! Each of these boxes represents a common word or phrase. For example, in the first one, the word *EGGS* is over the letters *EZ*. The answer is *EGGS OVER EASY*. See if you can figure out the rest.

1

EGGS
EZ

ANSWER:
EGGS OVER EASY

2

BsickED

ANSWER:

3

HORSING

ANSWER:

4

SETTLE

ANSWER:

5

DON'T COUNT YOUR CHICKENS they hatch

ANSWER:

How do spiders learn definitions?

They use Webster's Dictionary.

6

RUNNER RUNNER
BASE

ANSWER:

7

A W A K E

ANSWER:

8

MINUTE MINUTE

ANSWER:

9

JACKET

ANSWER:

April 21, 753 BCE
2,775 YEARS AGO, ROME IS SAID TO HAVE BEEN FOUNDED.

According to legend, twins Romulus and Remus were the children of Mars, the Roman god of war. Their uncle, who had stolen the throne of Alba Longa, was afraid his nephews would overthrow him to take their rightful place as kings. He commanded them to be drowned. Miraculously, they survived and were found by a wolf. She watched over the babies until a shepherd happened upon the boys and adopted them. Once grown, Romulus and Remus went back to the place where the wolf rescued them and founded the city of Rome.

Mars was just one of many gods that the Romans worshiped. Match each god with their mythological responsibility. Then find each god's name in the word search below.

ROMULUS.

MYTHOLOGICAL RESPONSIBILITY

1. GODDESS OF LOVE AND BEAUTY
2. GOD OF SUN
3. GOD OF WAR
4. GODDESS OF THE HUNT
5. GOD OF HEALING
6. GODDESS OF WISDOM
7. GOD OF TIME AND AGRICULTURE
8. GODDESS OF AGRICULTURE
9. GOD OF THE VINE
10. GODDESS OF THE DAWN
11. GOD OF LOVE
12. GOD OF FIRE AND METALWORK
13. GODDESS OF WOMEN AND MARRIAGE
14. MESSENGER OF THE GODS
15. GODDESS OF HOME AND HEARTH
16. GOD OF SLEEP
17. GOD OF NATURE AND WILDLIFE
18. GODDESS OF SPRING
19. GOD OF THE UNDERWORLD
20. GOD OF THE SEA
21. GODDESS OF THE MOON
22. RULER OF THE GODS

ROMAN GOD

A. AESCULAPIUS
B. JUNO
C. VESTA
D. APOLLO
E. DIANA
F. LUNA
G. FAUN
H. CUPID
I. AURORA
J. CERES
K. VENUS
L. NEPTUNE
M. VULCAN
N. BACCHUS
O. MARS
P. PROSERPINE
Q. SOMNUS
R. MINERVA
S. PLUTO
T. JUPITER
U. SATURN
V. MERCURY

```
A T N G T Z S D V A
R F A R Y R U I M S
O R N Y U X I A H R
R S Q E S T P N A M
U L O L P N A A V B
A M U M L T L S A M
A N D Q N G U C G I
A P K P S U C N A N
Y W O E F H S E E E
R T R L U F E D T R
U E O S L O A U V V
C S R A M O L V U A
R E T I P U J R L Q
E D V E S T A L C G
M P I F K T N U A F
G L T P J N Q M N E
I U D V U N H E X T
I T Z W U C Z J Y Q
G O L J V E N U S F
P R O S E R P I N E
```

April 2023
OPENING DAY OF THE MAJOR LEAGUE BASEBALL SEASON

The first baseball game at Yankee Stadium in New York City was played on **APRIL 18, 1923— 100 YEARS AGO!**

PLAY BALL!
Use the clues to fill in the batting order on each player's card.

CLUES

A. The kids wearing glasses do not bat 1st or 9th.

B. The boy with braces bats 1st.

C. The 8th and 9th batters have the same first initial.

D. The number on the jersey of the boy batting 2nd is twice as much as the number of the kid batting 4th.

E. Batter 6, a girl, has the same color hair as batter 7.

F. The girl outfielder bats 3rd.

Cards: Lindsey pitcher 60, Seth center field 22, Cody 3rd base 47, Laura 1st base 55, Claudia right field 10, Hector catcher 44, Ariel shortstop 20, Jacob 2nd base 35, Troy left field 29

The first recorded baseball game took place in 1845 between teams from New York and Brooklyn.

♪ "TAKE ME OUT TO THE BALL GAME"

Write the words below in any order in the blank spaces to create silly lyrics to this famous baseball song:

house, car, pigeons, cheese, football, crayons, email, turtle, sneaker, eyeball

Take me out to the ball_____,

Take me out to the _____.

Buy me some_____ and cracker_____,

I don't care if _____ never get back.

So it's root, root, root for the _____ _____,

If they don't _____ it's a shame.

For it's one, two, three _____ you're out

At the old _____ game.

HOME RUN!
Batter up! Can you find the right path to home plate? The symbols will tell you which way to move.

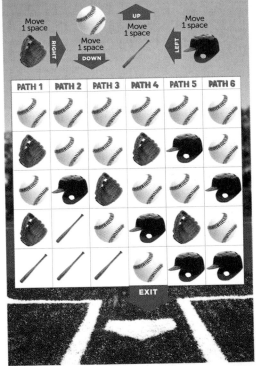

Move 1 space — RIGHT
Move 1 space — DOWN
UP — Move 1 space
Move 1 space — LEFT

PATH 1 | PATH 2 | PATH 3 | PATH 4 | PATH 5 | PATH 6

EXIT

April 6
WORLD TABLE TENNIS DAY

Your serve! Todd and Samantha have been playing so long, they're starting to see double! Can you find at least 20 differences between these two pictures?

April 17, 2023
THE BOSTON MARATHON

The Boston Marathon takes place on Patriots' Day. Only a few states celebrate this holiday, including Massachusetts. The holiday commemorates the Battles of Lexington and Concord, which were the first battles of the Revolutionary War.

THE RUNDOWN These five racers are poised and ready to race for their prize. Who will get the first-place trophy? Follow each runner's path to find out, and to see what the other runners place.

April 23-29, 2023
NATIONAL LIBRARY WEEK

This is a weeklong celebration of all that libraries have to offer. And there are plenty of them to celebrate: the U.S. has about 116,000 libraries of all kinds.

National Librarian Day is on April 16.

SHELF SHUFFLE

Figure out what the library books in each row (vertically, horizontally, and diagonally) have in common.

BOOK SMART

The head librarian wants to order 10 popular books for the library, but someone jumbled up the titles on her list. Can you figure out the correct titles?

1. *Anne of Witch*
2. *Charlotte's Stone*
3. *A Wrinkle in Chocolate*
4. *Diary of a Wimpy Cookie*
5. *The Lion, the Web and the Wardrobe*
6. *Harry Potter and the Sorcerer's Underpants*
7. *Charlie and the Sidewalk Factory*
8. *The Adventures of Captain Time*
9. *Where the Kid Ends*
10. *If You Give a Mouse a Green Gables*

April 8
DRAW A BIRD DAY

This day was inspired by a little British girl who visited an uncle wounded in World War II. To cheer him up, she asked him to draw a picture of a bird. Soon after, whenever the girl visited, the uncle and other wounded soldiers competed to see who could draw the best picture of a bird.

THERE ARE ABOUT **9,000** DIFFERENT SPECIES OF BIRDS. About 1,200 of those species may become extinct by the end of the century.

JUST WING IT Fill in the squares by drawing or writing the name of each bird. Every type of bird should appear only once in each row, column, and 2 x 3 box.

WORLD ART DAY

The birthday of Leonardo da Vinci is the perfect day to celebrate art and creativity in all its forms. Da Vinci was not only a great painter but also an incredible mathematician, architect, engineer, and inventor.

CRAFT A SUPER SPACESHIP

Leonardo da Vinci designed plans for lots of different flying machines. Now it's your turn—create your own spaceship!

1. Decorate a cardboard tube. We used paper and a marker. You might use stickers or paint.

2. Cut two right triangles for the wings from paper. Cut a partial circle.

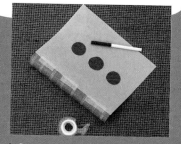

3. Fold one side of each triangle. Tape them to the bottom of the tube. Wrap the partial circle into a cone and tape it to the top.

4. Layer tissue paper. Pinch it near the top and tape it. Snip the ends, then crumple. Tape inside the tube.

April 4
INTERNATIONAL CARROT DAY

CARROT-RAISIN SALAD

1. Put 1 pound **shredded carrots** into a bowl. Add 1 cup **raisins**.

2. Squeeze the juice from half of a **lemon** and half of an **orange** into the carrot-and-raisin mixture.

3. Add ¼ cup **brown sugar** and a pinch of **salt**. Mix well. Refrigerate until you're ready to eat.

National Raisin Day is on **APRIL 30.**

Carrots have more natural sugar than any other vegetable except beets!

Carrots are orange because they contain the chemical beta-carotene, which our bodies turn into vitamin A.

How can you make a soup rich?

Add 14 carats to it.

April 6, 2023
NATIONAL BURRITO DAY

Made in Mexico in 2010, the world's largest burrito weighed 12,785 pounds. It was wrapped in a flour tortilla that measured nearly a mile and a half.

The word *burrito* **means "little donkey" in Spanish.** Some say that long ago a food vendor carried the food on his donkey, and customers asked for his burrito, meaning the donkey holding the food. Others say it got the name because it looks like the bedrolls carried on a donkey. Either way, this sandwich of rice, vegetables, cheese, and meat wrapped in a tortilla is a popular taste sensation.

BOBBIE'S BURRITOS

Bobbie the Burrito Maker wanted to share the recipe for her famous fiery-hot burritos. She drew pictures of the steps involved, but as she was hanging the pictures, the wind blew them onto the floor. **Can you help Bobbie put these pictures back in order?**

April 12

NATIONAL GRILLED CHEESE SANDWICH DAY

Ask for an adult's help with anything sharp or hot.

SWEET GRILLED CHEESE

1. Cut half of a peeled, baked **sweet potato** into slices.

2. **Butter** one side of two pieces of **bread**.

3. Between the two unbuttered sides, place **cheddar cheese**, sweet potato slices, and **provolone cheese**.

4. Ask an adult to heat a skillet over medium-low heat. Cook the sandwich for 5–6 minutes on one side. Flip it and cook it for 3–4 minutes. Remove from heat.

April 22

NATIONAL JELLY BEAN DAY

TONGUE TWISTER
Jason enjoys sorting jelly beans into jars.

IT CAN TAKE 7 TO 21 DAYS TO MAKE ONE JELLY BEAN.

Can you find these seven jigsaw pieces in this photo of jelly beans?

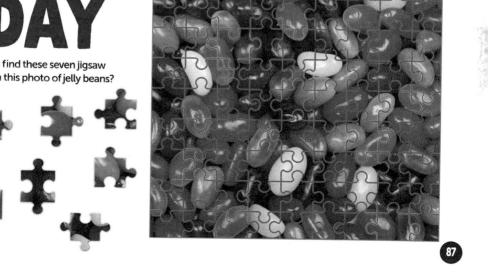

APRIL FOOLS' DAY

Why is everyone so tired on April Fools' day?

Because they just finished a 31-day March.

Here's one theory on how April 1 became April Fools' Day. New Year's Day was once celebrated on April 1 in Europe. In 1582, it was decided that New Year's would start on January 1. The people who hadn't heard about this switch continued to celebrate the holiday on April 1, which gave them the reputation of being foolish and easy to trick.

CUP O' LAUGHS

Build the perfect prank for April Fools'. If someone fills this cup too high, it will spill all over them. Whoops!

1. Use a **pushpin** to make a small hole in the bottom of a **plastic cup**.

2. Widen the hole with a **pencil** until a **bendy straw** can just fit through.

3. From the bottom, pull the straw partway through the hole. Bend the short section of the straw so it stays down.

4. Cut off the end that sticks out of the bottom of the cup.

5. To test it, fill the cup with water over a sink.

Why do eggs like April Fools' day?

They love practical yolks.

What monster plays the most April Fools' jokes? Prankenstein

1. Just right. 2. Too much! 3. Everything spills.

OLD-SCHOOL PRANKS

yum!

- Place vanilla pudding in an empty mayonnaise jar. Eat a big scoop in front of other people and watch their expressions of horror.

- Put a piece of plastic wrap under the lid of a saltshaker. Screw the lid back on, trim off any extra wrap, and watch your family try to shake out the salt.

- Glue a coin to the ground and grin as people try to pick it up.

- Place a leek in your sink and tell your family, "Oh, no! There's a leek in the sink."

- Call a friend and ask for Jess a few times. At the end of the day, call your friend, pretend you're Jess, and ask for messages.

PASSOVER

Every spring, a special meal called a *seder* occurs on the first night of the Jewish holiday of Passover. At the seder, everyone at the table takes part in telling the story of how the Jewish people escaped slavery, using a guide called the *Haggadah*. There is food and song. There are prayers for remembering what happened long ago and prayers that there will be no slavery anywhere at any time for any people.

In the 1930s, a rabbi lobbied Coca-Cola to make a kosher version of its soda for Passover. He was successful, and the company still makes kosher Coca-Cola today.

1 ROASTED EGG The roasted egg symbolizes life.

2 MAROR This bitter root represents the bitterness of slavery. Horseradish is often used.

3 ROASTED LAMB BONE This bone symbolizes the lamb eaten quickly when the Jews fled Egypt.

4 CHAROSET (hah-ROH-set) An apple-and-nut mixture represents the mortar made by the Jews when they toiled as slaves in Egypt. The sweetness of the apple symbolizes the promise of a better world.

5 KARPAS These greens, usually parsley, symbolize freedom. The parsley is dipped in salt water, which stands for the tears of slavery. In addition, karpas represent spring, because Passover is also a celebration of the spring harvest.

6 PESACH These three Hebrew letters spell *Pesach*, or *Passover*.

The youngest child traditionally asks four questions at a Passover seder. The last one is, "Why do we lean on pillows tonight during dinner?" In ancient times, only free people reclined while eating. Using pillows reminds everyone of freedom's gifts and the end of the Jews' enslavement in ancient Egypt.

MAKE A MATZO PILLOW

1. Trace around a large **cereal box** twice onto **muslin fabric**. Cut out the two rectangles.

2. Thread **brown yarn** through a **large-eyed needle**. Knot the end of the yarn. Sew the two pieces of muslin together on three sides. Make a second knot. Cut off the extra yarn.

3. Fill the pocket with **polyester fiberfill**. Sew the open end closed.

4. Draw lines on the pillow with a **marker**.

April 9, 2023

EASTER 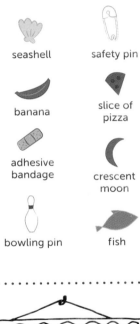 SUNDAY

Easter is the most important holiday in the Christian religion. This holiday celebrates the day Christians believe Jesus Christ rose from the dead on the third day after he was crucified on Good Friday. Western churches celebrate Easter on a Sunday between March 22 and April 25. The exact date depends on the date of the first full moon after the first day of spring.

These woodland creatures are decorating eggs for their annual Easter egg hunt. Before they hunt for their eggs, can you hunt for the eight objects in the scene?

seashell

safety pin

banana

slice of pizza

adhesive bandage

crescent moon

bowling pin

fish

DRAW YOUR OWN EASTER RABBIT!

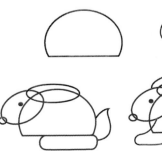

Want to create a bunny sketch to add to your Easter decorations? Hop to it, using the steps below.

EID AL-FITR

During the month of Ramadan, Muslims do not eat or drink from dawn to sunset. When Ramadan ends, Muslims everywhere celebrate Eid al-Fitr, the festival of fast-breaking.

They prepare special foods for friends and family. One dish common in India and Pakistan is a sweet noodle pudding called *sheer khurma*, which simply means "milk with dates." In some countries, this joyous holiday goes on for three days!

SWEET NOODLE PUDDING

1. With a parent's help, heat 3 cups **milk**, 1 cup **whipping cream,** and ½ cup **sugar** in a pan on the stove. Stir it until the mixture starts to foam.

2. Add 1 cup **uncooked vermicelli or angel-hair pasta** (broken into 3-inch pieces) and lower the heat. Stir for 15 minutes, or until the milk and cream thicken. Add ¼ cup **chopped dates**.

3. If serving warm, stir in ½ cup **nuts**, such as almonds or pistachios, and ¼ cup **raisins**.

4. If serving cold, add 1 small can **fruit cocktail**, drained, and ⅓ cup **shredded coconut**. Chill the pudding in the refrigerator.

On the Islamic calendar, a new month starts with a new moon. Every year, Eid al-Fitr falls about 11 days earlier than the previous year.

Eid al-Fitr begins when local "moon sighters" report seeing the new moon. The Judicial High Court then decides if Eid has arrived. When the sighting has been verified, Eid is declared on televisions, radio stations, and at mosques.

Children honor elderly relatives or neighbors by kissing their right hand and placing it on their forehead while greeting them.

During Eid al-Fitr, Muslim children in Egypt dance in the streets, swinging *fanous* of all sizes. Below are some countries that celebrate Eid. Read the letters in **red** from top to bottom to find out what a *fanous* is.

MALAYSIA

THAILAND

JORDAN

KUWAIT

INDONESIA

QATAR

BAHRAIN

April 8
ZOO LOVERS' DAY

ZOOKEEPER'S BYE-BYE

When he left for home, the head zookeeper accidentally scrambled the names of the animals he said goodbye to. Help him straighten out their names. When you do, each name will rhyme with his goodbye phrase.

1. After awhile, DOCCOREIL _____
2. See you soon, you big NABBOO _____
3. Got to go, FABFULO _____
4. Time to sleep, bighorn PEESH _____
5. Cheerio, KECGO _____
6. Bye-bye, FEBLUTTRY _____
7. Toodle-oo, AKNARGOO _____
8. Take good care, RAPLO EBAR _____
9. That's all for me, PENCHEZAMI _____
10. Take a break, TRANTELSAKE _____

FIVE MOST-VISITED ZOOS IN THE U.S.

1. San Diego Zoo, San Diego, CA
2. Lincoln Park Zoo, Chicago, IL
3. Saint Louis Zoo, Saint Louis, MO
4. Columbus Zoo and Aquarium, Columbus, OH
5. Brookfield Zoo, Brookfield, IL

The oldest zoo in the world was founded in 1752 in Vienna, Austria.

April 18
NATIONAL *VELOCIRAPTOR* AWARENESS DAY
KIDS' SCIENCE QUESTIONS

Could a *Velociraptor* pack really kill a *T. rex*?

Velociraptor could not have killed *T. rex*. For one thing, the two never met. *Velociraptor* lived in Asia about 80 million years ago. *T. rex* lived in North America about 65 million years ago. But even if they had met, a *Velociraptor* pack probably couldn't have even scared a forty-foot-long *T. rex*. That carnivore could have swallowed two of those wolf-sized raptors in a single bite!

Velociraptor is Latin for "swift robber."

What do you call a sleeping dinosaur?

A dino-snore

April 28, 2023

ARBOR DAY

There weren't a lot of trees in Nebraska in the 1800s, so J. Sterling Morton proposed a holiday called Arbor Day that called for people to plant them. They would provide fuel, building material, and shade. More than one million trees were planted in Nebraska on the first Arbor Day in 1872.

The Arbor Day Foundation has planted more than **250 MILLION TREES** since 1872.

THAT'S ONE OLD TREE!

The oldest living organism that doesn't clone itself is a bristlecone pine located in the White Mountains of California, in Inyo National Forest. Scientists estimate that the tree is more than five thousand years old. It started growing around the time humans invented writing and the wheel! Its location is kept secret to keep people away from it. That way, it might live another five thousand years!

What did the tree wear to the pool party?

Swimming trunks

There are about **5.5 BILLION** trees in urban areas of the U.S.

TREEMONTON TOWERS

The animals of Treemonton are celebrating in their town's twin treehouses after a day of planting trees. Can you figure out how to go from the ground to the top floor without waking any bats?

April 9
NATIONAL UNICORN DAY

Take a splash at finding the pencil, pine cone, pail, paddle, pickle, pear, parasol, and paintbrush hidden in this scene.

SATURDAY, APRIL 29, 2023, is National Pool Opening Day!

April 13
NATIONAL SCRABBLE DAY

What is the highest-scoring word you can make from these Scrabble letters? Your score is the sum of the numbers on the tiles. You can use each letter only once.

10 TRICKY HIGH-SCORING
SCRABBLE WORDS

1. Oxyphenbutazone
2. Muzjiks
3. Zax
4. Quetzals
5. Quixotry
6. Gherkins
7. Quartzy
8. Xu
9. Syzygy
10. Za

TAKE OUR DAUGHTERS AND SONS TO WORK DAY

More than 37 million Americans at over 3.5 million workplaces take part in this special day. The object is for kids to think about their careers. It also helps them appreciate what their parents do every day to help their family.

At this job fair, the participants brought things to help show kids what they do at work. Your job is to match each person to the correct object. When you're done, one object will be left. Use it to guess who hasn't arrived yet.

April 28
NATIONAL SUPERHERO DAY

This day was created in 1995 by workers at Marvel Comics. It honors the people who protect us from the bad guys, whether comic-book superheroes or real, everyday heroes.
If you were a superhero, what would your name be?

CHOOSE YOUR BIRTHDAY MONTH

JANUARY: The Great
FEBRUARY: Captain
MARCH: The Amazing
APRIL: Doctor
MAY: The Fantastic
JUNE: Professor
JULY: The Flying
AUGUST: Commander
SEPTEMBER: The Unstoppable
OCTOBER: Agent
NOVEMBER: The Invisible
DECEMBER: The Mysterious

THEN CHOOSE THE FIRST LETTER OF YOUR FIRST NAME

A: Guinea Pig
B: Green Bean
C: Cheese Stick
D: Marshmallow
E: Hullabaloo
F: Sandwich
G: Spinach
H: Jelly Bean
I: Sock
J: Broccoli
K: Kerfuffle
L: Puppy
M: Walrus
N: Cactus
O: Armadillo
P: Malarkey
Q: Pinecone
R: Platypus
S: Kitten
T: Waffle
U: Shenanigan
V: Scrambled Egg
W: Sloth
X: Gecko
Y: Guacamole
Z: Flapjack

Take a spin around the globe to see ho...

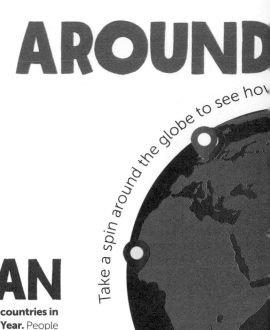

April 13–15, 2023

⚲ SONGKRAN

For three days, people in Thailand and other countries in Southeast Asia get wet to celebrate the New Year. People sprinkle water on statues of Buddha for good luck and on the hands of older relatives and friends as a sign of respect. It is a Buddhist tradition to drizzle water on people; it symbolizes rinsing away the bad luck of the old year and starting over pure for the new one.

April 23, 2023

⚲ ST. GEORGE'S DAY

Legend has it that a knight named George killed a dragon to free the city of Silene, which is in modern-day Libya. For that feat of derring-do, George was made a saint and is honored not only in England, but in parts of Italy, Portugal, and Spain.

Do You Know That Dragon?
Match the dragon to the movie or book it appears in.

1. Toothless
2. Haku
3. Smaug
4. Maleficent
5. Mushu
6. Falcor
7. Draco
8. Hungarian Horntail

a. *Sleeping Beauty*
b. *Dragonheart*
c. *Spirited Away*
d. *Mulan*
e. *The Hobbit*
f. *How to Train Your Dragon*
g. *Harry Potter and the Goblet of Fire*
h. *The Neverending Story*

An Australian lizard

These real animals may have inspired the belief in dragons:
• Dinosaur fossils
• Nile crocodile
• Goanna
• Whales

THE WORLD

April 27
⚲ KONINGSDAG

Koningsdag means "King's Day," a Netherlands' national holiday that celebrates the birthday of King Willem-Alexander. Before it was King's Day, the holiday was called Queen's Day to honor the female rulers of the Netherlands. Dutch people celebrate by wearing orange and riding through Amsterdam's canals on boats.

Somalian Flag

Gabonese Flag

Nigerian Flag

April 27
⚲ INDEPENDENCE DAY

On this day, Sierra Leone celebrates its independence from Great Britain in 1961. Back then, the new nation unveiled its own flag, and today citizens are encouraged to wave it proudly.

Fly It High

Can you figure out the three colors of the Sierra Leone flag?

Clues:

1. The top stripe of the flag has a color found in the flags of both Nigeria and Gabon, but not in Somalia's flag.

2. The middle stripe has a color found in both the Nigerian and Somalian flags, but not in the Gabonese flag.

3. The bottom stripe has a color found in the flags of both Somalia and Gabon, but not in the Nigerian flag.

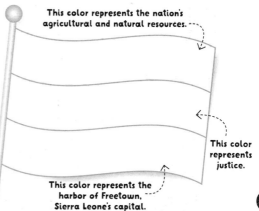

This color represents the nation's agricultural and natural resources.

This color represents justice.

This color represents the harbor of Freetown, Sierra Leone's capital.

97

SUNDAY	MONDAY	TUESDAY	WEDNESDAY
BIRTHSTONE EMERALD	**Mother Goose Day** Reread a favorite story, then write your own. **1**	**NATIONAL BABY DAY** In their first year, babies sleep 5,400 hours on average and use roughly 3,360 diapers. **2**	**Święto Konstytuc 3 Maja (Poland)** The Polish Parliament passed the country's Constitution on May 3, 1791. Today, Poles celebrate with parades, concerts, and speeches.
NATIONAL TOURISM DAY Take time today to plan a vacation with your family! **7**	**No Socks Day** Free your toes! **8**	**National Sleepover Day** Break out the sleeping bags! **9**	*All aboard!* In 1869, a golden spike was driven into the tra at Promontory Summ Utah, to complete the first coast-to-coast railroad in the United States. **10**
MOTHER'S DAY **14**	**International Day of Families** Learn about families that may be different than yours. **15**	*"I'd like to thank the Academy . . ."* On this day in 1929, the first Academy Awards ceremony (also known as the Oscars) was held. **16**	*Off to see the Wiza* In 1900, the first cop *The Wonderful Wiz of Oz,* by L. Frank Ba was printed. **1**
National Waitstaff Day Restaurant servers work hard to give you a pleasant dining experience. Thank them and give them a big smile— and tip! **21**	**National Solitaire Day** Go old school—pick up a deck of cards. How many variations do you know? **22**	**World Turtle Day** **23**	**National Scaveng Hunt Day** **24**
National Brisket Day Grab the barbecue sauce and dig in! **28**	**MEMORIAL DAY** **29**	**National Water a Flower Day** Drink up! **30**	**National Macarc Day** **3**

MAY

International Firefighters' Day

...nk a brave firefighter ...day for their service.

4

CINCO DE MAYO

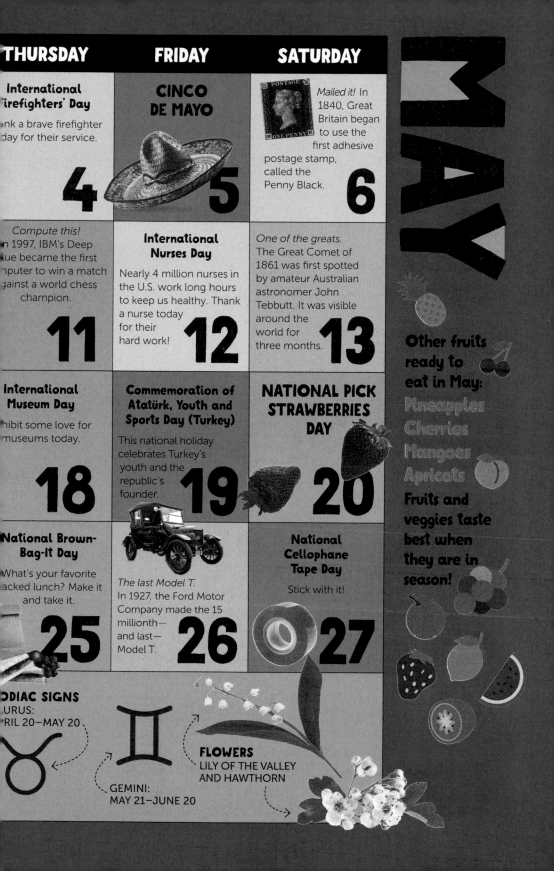

5

Mailed it! In 1840, Great Britain began to use the first adhesive postage stamp, called the Penny Black.

6

Compute this! ...n 1997, IBM's Deep ...ue became the first ...mputer to win a match ...ainst a world chess champion.

11

International Nurses Day

Nearly 4 million nurses in the U.S. work long hours to keep us healthy. Thank a nurse today for their hard work!

12

One of the greats. The Great Comet of 1861 was first spotted by amateur Australian astronomer John Tebbutt. It was visible around the world for three months.

13

International Museum Day

...hibit some love for ...museums today.

18

Commemoration of Atatürk, Youth and Sports Day (Turkey)

This national holiday celebrates Turkey's youth and the republic's founder.

19

NATIONAL PICK STRAWBERRIES DAY

20

National Brown-Bag-It Day

What's your favorite ...acked lunch? Make it and take it.

25

The last Model T. In 1927, the Ford Motor Company made the 15 millionth— and last— Model T.

26

National Cellophane Tape Day

Stick with it!

27

Other fruits ready to eat in May:

Pineapples
Cherries
Mangoes
Apricots

Fruits and veggies taste best when they are in season!

...ODIAC SIGNS

...URUS:
...RIL 20–MAY 20

GEMINI:
MAY 21–JUNE 20

FLOWERS

LILY OF THE VALLEY AND HAWTHORN

Kalpana Chawla

ASIAN/PACIFIC AMERICAN HERITAGE MONTH

Pay tribute to the generations of Asian/Pacific Americans who have uplifted American history, society, and culture. Match each person to their historic accomplishment.

1. At 17, she was the youngest woman to win a snowboarding gold medal, at the 2018 Winter Olympics in PyeongChang.

2. At the age of 21, this architect and sculptor designed the Vietnam Veterans Memorial in Washington, D.C.

3. This actor was the first Asian American to play a major character on an American TV show, as the original Mr. Sulu on *Star Trek*.

4. This two-time Olympian is the most-decorated figure skater in U.S. history.

5. This Pulitzer Prize–winning journalist, filmmaker, and immigration activist was born in the Philippines and raised in the U.S.

6. This Olympic gold medalist, who was considered the greatest freestyle swimmer in the world, helped popularize surfing.

7. An advocate for equal rights, this lawyer and politician was the first woman of color and the first Asian American elected to Congress.

8. This astronaut was the first Indian American woman to go into space.

The U.S. Pacific Islands region includes our 50th state, Hawaii, as well as the territories of Guam, the Commonwealth of the Northern Mariana Islands, the Republic of the Marshall Islands, the Federated States of Micronesia, the Republic of Palau, and American Samoa.

George Takei

Michelle Kwan

Patsy Mink

Chloe Kim

Duke Kahanamoku

Jose Antonio Vargas

Maya Lin

NATIONAL STRAWBERRY MONTH

SWEET STRAWBERRY PIZZA

1. Line a large baking sheet with parchment paper.

2. Have an adult preheat the oven to 375°F.

3. Stretch or roll 12 ounces of fresh **pizza dough** into a large oval and place it on the baking sheet.

4. Brush the dough with 2 tablespoons of unsalted, melted **butter**.

5. Slice 10–12 **strawberries** and arrange them on top. Combine 2 tablespoons **sugar** and ⅛ teaspoon **cinnamon** and sprinkle it over the pizza.

6. Bake the pizza for 20–25 minutes or until the dough is golden and the strawberries begin to bubble.

Ask for an adult's help with anything sharp or hot.

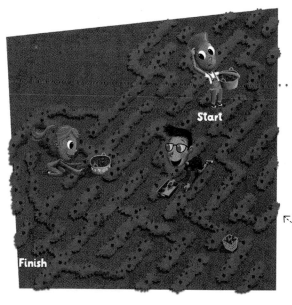

STUCK IN THE STRAWBERRIES

Help Carter find his way out of the strawberry field.

Start

Finish

INTERNATIONAL
DRUM MONTH

Drums have been played for centuries all over the world. Early drums were sections of hollowed tree trunks covered at one end with reptile, fish, or other animal skins. Today, drum "skins" are usually made of a plastic called *Mylar*.

The oldest drum was found in China. Made from clay and alligator hides, it dates back as early as **5500 BCE**.

The largest drum—**18 feet 2 inches in diameter, 19½ feet tall, and weighing 15,432 pounds**—was created in South Korea in 2011. The drum is a traditional Korean CheonGo drum.

crash cymbal · ride cymbal · snare drum · hi-hat cymbals · high tom · mid tom · floor tom · bass drum · drum throne (seat)

DRUM MATCH

Match each of these drums to its region of origin.

1. Adufe
2. Bodhrán
3. Conga
4. Djembe
5. Pandeiro
6. Steel Pan
7. Taiko

A. Brazil
B. Cuba
C. Ireland
D. Japan
E. Portugal
F. Trinidad and Tobago
G. West Africa

ANIMAL ACTS

• **Rabbits, kangaroo rats, and other rodents** use their paws to drum the ground, warning others of approaching predators.

• **Palm cockatoos** of Australia break off a stick or seedpod, hold it in their feet, and rap against a hollow tree branch to attract a mate.

• **Macaque monkeys** drum objects to show strength. The louder the drumming, the bigger and stronger the macaque probably is.

NATIONAL PET MONTH

What odd, weird, or wacky things can you find in this pet shop?

More than 63 million households own dogs. More than 42 million have cats. And 6 out of 10 households have more than one pet. Circle sets of four emojis together that have two cats and two dogs. One side of each square must touch a side of another square in the same set. You are done when all the squares are circled.

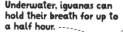
Dogs keep cool by panting. They also sweat through their foot pads.

Cats can spend up to half their awake time grooming themselves.

A goldfish named Tish lived 43 years. It was won at a fair in 1956.

Underwater, iguanas can hold their breath for up to a half hour.

A group of ferrets is called a *business*.

Christopher Columbus brought back two parrots as pets for Queen Isabella when he returned from his journey to the Americas.

Pigs are really clean animals and only roll in the mud to cool off. They're also smarter than other pets.

What did the cat say when the dog ran away from home?

"This is the best dog-gone day ever!"

Where do cats and dogs go on vacation?

Pets-ylvania

May 20, 1873

150 YEARS AGO, LEVI STRAUSS AND JACOB DAVIS PATENTED DENIM PANTS WITH METAL RIVETS—WHAT WE CALL JEANS TODAY.

Businessman Strauss and tailor Davis went in together on the patent. Davis had the idea to use metal rivets to hold denim fabric together to make more durable work pants. Strauss sold Davis the fabric to make this revolutionary piece of clothing. Since then, blue jeans have grown to be a favorite of people all over the world.

LAUNDRY DAY

Jeans, T-shirts, socks . . . they all have to get cleaned. But socks have a mysterious way of disappearing! Head to this laundromat and see if you can find the 20 missing socks hidden in this scene.

Denim originated in Nimes, France—which is where the fabric got its name. The French words *de Nimes* mean "of Nimes" in English.

A MESSY MAZE

Carly has left her favorite pair of jeans, as well as some other items, on her floor. Can you help her get to her laundry basket so she can tidy her room?

May 3 is National Textiles Day. It's a great day to learn about the history of other fabrics!

May 29, 1953

70 YEARS AGO, EDMUND HILLARY AND TENZING NORGAY WERE THE FIRST PEOPLE TO REACH THE TOP OF MOUNT EVEREST.

Edmund Hillary

Tenzing Norgay

At 29,032 feet above sea level, the top of Mount Everest is one of the highest points on Earth. The journey up this hulking peak is dangerous—climbers must deal with little oxygen, intense cold, and the threat of avalanches.

TEN YEARS AFTER Hillary and Norgay's historic climb, James Whittaker became the first American to summit Mount Everest.

These kids are making a climb of their own—although the wall they're scaling isn't quite as tall or treacherous as Mount Everest!

Can you find all 14 objects hidden in the scene?

banana

pencil

teacup

mushroom

ice-cream cone

bird

turtle

artist's palette

wedge of orange

toothbrush

bean

jellyfish

lemon

eggplant

May 6, 2023

KENTUCKY DERBY

Every first Saturday in May since 1875, the Churchill Downs racetrack in Lexington, Kentucky, has hosted a special Thoroughbred-horse race, the Kentucky Derby. The Derby is the first of three races known as the Triple Crown of Racing, which also includes the Preakness Stakes race and the Belmont Stakes race. **What do the horses in each row—down, across, and diagonally—have in common?**

HATS ON!

Since the 1960s, spectators at the Kentucky Derby have been known for their fancy hats.

What would your Kentucky Derby hat look like? Draw it here.

May 28, 2023

INDY 500

Called the "Greatest Spectacle in Racing," this competition at the Indianapolis Motor Speedway takes place on the last Sunday of May. Thirty-three drivers zoom 200 laps around a 2½-mile track for a total of 500 miles.

Which things in this picture are silly? It's up to you!

In 2013, Tony Kanaan had the fastest average winning speed: **187.433 MPH.** He had the fastest time, too: 2 hours, 40 minutes, and 3.4181 seconds.

INDY TRADITIONS

Drink the Milk: Three-time Indianapolis 500 winner Louis Meyer drank a glass of buttermilk after winning the 1936 race. Except for the years between 1947 and 1955, a bottle of milk has been presented to the winner ever since.

The first Indy 500, in 1911, took winner Ray Harroun **6 HOURS, 42 MINUTES.**

Kiss the Bricks: The Speedway became known as "the Brickyard" after it was paved with 3.2 million paving bricks in 1909. Later, asphalt was laid over the track, except for one yard of brick at the start-finish line. After NASCAR champion Dale Jarrett won a race in 1996, he knelt down and kissed the Yard of Bricks. Now other winners do it, too.

NATIONAL CARTOONISTS DAY

Today marks the first appearance of a newspaper comic strip: *Hogan's Alley*, created by Richard Felton Outcault in 1895. This Sunday comic featured Mickey Dugan, known as the Yellow Kid, who starred in various versions of the strip until January 1898.

Find the funny! Write a caption for each cartoon.

How to Draw a Grumpy Cartoon Bear

1. Start with a circle for the skull. Draw a large oval behind it for the jaw. Add the nose.

2. Define the snout by drawing a circle around the nose. Add eyes.

3. Draw a downturned mouth and slanting eyebrows. Don't forget ears!

4. Flatten the top of the head a little bit. Finish up with a furry coat and other details. Ta-da!

Do cartoons make you laugh? Good news— **WORLD LAUGHTER DAY** is the first Sunday in May. Try laughing in a different language. Instead of texting *hahaha*, type *55555* (Thai, because 5 is pronounced "ha"), *jajaja* (Spanish), or *MDR* (French for *mort de rire*—"dying of laughter").

May 7 is **FREE COMIC BOOK DAY!** On the first Saturday in May, participating comics stores around the world give away at least one FREE book to anyone who visits.

The longest-running newspaper comic in history is *The Katzenjammer Kids*. The main characters, Hans and Fritz, have been getting into cartoon trouble since 1897.

Bake a giant chocolate-chip cookie.
Roll out cookie dough into one pizza-sized cookie!

Create doodles from ink fingerprints.

May 30

Do stuff with tiny stones.
Pile them high, paint them, create a drawing around them, or use them as the pieces in a game of jacks.

NATIONAL CREATIVITY DAY

Today is the day to try something new. Tap into your creative side and create something special. Here are some ideas to get you started!

Draw a chameleon!
What color will you make it?

Vtrsyr s vpfr
That's "Create a code" in code (if you shift your hands to the right on a keyboard to type it).

What kind of code will you make up?

Dance it out!
Make up a dance move that uses only your legs. Then make up one that uses only your arms. What do they look like when you put them together?

Do a new hairdo.
With permission, use gel or a styling tool to give yourself a different hairstyle. Then name it.

109

May 11
EAT WHAT YOU WANT DAY

Grab your favorite snack to celebrate today. Then solve this food puzzle! These food phrases and pictures are all mixed up. **Can you match each food with the correct phrase?**

1. **The**  **of my eye.**

2. **A couch** .

3. **Like two** **in a pod.**

4. **As cool as a** .

5. **Don't cry over spilled** .

6. **One smart** .

7. **Don't put all your** **in one basket.**

8. **Spill the** .

9. **Bigger** **to fry.**

10. **The big** .

May 17
WORLD BAKING DAY

HOMEMADE BROWNIES

1. Have an adult preheat the oven to 350°F. Spray a 9-inch baking pan with nonstick cooking spray.
2. In a large bowl, mix together 1 cup **sugar**, 1/3 cup **unsweetened cocoa powder**, 1/2 cup **flour**, 1/4 teaspoon **baking powder**, and 1/4 teaspoon **salt**.
3. Add 1/2 cup melted **butter**, 2 **eggs**, and 1 teaspoon **vanilla extract**. Stir until well blended. Optional: Fold in 1/4 cup **mini chocolate chips**,
4. 1/4 cup **mini marshmallows**, and 1/4 cup finely chopped **pecans**. Spread the mixture in the prepared pan.
5. Bake 20–25 minutes, or until a toothpick put in the center comes out clean.
6. Cool in the pan on a wire rack, then cut into squares. Recipe makes 16 brownies.

Ask for an adult's help with anything sharp or hot.

NATIONAL HAMBURGER DAY

Ground-beef-and-onion patties cooked up by immigrants in the U.S. were named after the German city of Hamburg. "Hamburg steak" was served in New York restaurants as early as 1837. Build your own buns puns by using the picture code to fill in the letters and finish these three jokes.

Can't get enough beef on a bun? May is also National Hamburger Month!

Americans eat about **13 BILLION BURGERS** each year—enough to circle Earth 32 times!

A	B	C	E	I	K	L	M	P	T	Y

What did Mr. and Mrs. Hamburger name their daughter?

__ __ __ __ __

The record for the largest hamburger weighs in at more than **2,566 POUNDS**, set in Pilsting, Germany, in 2017.

How do you make a hamburger laugh?

__ __ __ __ __ __ __ !

What kind of dance does a hamburger go to?

__ __ __ __ __ __ __

TOP THIS!

A food-ordering app reports America's top burger toppings in this order:

Condiments
1. Mayo
2. Ketchup
3. Mustard

Cheeses
1. American
2. Cheddar
3. Swiss
4. Provolone
5. Pepper Jack

Add-ons
1. Pickles
2. Tomatoes
3. Lettuce
4. Onions
5. Bacon

What do you like on your burger?

THE FRIED ONION BURGER DAY FESTIVAL is held every year on the first Friday and Saturday in May in El Reno, Oklahoma. Chefs cook up the world's largest hamburger topped with fried onions. The current record holder is an 850-pound burger—complete with a massive bun and heaps of onions—measuring 8½ feet across.

May 5
CINCO DE MAYO

Today marks Mexico's victory over an invading French army in the Battle of Puebla in 1862. In the U.S., Cinco de Mayo (*Fifth of May*) spotlights Mexican heritage and culture with parties, parades, piñatas, and plenty of *deliciosa* food. Although it's a pretty minor holiday in Mexico, it became an official U.S. holiday in 2005, to celebrate Mexican culture and heritage.

MOLE POBLANO, a sauce containing chili pepper, chocolate, and spices, is the official dish of Cinco de Mayo.

Cinco de Mayo is NOT Mexico's Independence Day. That's September 16.

Match these Spanish words with their English translations.

1. La familia
2. El amigo
3. La fiesta
4. El país
5. El desfile
6. La comida

A. Friend
B. Country
C. Food
D. Family
E. Parade
F. Party

MINI PIÑATAS

1. For each piñata, collect four short **paper tubes**. For legs, cut two of the tubes in half. **Tape** the legs to a full-sized tube. If you like, fill the tubes with **wrapped candy** (or leave them empty and use the mini piñata as a table decoration). Tape over the ends.

2. For the head, cut off the end of the fourth tube and tape it back on sideways, as shown. Tape the head to the body.

3. Wrap the piñata with **masking tape**. Shape ears from the tape.

4. Cover the piñata with **crepe-paper strips**. Add **wiggle eyes**.

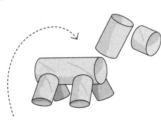

Although piñatas are most commonly associated with Mexico, they may be Chinese in origin. In the 14th century, the tradition of smashing clay pots came to Europe. The Italians called it *pignatta*, meaning "earthenware cooking pot." In the 16th century, Europeans brought the tradition to Mexico, although Mayans and Aztecs had previously decorated clay pots with feathers to be broken. Today, piñatas are made from paper and cardboard rather than clay pots, for safety.

May 14, 2023
MOTHER'S DAY

In 1868, Ann Jarvis tried to establish "Mother's Friendship Day" between mothers on both sides of the Civil War. But it was her daughter, Anna Jarvis, who was able to convince President Woodrow Wilson to sign a bill in 1914 recognizing Mother's Day as a national holiday, celebrated on the second Sunday in May.

BOUQUET BANNER FOR MOM

1. From **cardstock**, cut out flowers, leaves, three triangle shapes, and the letters M, O, M.

2. Decorate them with **glitter glue**, **craft gems**, and **markers**.

3. Glue a letter and a bouquet to each triangle. **Tape** them to a long piece of **ribbon**.

MOM MATCH

Every year, about 113 million Mother's Day cards are sent. Match each card to the baby animal that sent it.

Mother's Day is celebrated in nearly 50 countries, though some on different days. The United States, Italy, Australia, Belgium, Denmark, Finland, and Turkey all celebrate it on the second Sunday of May.

Anna Jarvis hated how commercialized Mother's Day had become by the 1920s, and she tried to get people to stop buying flowers, cards, and other gifts.

I really look up to you, Mama!

Mommy, you really bring me out of my shell!

To my mother, who makes our den such a cozy place!

Ewe really raise the baaaa, Maaaa!

Even though I'm in a great school now, I'll always be your small fry, Mom!

MAY DAY

People have celebrated May Day for thousands of years. Giving bouquets of wildflowers (often anonymously) and dancing around a maypole decorated with streamers are two May Day traditions. The celebration welcomes spring and new life. Get in the May Day spirit with these flower puzzles. Then go outside and enjoy real-life flowers.

JUMBLED FLOWERS

Unscramble each set of letters to get the name of a flower.

YILL __ __ __ __

LITUP __ __ __ __ __

ICALL __ __ __ __ __ __

LOVEIT __ __ __ __ __ __

FADIFOLD __ __ __ __ __ __ __ __

FLOWER OR NOT?

Each pair of words has one flower and one faker. **Circle the flowers.**

Bluebell **or** Barbell?

Snapdragon **or** Snickerdoodle?

Chrysalis **or** Chrysanthemum?

Rhododendron **or** Rapscallion?

Gladiolus **or** Gondola?

Clementine **or** Clematis?

Hydra **or** Hydrangea?

Foxglove **or** Bearclaw?

Scotland's national flower is the thistle. Legend says it became the national flower after saving the lives of an army of Scots. Invading Vikings stepped on the poky plants and yelled in pain, waking the Scottish warriors and giving them time to escape.

In Hawaii, May 1 is called LEI DAY. On this day, people honor the custom of weaving and wearing flower leis.

COUNT THE CODE

Count the number of petals on a flower. Then write the matching code letter in the center of the flower. Fill in the rest of the flowers to find the answer to this riddle.

WHAT DID THE DOG DO AFTER HE SWALLOWED A FIREFLY?

KEY

3 - E	9 - K
4 - D	10 - A
5 - I	11 - T
6 - R	12 - B
7 - H	13 - W
8 - G	14 - L

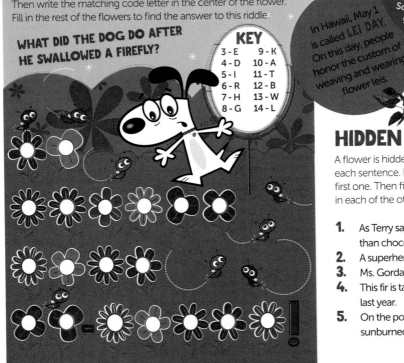

HIDDEN FLOWERS

A flower is hidden in the letters of each sentence. Find **ASTER** in the first one. Then find a different flower in each of the others.

1. As Terry says, vanilla is better than chocolate.
2. A superhero seldom fails.
3. Ms. Gorda is your new teacher.
4. This fir is taller than it was last year.
5. On the porch, I don't get sunburned.

MEMORIAL DAY

Originally called Decoration Day, Memorial Day is a day to remember soldiers and their sacrifices. The first national celebration took place in 1868 at Arlington National Cemetery. Today, many towns celebrate with a parade to honor and remember soldiers.

SEARCHING FOR STARS

Mark is making a wreath for Memorial Day. Can you find 11 extra stars hidden in the scene around the wreath?

POPPY POWER

*In Flanders fields the **poppies** blow*

Between the crosses, row on row,

That mark our place; and in the sky

The larks, still bravely singing, fly

Scarce heard amid the guns below.

—FROM "IN FLANDERS FIELDS"

Lieutenant Colonel John McCrae, a Canadian doctor, wrote the poem quoted above on May 3, 1915, while treating soldiers on the battlefields of Flanders in Belgium during World War I. His poem inspired a Georgia schoolteacher, Moina Belle Michael, in 1919 to wear and hand out red silk poppies in soldiers' honor. Today, American Legion volunteers distribute more than 2.5 million red crepe-paper poppies each year, with donations used to assist veterans and military families.

MAKE A POPPY BOUQUET

Cut a flower from **red craft foam**. Hold a **black button** to the flower's center. Poke a **green fuzzy stick** through the back of the flower and thread it through the buttonholes. Poke it back through the flower. Twist the end around the stem. Fill a vase with your poppies.

SPACE DAY

The first Friday in May is all about future astronomers, astronauts, and out-of-this-world explorers. This day encourages kids to study science, technology, engineering, and math, so you can reach for the stars—and the planets!

ASTRONOMY is the study of space, the universe, and all the objects in them. Which three celestial objects can you spell from the letters in ASTRONOMY? What other words can you find?

See how stellar your knowledge of space is with this quiz.

1. Pluto is known as this.
   a. A dwarf planet
   b. A baby planet
   c. A puppy planet

2. Which planet is closest to the sun?
   a. Earth
   b. Venus
   c. Mercury

3. How much bigger is the sun's diameter than that of Earth's?
   a. 19 times bigger
   b. 109 times bigger
   c. 19 million times bigger

4. What are Saturn's rings made up of?
   a. Fiery gas
   b. Gold and diamonds
   c. Ice, dust, and rocks

5. What is a common nickname for Mars?
   a. The Red Planet
   b. The Green Planet
   c. E.T.'s Home Planet

6. What year did astronauts first walk on the moon?
   a. 1949
   b. 1969
   c. 1999

KIDS' SCIENCE QUESTIONS

How do astronomers discover other galaxies?

Astronomer Dr. Ken Croswell says the trick is to find the galaxies among the many objects in the sky. If an object shows as a point of light, it's probably a star, not a galaxy. If the object looks like a pinwheel, it's a galaxy. Each galaxy is made up of many stars swirling around, so only a galaxy can take this swirly shape. If the object is a fuzzy patch whose light is moving faster than 500 kilometers per second, then it's probably a galaxy. It can't be part of our galaxy because it's moving too fast for our galaxy to hold it. So, if it's that far away and still bright enough to see, it's probably another galaxy. But astronomers still make mistakes. If the galaxy is compact, they may think, at first, that it's a star!

Halley's Comet passes by Earth only every 75 to 76 years. The last time was 37 years ago. So, get ready for the next sighting—in **2062!**

May 26
NATIONAL PAPER AIRPLANE DAY

Test out the aerodynamic skills of this aerobatic airplane.

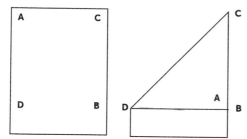

1 Put the paper down on a surface, as shown. Fold corner *A* down to meet *B* so the edges line up.

2 Fold *C* down to *D* so the paper looks like this.

3 Fold *E* down toward *F*.

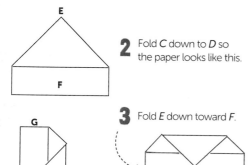

4 Turn the paper clockwise. Fold *H* up to *G* so the edges line up.

5 To make wings, fold down the top layer along the dotted line *I*. Turn the paper over and fold down in the same way.

6 To make the wing tips, fold the wings up about a quarter of an inch, as shown by the dotted lines.

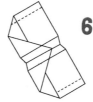

7 Fold the tail in at an angle, as shown by the arrow and dotted lines.

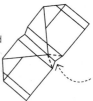

8 Give it a test flight. Grip the bottom of the plane and throw it hard. The plane will glide in large circles.

KIDS' SCIENCE QUESTIONS

How do airplanes stay in the sky?

The key to keeping an airplane flying is the wings. As the jet engines or propellers move the plane forward, the wing splits the air. Some air flows fast over the wing and the rest flows under it slowly.

Here is where the experts disagree. Some say that the faster flow of air over the wing lowers the air pressure above it. Then the higher pressure of the slow-moving air underneath pushes upward on the wing.

But other scientists say the explanation is simpler than that: The plane flies because the wing is set at an angle that pushes downward on the air.

May 8
NO SOCKS DAY

Can't decide on a pair to wear? Free up your toes and your laundry load by going without socks. But first help Henry find a match for each of the socks numbered 1 through 7. *P.S. Henry: May 10 is Clean Up Your Room Day.*

May 13
NATIONAL FROG JUMPING DAY

Mark Twain's famous short story "The Celebrated Jumping Frog of Calaveras County," published in 1865, inspired this special day.

Three friends have entered their frogs in the annual Calaveras jumping contest. Using the clues provided, can you figure out whose frog is whose and what place each frog took in the contest?

Use the chart to keep track of your answers. Put an X in each box that can't be true and an O in boxes that match.

	Tad	Pollie	Hoppy	1st	2nd	3rd
Jordan						
Skyler						
Riley						

1. Jordan's frog finished after Hoppy.
2. Skyler's frog finished before Riley's frog and Pollie.
3. Tad finished second.

May 18
INTERNATIONAL MUSEUM DAY

Dina is visiting the National History Museum to see her favorite carnivore: *T. rex.*
Help her by finding a clear path from **START** to **FINISH**. Don't get lost in the crowd!

May 24
NATIONAL SCAVENGER HUNT DAY

Grab a friend and try out these scavenger hunts that are easy to do close to home. See who can collect all of the objects first.

5 SENSORY SCAVENGER HUNTS

1. Taste 5 foods you've never tried before.
2. Look for 5 objects around your house that are the same color.
3. Feel 5 objects that each have a different texture.
4. Sniff out 5 unique smells outside.
5. Listen for 5 different sounds in your home.

SCAVENGE FOR 7 SOMETHINGS

A LEAF
SOMETHING ROUND
A BOOK WITH MORE THAN 200 PAGES
A BRUSH
SOMETHING SMOOTH
A TOY WITH WHEELS
SOMETHING WITH SPOTS

For an added challenge, think of seven more items to hunt for!

Take a spin around the globe to see how

Many countries celebrate Labor Day with parades like this one, held in Belgium.

May 1

LABOR DAY

In the United States and Canada, Labor Day falls in September. But for roughly 90 other countries, the day to celebrate workers is May 1. Several Asian, European, South American, and African countries remember their workers on this day and celebrate the rights that they have.

May 5

KODOMO NO HI

In Japan, *Kodomo no Hi*, or Children's Day, is all about wishing kids health and happiness. Carp streamers made from brightly colored paper or cloth, called *koinobori*, are hung from the rooftops and public buildings as a symbol of children's determination and strength.

Japanese Carp Kite

1. For the body, cut a vase shape from a **paper bag**. Tape a **fuzzy stick** to the body's widest part. Leave 1 inch of the fuzzy stick hanging off each edge.

2. For scales, cut up **cupcake liners** and glue them to the narrow part of the body. Use pieces of **coffee filters** for the tail and fins.

3. Decorate the head with **colored paper**.

4. Punch two holes in the head and tie **yarn** through them for a hanger. Twist the ends of the fuzzy stick together.

Carp, or koi fish, are thought to be strong and spirited, overcoming all obstacles to swim upstream.

THE WORLD

people around the world celebrate in May.

May 9
○ VICTORY DAY

This Russian holiday marks Nazi Germany's surrender to the Soviet Union in 1945. It honors the millions of people who lost their lives in World War II, known in Russia as the Great Patriotic War. Military parades are held in major cities, with the largest one in Moscow's Red Square. It ends with fireworks displays set off in 15 parks around the city. **Can you find where the three jigsaw pieces fit into this photo of the Red Square fireworks?**

May 17
○ CONSTITUTION DAY

Norway's celebration of its independence in 1814 is known as *syttende mai* (seventeenth of May). But kids know it as a day when they can have as many *pølser med lompe* (hot dogs in a potato tortilla) and as much *is krem* (ice cream) as they like!

Norwegians eat as much as 10 times more ice cream on May 17 than on any other spring day.

SUNDAY	MONDAY	TUESDAY	WEDNESDAY

ZODIAC SIGNS
GEMINI: MAY 21–JUNE 20

CANCER: JUNE 21–JULY 22

BIRTHSTONES
PEARL, ALEXANDRITE, AND MOONSTONE

NATIONAL HUG YOUR CAT DAY 4

Hot-Air Balloon Day
The highest hot-air balloon flight reached 68,986 feet. 5

National Day (Sweden)
Swedes celebrate this day with special ceremonies welcoming new Swedish citizens. 6

National Oklahoma Day 7
Oklahoma is OK!

A wonder of the world. In 1770, explorer Captain James Cook discovered the Great Barrier Reef off the coast of Australia. His studies of the reef introduced the scientific community to this living marvel. 11

NATIONAL RED ROSE DAY 12

National Sewing Machine Day
A stitch in time . . . 13

FLAG DAY 14

FATHER'S DAY 18

National Watch Day
Got the time? 19

Vanilla Milkshake Day
Cool off with a refreshing treat. 20

FIRST DAY OF SUMMER 2

Was it called New Dominion back then? In 1788, Virginia became a state. 25

National Canoe Day
Grab a paddle. 26

NATIONAL ICE-CREAM CAKE DAY 27

EID AL-ADHA
begins at sunset. 28

THURSDAY	FRIDAY	SATURDAY

Say Something Nice Day

"u're the best!"

ve your style!"

glad you're friend!"

u're hilarious!"

1

National Rotisserie Chicken Day

Drumstick or white meat?

2

He really was walking on air. In 1965, Edward Higgins White II became the first American astronaut to walk in space.

3

WORLD OCEANS DAY

8

Oh boy, oh boy, oh boy. On this day in 1934, Donald Duck appeared for the first time.

9

National Ballpoint Pen Day

Jot down a note, story, or letter with your favorite pen.

10

asten your seatbelts! In 1921, Bessie Coleman was the first African American to receive a pilot's license.

15

Wheeeeee! In 1884, the first roller coaster in America opened.

16

Welcome home! In 1885, the Statue of Liberty arrived at New York Harbor after a long boat journey from France, where it was made.

17

Teacher's Day (El Salvador)

ive *una manzana* to your teacher today.

22

National Pink Flamingo Day

Try standing on one leg today.

23

Swim a Lap Day

Dive in!

24

International Mud Day

Make some mud pies to celebrate.

29

Don't look down! On this day in 1859, daredevil French acrobat Charles Blondin crossed Niagara Falls on a tightrope.

30

JUNE

FLOWERS
HONEYSUCKLE
AND
ROSE

NATIONAL OCEAN MONTH

What things look silly in this image? It's up to you!

TRUE or FALSE?

Which of these ocean facts are true and which are all wet? Circle T or F.

T F The ocean is home to most of Earth's plants and animals.

T F Whales have belly buttons.

T F The world's most active volcanoes are found beneath the Pacific Ocean.

T F A jellyfish's body is made up of water, sugar, and grape flavoring.

T F The seafloor of the Southern Ocean is lined with ceramic bathroom tile.

June 8 is World Oceans Day.

The United Nations says, "The purpose of the Day is to inform the public of the impact of human actions on the ocean, develop a worldwide movement of citizens for the ocean, and mobilize and unite the world's population on a project for the sustainable management of the world's oceans."

Why do seahorses like only salt water?

AHCHOOO!

Because pepper water makes them sneeze

Where did the whale play his musical instrument?

In the orca-stra

What kind of fish goes well with peanut butter?

Jellyfish

AFRICAN AMERICAN MUSIC APPRECIATION MONTH

African American musicians have created some of the most innovative music styles, such as jazz. Unscramble the names of musical instruments used in a New Orleans jazz band. Then copy the circled letters in order onto the blanks at the bottom of the page to answer the riddle.

1. JOBAN: __ __ __ __ ⃝

2. BOMTRONE: __ __ __ __ __ __ ⃝ __

3. BUTA: ⃝ __ __ __

4. XOOPHENSA: __ __ __ __ ⃝ __ __ __ __

5. TUPTREM: __ __ __ ⃝ __ __ __

6. CARLNITE: __ __ __ __ __ ⃝ __

7. IPNOA: __ ⃝ __ __ __

8. SURMD: __ ⃝ __ __ __

9. SABS: __ __ ⃝ __

10. ATGUIR: __ __ __ __ __ __

Why do farmers play soft jazz for their corn stalks?

It's easy ____ _____ _____.

NATIONAL CANDY MONTH

Cotton candy was called fairy floss until 1920.

M&M's are one of astronauts' favorite candies to bring to space.

Everyone knows candy is made with sugar. But did you know it can contain acid or oil, too? Try these two simple experiments to unlock the secrets inside your favorite candy.

ACID: Candy that tastes sour contains acid. Most fruit-flavored candy contains citric acid, the sour chemical in lemons. To test a sour candy for acid, try this:

• Dissolve the **candy** in a half-cup of **water**. (WARHEADS and SweeTARTS work well.)

• Sprinkle in a spoonful of **baking soda**.

• If you see bubbles, the candy water contains acid.

What's happening? Baking soda reacts with acid to form the gas carbon dioxide. The gas makes bubbles in the water.

bubbles

shiny puddles

OIL: Many kinds of chewy candy, like taffy, are made with oil. The oil helps keep the candy smooth, soft, and chewy. To test a chewy candy for oil, try this:

• Dissolve the **candy** in a cup of hot tap **water**. (Try Starburst candy.)

• Look for shiny puddles floating on the surface.

• When the water cools, you may see a white, waxy layer on top.

What's happening? The kinds of oils used in these candies melt in hot water, forming the shiny puddles. In colder water, the oil can cool into a white, waxy solid. Since oil is lighter than water, it floats.

NATIONAL FRESH FRUIT AND VEGETABLE MONTH

Can you spot a fruit or vegetable hiding in each sentence?
Example: The ship eased into port.

1. In the showroom, a car rotated on a platform.
2. Maya looked up each book Liam recommended.
3. The dog's bark alerted the cat.
4. "I'm getting a new bicycle Monday," said Darnell.
5. Adrianna gets up early every morning.
6. I bought a teapot at Oscar's sale.
7. Pete and his mom baked his teacher rye bread.
8. That clown can spin a chair on his hand.

GREAT OUTDOORS MONTH

Without showing this page to anyone, ask friends or family members for the words in parentheses. Then read the story out loud.

Today I went camping. I filled my backpack with _____ (PLURAL NOUN) and headed out. I enjoyed seeing nature, like the _____ (PLURAL NOUN) growing on a tree. Then I suddenly heard a noise! It sounded like an angry _____ (WILD ANIMAL). Or was it a _____ (TYPE OF MONSTER) from _____ (NEARBY TOWN)? I got my answer soon enough when I came face to face with a terrifying _____ (INSECT). Thinking quickly, I threw it some _____ (FOOD) and was lucky to escape with my life! I was feeling hungry, so I started roasting some _____ (PLURAL NOUN) on a stick when I heard another noise. Was it a herd of _____ (ADJECTIVE) _____ (PLURAL NOUN)? No, it was Mom on the back deck, calling my name. I happily ended my scary, _____ (ADJECTIVE) camping trip in the backyard and went in for dinner.

FISHING FOR HIDDEN WORDS

Celebrate by finding these six words (not pictures) in the scene. Can you find BOY, FISH, HOT, NICE, TREE, and WAVE?

TONGUE TWISTERS

The wretched runner ran around the rough and rugged rock.

A flabby flounder fouled Flanders's fishing feast.

The harried hiker helped heat the honeyed ham.

Floyd found a fish before Fran found a fish.

June 6, 1933
90 YEARS AGO, IN CAMDEN, NEW JERSEY, THE FIRST DRIVE-IN MOVIE THEATER OPENED.

Richard Hollingshead set up the first drive-in movie theater and called it Park-In Theaters. It cost 25 cents per car and 25 cents a person to watch a movie. Drive-in theaters became so popular that 5,000 of them popped up around the country over the next three decades.

There are lots of silly things happening at this drive-in theater. How many silly things do you see?

June 16, 1963

60 YEARS AGO, THE FIRST WOMAN TRAVELED TO SPACE.

Valentina Tereshkova, a cosmonaut from the Soviet Union (now Russia), launched into space in a capsule called Vostok 6. She spent nearly three days high above Earth, orbiting the planet a total of 48 times before coming back down.

This astronaut is out on a spacewalk. Can you find at least 17 differences between these two photos?

A COSMONAUT and an **ASTRONAUT** are very similar. The difference between them comes down to where they train. An astronaut is someone trained by NASA, the European Space Agency (ESA), the Canadian Space Agency (CSA), or the Japanese Aerospace Exploration Agency (JAXA). A cosmonaut, on the other hand, is trained by the Russian Space Agency.

What do astronauts use to brush their teeth?

Tooth-space

What do astronauts like to drink?

Gravi-tea

STAR PILOTS GAME

Want to play a game that's out of this world? First craft a space station and astronaut for the game. Then read the rules on how to play.

1. For the space station, decorate a short **cardboard tube** with **paint** and **markers**.

2. For a solar panel, cover a thin **cardboard rectangle** with **black paper**. Decorate it with a **silver marker**. Cut two slits in one end of the space station. Slide the solar panel into the slits.

For the astronaut, paint a **clothespin** white. After it dries, tie a **string** around its middle. **Tape** the other end of the string to the space station.

Glue **paper** arms and a head to the clothespin. Decorate the astronaut with markers.

TO PLAY: Player A holds the space station in the air with the tube opening facing Player B. Player B closes his or her eyes while holding the astronaut. Using the words *up, down, right, left, forward, back,* and *stop,* Player A helps Player B guide the astronaut safely back to the space station.

INTERNATIONAL DAY OF YOGA

Breathe in . . . breathe out. Take a few moments today to try some yoga stretches. Then look for the 16 objects hidden in this yoga studio.

Although we don't know exactly when yoga was invented, we do know its origin was in NORTHERN INDIA AT LEAST 5,000 YEARS AGO. Its purpose was to encourage physical, mental, and spiritual discipline.

magnet

candy corn

mitten

chocolate-chip cookie

ruler

baseball bat

toothbrush glove

recorder

comb

hat

snail

crescent moon

bowl

bow tie

fried egg

NATIONAL HOCKEY LEAGUE
STANLEY CUP FINAL

The Stanley Cup is named after Lord Stanley of Preston, the governor general of Canada in 1892. He bought the first cup for the league.

Take a shot at the correct answer and score a point for each one you get right.

1. **When ice hockey first began, what did players use for a puck?**
   a. A frozen hamburger patty
   b. A frozen patty of cow manure
   c. A crushed soda can

2. **What was the first hockey mask made of?**
   a. Leather
   b. Wood
   c. A carved pumpkin

3. **On September 23, 1992, how did goalie Manon Rhéaume make sports history?**
   a. Manon caught a puck blindfolded.
   b. Manon performed a figure skating routine during a game.
   c. Manon became the first woman to play in the NHL in a preseason game.

4. **What is written on the Stanley Cup?**
   a. Famous quotes by people named Stanley
   b. The names of the teams and players who have won the NHL championship
   c. The recipe for Stanley's Cup of Noodles soup

5. **When a hockey player scores three goals in a game, what do fans throw on the ice?**
   a. Hats
   b. Frozen fish sticks
   c. Hockey pucks

FINAL SCORE:

You scored _____ times!

A new Stanley Cup isn't made every year. The same cup is given to the championship's winning team for 100 days during the off-season.

CHAMPIONSHIP
CHAMPS

These teams have won the Stanley Cup the most times since the NHL took over the championship in 1927:

1. Montreal Canadiens

2. Toronto Maple Leafs

3. Detroit Red Wings

4. Boston Bruins

5. Chicago Blackhawks

Why did the hockey rink melt after the game?

Because all the fans left.

Why do hockey players make the best birthday cakes?

Because they know all about icing.

What did the hockey goalie say to the puck?

"Catch you later."

June 15
NATURE PHOTOGRAPHY DAY

Find the 16 objects hidden in this canyon photo.

fish   bird   crown   trowel   carrot   shoe   ice-cream cone   pencil

candle   mushroom   rocket   ladle   dog's bone   sock   toothbrush   bowling pin

PICTURE THIS!

Here are some tips for taking photos of animals.

- **Wait It Out:** Animals won't follow directions. You'll have to wait patiently to get a good shot.

- **Focus on the Eyes:** Humans often connect with others through eye contact, so focus on the animal's eyes or head.

- **Get Low:** Instead of pointing your camera downwards, kneel or lie down (from a safe distance) so you're on the animal's level.

- **Zoom In:** Close-up photos show a lot of detail about an animal's face, eyes, or fur. Use the camera's zoom feature to get a detailed photo.

- **Snap, Snap, Snap:** Don't expect every photo to be perfect. Photographers often take 100 pictures to end up with one they really like.

- **Practice!** To practice your skills, take plenty of pictures of pets, birds, or insects, or visit a zoo or aquarium.

National Camera Day is June 29!

June 21
WORLD MUSIC DAY

Melody's Music Shop is having a sale! Name the eight instruments on the sale wall, then unscramble their first letters to solve the riddle. We've placed the *A* for *acoustic guitar* in the correct spot to get you started.

Tongue Twisters for Singers

Singers often warm up their mouths, lips, and tongues with tongue twisters. How fast can you say these tricky phrases?

If Stu chews shoes, should Stu choose the shoes he chews?

Wayne went to Wales to watch walruses.

Four furious friends fought for the phone.

Six sleek swans swam swiftly southward.

Five frantic frogs fled from fifty fierce fishes.

June 2, 2023

NATIONAL DOUGHNUT DAY

Each doughnut has an exact match—
except one. Can you find it?

June 10

NATIONAL HERBS AND SPICES DAY

Spice up your day with this word search. **Can you find all 18 of these popular herbs and spices?**

WORD LIST

ALLSPICE
ANISE
BASIL
CARDAMOM
CAYENNE PEPPER
CHIVES
CINNAMON
CURRY
DILL
FENNEL
NUTMEG
OREGANO
PAPRIKA
PARSLEY
SAFFRON
SAGE
THYME
TURMERIC

```
R  E  P  P  E  P  E  N  N  E  Y  A  C  P  E
A  U  N  H  K  L  S  Q  A  G  X  Y  S  C  A
B  N  L  S  E  K  M  E  H  D  Y  O  I  N  K
X  A  A  N  I  S  E  Y  V  R  T  P  G  O  I
C  G  S  D  I  L  L  F  R  I  S  K  R  M  R
E  M  E  I  T  X  U  U  E  L  H  B  V  A  P
S  C  E  G  L  C  C  V  L  N  D  C  O  N  A
A  I  B  R  C  J  A  A  N  H  N  Q  N  N  P
F  R  V  Z  A  P  L  C  U  K  C  E  J  I  V
F  E  E  R  R  V  Y  S  T  T  V  T  L  C  X
R  M  H  M  D  Y  O  R  M  Q  B  F  W  S  U
O  R  I  P  A  R  S  L  E  Y  T  X  Z  H  T
N  U  Y  Y  M  O  N  A  G  E  R  O  J  Q  G
N  T  B  L  O  Y  J  K  P  Y  E  M  Y  H  T
S  Q  U  J  M  F  T  O  B  B  W  I  N  H  Q
```

Celebrate more delicious foods with these four holidays.

June 11

NATIONAL CORN ON THE COB DAY

A typical ear of corn has about 800 kernels.

June 21

NATIONAL SMOOTHIE DAY

Mashed beans will make a smoothie thicker without adding any bean flavor.

June 22

NATIONAL ONION RING DAY

Americans eat an average of 22 pounds of onions per person per year.

June 26

NATIONAL CHOCOLATE PUDDING DAY

The first known recipe for chocolate pudding appears in a cookbook from 1730.

FATHER'S DAY

Make a card for your father or someone you'd like to celebrate on Father's Day.

GOLF BAG

1. For the golf bag, cover a **short cardboard tube** with **paper**. Add a handle.

2. For golf clubs, bend one end of three **fuzzy sticks** and cover each with **foil**. Glue the clubs into the golf bag.

3. Fold **cardstock** in half to make a card. Glue on the golf bag. Add a paper flag and a message.

LAWN MOWER

1. Fold **cardstock** in half to make a card.

2. Use **paper** to cover a **small box** (such as a raisin box). Add a message. Glue it to the front of the card.

3. **Tape** on paper wheels, a strip of paper "grass," and a **fuzzy-stick** handle.

4. Add a message on the "grass" inside.

BARBECUE

1. Fold **cardstock** in half to make a card.

2. For the grate, glue **fuzzy sticks** across the front.

3. Add **paper** food and handles.

4. Write a message on paper inside.

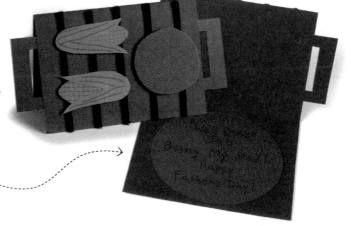

FLAG DAY

Flag Day celebrates the official adoption of the stars and stripes by the Second Continental Congress on June 14, 1777. Flag Day was first celebrated in 1885 at the Stony Hill School, a one-room school in Waubeka, Wisconsin.

MAKE RED, WHITE, AND BLUE NACHOS

Before you begin, ask an adult to set the oven to broil.

1. Open and spread a 6-ounce bag of **blue tortilla chips** evenly on a 9-by-13-inch pan.

2. Spoon 1 cup **salsa** over the chips.

3. Sprinkle 1 cup shredded **white cheddar cheese** on top. Add toppings, such as **chopped tomatoes, sliced olives**, and **black beans**, if you'd like.

4. Ask an adult to broil the nachos for 3 minutes. Let stand for 3 minutes before eating.

ON JUNE 14, 1777, Congress decided the U.S. flag would have 13 stripes, alternating in red and white, plus 13 white stars in a blue field. The number 13 was chosen because there were 13 colonies.

After Vermont and Kentucky became the 14th and 15th states, the flag was changed to 15 stars and 15 stripes in 1795.

As new states joined the country, there wasn't enough room to keep adding stripes. So in 1818, Congress decided the flag would go back to 13 stripes and have one star for every state.

The arrangement of the 50 stars on today's flag was created by a high school student. Robert Heft of Ohio created the flag for a class project when Alaska and Hawaii were about to become states. He also sent his design to the White House. Heft got a B- on the project, but the teacher changed it to an A after President Eisenhower chose Heft's design as our new flag.

June 21, 2023

Kick off summer with these fun activities!

FIRST DAY

3 SUNNY-DAY CRAFTS

- **Create a suncatcher** using colored paper, yarn, and tissue paper.
- **Build a sculpture** using objects from nature.
- **Make your own bubble wands** from fuzzy sticks. Dip them in some bubble solution, and blow!

3 WAYS TO USE SIDEWALK CHALK

- **Create a story** just by drawing pictures.
- **Create a life-sized board game,** drawing the game spaces with chalk.
- **Write funny jokes** or cheerful messages on your sidewalk.

3 WATER BALLOON GAMES

- **Yard Toss.** Place four rulers (or other markers) at varying distances. See who can toss a water balloon the farthest without bursting it.
- **Exploding Tag.** Fill a few water balloons and set them aside. Instead of tagging another player, *It* lightly tosses a water balloon at that person (below the neck). If it doesn't pop, that person becomes *It*!
- **Balloon Bowling.** Use empty cans and plastic bottles as pins and a water balloon as the ball. Set the pins on a flat surface outdoors and see how many you can knock down.

For people in Australia, Argentina, and the rest of the Southern Hemisphere, today is the first day of winter.

The first day of summer is also called the summer solstice. It's the day with the most daylight hours in the Northern Hemisphere.

In northern Alaska, the sun never fully sets today, and in 1906, locals began celebrating by playing baseball in the midnight sun. The Alaska Goldpanners baseball team took over the tradition in 1960. Their annual summer solstice game starts at 10:30 p.m. and finishes by 2 a.m.—in the sunlight.

Be sure to throw away the pieces after the balloons pop!

OF SUMMER

$24
BUY THESE SANDALS GET GLASSES FREE!

$24 $10 OFF!

$20 $8 OFF!

$24 50% OFF!

Slip on your flip-flops on June 16— IT'S NATIONAL FLIP-FLOP DAY!

$20 50% OFF!

$20 BUY THESE GLASSES GET SANDALS FREE!

Summertime is beach time! Rey wants to buy one pair of sandals and one pair of sunglasses at Sally's Sea Store. Can you help her find the best deal?

WORLD REEF DAY

How well do you know coral reefs?
Take this quiz and find out!

1. The _____, off the coast of Australia, is the largest coral reef. It can be seen from space!
   a. Great Barrier Reef
   b. Colossal Coral Reef

2. Coral reefs make up less than 2 percent of the ocean floor, but scientists estimate that _____ of all ocean species depend on reefs for shelter and food.
   a. 5 percent
   b. 25 percent

3. A coral colony is made up of tiny, interconnected _____ that together secrete the coral's hard "skeleton."
   a. Parsnips
   b. Polyps

4. Zooxanthellae (zo-zan-THELL-ee) are . . .
   a. Algae that live in corals and give them food in exchange for a home.
   b. Underwater zoos that can be visited only by submarine.

5. True or false: Coral reefs grow where there are strong waves and currents.
   a. True. The waves and currents bring food to the reefs.
   b. False. Waves and currents would wash the reefs away.

6. Sharks, turtles, crabs, starfish, octopuses, and many other animals live in or visit coral reefs. Which animal does NOT visit coral reefs?
   a. Humpback whale
   b. Poison dart frog

7. Are corals plants or animals?
   a. Plants. They're relatives of seaweed.
   b. Animals. They're relatives of jellyfish and anemones.

8. True or false: The bright colors of some corals help protect them from the sun's rays— like the way sunscreen protects humans.
   a. True
   b. False

9. Pollution, overfishing, and rising ocean temperatures are threatening coral reefs. What's one thing scientists are doing to try to save them?
   a. Dumping ice cubes into the oceans to cool them down.
   b. Breeding super-strong corals that can survive the changes to their environment.

> What did the fish say to the coral reef?

> "You're my worst anemone."

DIVE IN!

The Great Barrier Reef is the world's largest coral reef. Lots of fish can be found in it—and so can lots of words! How many words can you make from the letters in

GREAT BARRIER REEF?

_____   _____   _____
_____   _____   _____
_____   _____   _____
_____   _____   _____

June 30
ASTEROID DAY

Asteroid Day marks the anniversary of the 1908 Tunguska impact, in which an asteroid hit the earth in Siberia, destroying 800 square miles of forest. The goal of Asteroid Day is education and awareness.

ORBITING A SPACE POTATO

Planets aren't the only bodies in space that can have moons orbiting them. The potato-shaped asteroid shown here, which is named **Ida** (EYE-duh), is just one of many asteroids massive enough to have their own moons. Gravity keeps Ida's moon, Dactyl (DACK-tull), going around the asteroid, just as Earth's gravity keeps our moon in orbit around us.

Dactyl is just 1 mile wide. Our moon is 2,160 miles wide!

Like most asteroids, Ida isn't round. It contains so little material that its gravity isn't strong enough to pull it into a sphere shape.

Craters on Ida and Dactyl were caused by smaller asteroids that hit their surfaces over time.

Ida and Dactyl are in the asteroid belt, between the orbits of Mars and Jupiter.

Dactyl orbits Ida the long way.

KIDS' SCIENCE QUESTIONS
What is the difference between an asteroid and a meteor?

Asteroids are sometimes called *minor planets*. They are fairly small, rocky worlds. Like Earth and the other planets, asteroids orbit around the sun. Most asteroids are in a "belt"—a group of orbiting paths that lie between Mars and Jupiter.

A *meteor* is a streak of light we see in the sky when a much smaller bit of rock enters Earth's atmosphere and burns from the heat of friction as it falls through the air.

Two other important terms are *meteoroid* and *meteorite*. A meteoroid is a bit of rock that could burn up to create a meteor—before it enters the atmosphere. Meteorites are much more unusual. A meteorite is any part of a meteoroid that hits Earth's surface because it has not been completely burned up during its fall.

Meteorite

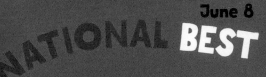

June 8
NATIONAL BEST DAY

How much do they know about you?

Answer these questions about yourself, then guess how a friend might answer them.
Have your friend do the same—then compare your answers!

1. How I'd spend the day if the power went out

3. The nickname I'd choose   4. My middle name   5. My favorite singer

7. A place I'd like to visit   8. My favorite team

9. My favorite foods

11. Something I do to make my friends laugh

12. Something I'm really good at   13. My favorite book

15. My favorite outdoor thing to do

16. My favorite color   17. Where I go when I want to be alone

19. The superpower I wish I had   20. Something I've always wanted

FUNNY FACE-OFF

Challenge one or more friends to this game of giggles!

IN ROUND ONE, take turns making funny faces.

IN ROUND TWO, take turns telling jokes or riddles.

IN ROUND THREE, take turns doing silly dances.

THE GOAL? Lots of laughs all around!

June 19
JUNETEENTH

On this day in 1865, a Union general announced to the people of Galveston, Texas, that slavery had been abolished in the United States, more than two-and-a-half years after the Emancipation Proclamation. The newly freed slaves in Texas erupted in a joyous celebration, and the event became known as Juneteenth.

Today people around the country celebrate this anniversary of the freedom from slavery with parades, festivals, and barbecues.

STRAWBERRY
BUBBLE LEMONADE

Put 1 cup **strawberries** into a blender. Blend until thick and smooth. Add 3 cups **lemonade** and 2 cups **seltzer**. Blend together and chill. Pour ¼ cup **maple syrup** onto one plate and 2 packs of **Pop Rocks** onto another. Dip the rims of 6 glasses into the maple syrup and then into the Pop Rocks. Add a few **ice cubes** to each glass and pour in the strawberry lemonade.

The color red is an important part of Juneteenth, and people eat and drink red foods, such as strawberry soda, hot sauce on barbecue, and red velvet cake.

June 27
NATIONAL
SUNGLASSES DAY

There are five pairs of sunglasses that match exactly in this beach scene. **Can you find them all?**

Reports suggest that someone in the U.S. loses, breaks, or sits on a pair of sunglasses every 14 minutes!

Take a spin around the globe to see how

June 12

⚲ DIA DOS NAMORADOS

Valentine's Day falls in February, but in Brazil the holiday honoring love is in June. *Dia dos Namorados* means "Boyfriend and Girlfriend's Day." Couples celebrate with cards, candy, and dinner.

These kids tangled up their balloon strings. Can you figure out whose is whose?

June 16

⚲ YOUTH DAY

South Africa's flag is unique in that it uses six main colors in the design.

Youth Day commemorates a protest by black students in South Africa in 1976.
At the time, the government discriminated against people who weren't white, and the students were peacefully protesting an unfair law. The police fired on the protesters and many students lost their lives. This terrible event eventually led to a change in the government. Today, South Africans honor those students on Youth Day by visiting museums, attending events about history, and by helping their communities.

THE WORLD

people around the world celebrate in June.

June 17
NATIONAL DAY

National Day in Iceland celebrates the country's independence from Denmark in 1944. In every town, a woman is chosen to read a poem or give a speech. She wears the national costume of Iceland, and many other people do, too. The whole country celebrates with parades, marching bands, carnivals, and concerts.

June 20
FLAG DAY

Día de la Bandera Nacional honors the flag of Argentina and the man who created it, Manuel Belgrano, a military leader who helped the country become independent from Spain. Every June 20, Argentina's president gives a speech and a big parade is held in the town where the flag was first flown.

The "Sun of May" was added to the flag in 1818, inspired by the sun on the first Argentine coin. It also honors an Incan sun deity, Inti.

The blue stripes are known as *celeste*, which means "sky blue."

Although Belgrano first raised the flag in 1812, it went through many variations until this official version was approved in 1861.

145

SUNDAY	MONDAY	TUESDAY	WEDNESDAY

ZODIAC SIGNS
CANCER:
JUNE 21–JULY 22

LEO:
JULY 23–AUGUST 22

BIRTHSTONE
RUBY

World UFO Day

Keep your eyes on the skies.

2

"We are the keepers of the flame of liberty." In 1986, after a two-year restoration, President Reagan lit the Statue of Liberty's torch in honor of its 100th anniversary.

3

INDEPENDENCE DAY

4

From books to billions. In 1994, Amazon.com was founded. It started as an online bookstore and has expanded into one of the most profitable businesses in the world.

5

National Sugar Cookie Day

Frosting, sprinkles, and lots of sugar—the recipe for a delicious cookie.

9

Don't Step on a Bee Day

10

World Population Day

The U.S. Census Bureau estimates there are 7.7 billion people on Earth.

11

NATIONAL EAT YOUR JELLO DAY

12

World Snake Day

Yesssssss.

16

There's a mouse in the house. In 1955, Disneyland opened in Anaheim, California.

17

NATIONAL SOUR CANDY DAY

18

Giving women a voice. In 1848, the first women's rights convention began in Seneca Falls, New York. One of their main goals was to get women the right to vote.

19

23
Gorgeous Grandma Day

Paperback Book Day
30

24
National Drive-Thru Day

National Mutt Day
31

Culinarians Day

From professional chefs to cooks in the home, today is a day to celebrate good food and the hard work put into making it.

25

It happened in a New York minute. In 1788, New York became the 11th state.

26

THURSDAY	FRIDAY	SATURDAY

JULY

FLOWERS
------ LARKSPUR AND WATER LILY

National Postal Worker Day

Deliver your thanks to your mail carrier.

1

Play ball!
In 1933, the first Major League Baseball All-Star Game was played.

6

Charge!
For one week, starting today, Pamplona, Spain, holds the Running of the Bulls as part of the San Fermin Festival (which begins on July 6).

7

National Video Game Day

Get your thumbs in shape.

8

International Rock Day

Don't take today for granite.

13

Far out!
In 2015, NASA's New Horizons probe became the first spacecraft to fly near Pluto.

14

National Give Something Away Day

Give something to someone less fortunate.

15

Summer is a great time to relax. How will you relax this month?

_____
_____
_____
_____
_____

ational Moon Day

What phase is the moon in today?

20

Liberation Day (Guam)

People celebrate with a carnival and parade with giant floats.

21

NATIONAL HAMMOCK DAY

22

National Walk on Stilts Day

How's the view up there?

27

NATIONAL SOCCER DAY

28

Global Tiger Day

Wear stripes today!

29

ICE CREAM MONTH

America's top 10 favorite ice-cream flavors are listed here. Can you crack the code and fill in their names? Each number stands for a different letter. Once you know one number's letter, you can fill in that letter in all the words.

We'll give you a hint—vanilla and chocolate take the first two spots!

1. __ __ __ __ __ __ __
   3 2 7 12 10 10 2

2. __ __ __ __ __ __ __ __ __
   8 1 11 8 11 10 2 19 6

3. __ __ __ __ __ __ __
   8 11 11 17 12 6 18
   __ __ __ __ __ __ __ __
   2 7 13 8 4 6 2 14

4. __ __ __ __
   14 12 7 19
   __ __ __ __ __ __ __ __ __
   8 1 11 8 11 10 2 19 6
   __ __ __ __
   8 1 12 9

5. __ __ __ __ __ __ __ __ __
   8 1 11 8 11 10 2 19 6
   __ __ __ __ __ __ __ __ __ __
   8 1 12 9   8 11 11 17 12 6
   __ __ __ __ __
   21 11 20 22 1

6. __ __ __ __ __ __   __ __ __ __ __
   5 20 19 19 6 4   9 6 8 2 7

7. __ __ __ __ __ __   __ __ __ __ __
   8 11 11 17 12 6   21 11 20 22 1

8. __ __ __ __ __ __ __ __ __
   18 19 4 2 16 5 6 4 4 15

9. __ __ __ __ __   __ __ __ __ __ __
   14 11 11 18 6   19 4 2 8 17 18

10. __ __ __ __ __ __ __ __ __ __
    7 6 2 9 11 10 12 19 2 7

This flavor is made up of #1, #2, and #8!

The average American eats more than 23 pounds of ice cream per year.

148

NATIONAL BERRY MONTH

July is also National Blueberry Month, National Blackberry Month, and National Raspberry Month. If you love berries, this is a great month for you!
Can you find the 22 hearts hiding in the fruit below?

The bumps on blackberries and raspberries are called *drupelets.*

TONGUE TWISTERS

Some berries will color your tongue, but these berry fun sentences will twist your tongue. Try saying each five times, fast!

Bumblebees pick black blueberries.

Barry's blueberry baklava beat Bob's blackberry bake at the bake-off.

Bridget's blueberry bucket is bigger than Brock's blueberry bucket.

WILD ABOUT WILDLIFE MONTH

With over 8.7 million wildlife species in the world, there's a lot to celebrate this month. Take some time to learn about a new animal or find out what animals live in your area.

JUMBLED ANIMALS

Unscramble each set of letters to get the name of a wild animal.

BRAZE   __ __ __ __ __

MELAC   __ __ __ __ __

ADNAP   __ __ __ __ __

TEACHHE   __ __ __ __ __ __

RAPLO RABE   __ __ __ __ __ __ __ __ __ __

GUESS WHO?

Can you figure out what these animals are?

LAND OR SEA?

Do you know which of these animals live on the land and which live in the water?

KOMODO DRAGON   STINGRAY
BRITTLESTAR   CHINCHILLA
ALPACA   BONGO
MANATEE   BARRACUDA

PENGUIN POSES

Most of the seventeen or so species of penguins live in the Southern Hemisphere. This group of emperor penguins is one of the seven or eight penguin species that make Antarctica their home. **Can you find 21 differences between these two photos?**

NATIONAL PARK AND RECREATION MONTH

This month was first celebrated in 1985!

It's a beautiful day at the park! But it looks like there are some silly shenanigans going down.
Can you spot what's silly?

PLASTIC FREE JULY

Water bottles, grocery bags, straws—too many plastic items are used only once and then thrown away. Plastic garbage is polluting the ground and turning up in rivers and oceans, where it's harming birds and fish.

Give the environment a break this month and stick with reusable water bottles, cloth tote bags, and paper straws. Try making it a habit that lasts past July.

Paper, cloth, and glass are reusable materials that are also reusable in this puzzle. Combine each word with one from the Word List to form a new word.

WORD LIST

back
dish
eye
hour
table
weight

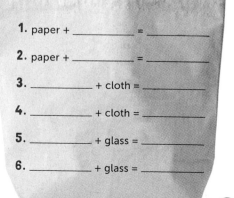

1. paper + _____ = _____
2. paper + _____ = _____
3. _____ + cloth = _____
4. _____ + cloth = _____
5. _____ + glass = _____
6. _____ + glass = _____

July 7, 1928

95 YEARS AGO, PRE-SLICED BREAD WAS INVENTED.

We may take it for granted now, but pre-sliced bread didn't exist until 1928, when Otto Frederick Rohwedder invented a machine that could easily slice bread loaves. Over time, sliced bread became overwhelmingly popular. When sliced bread was banned during World War II to conserve steel and wax paper, bread-eaters across the country revolted. Cutting their own bread? No, thank you! After two months, the ban was lifted, and the people had their sliced bread once again.

DEANNA'S DELI

When it comes to sandwiches, sliced bread is often a pretty important ingredient! Deanna uses it all the time to make BLTs, grilled cheeses, and other sandwich treats.
Decide what you want on your sandwich, then find the hidden objects.

crown

broom

mug

eyeglasses

button

crescent moon

nail   envelope   baseball   comb

spoon   bird

fish

The names of the hidden objects from Deanna's Deli are also hidden among the letters below.
Can you find them all? We found the first one for you.

```
H I M O D Y Y L B C
B S R D L K F L R R
U A I I X O G A O E
T Z A F Z E B B O S
T N U U C N C E M C
O S I O B V A S U E
N G M Y M E C A B N
T B T B Z L T B I T
B S L C R O W N R M
N P G H D P L S D O
L O M W A E N W P O
S O K M U G P W R N
H N M R B M T F R V
S E S S A L G E Y E
```

BOOKS NEVER WRITTEN

Best Inventions by Sly Sid Brett
How to Make Bread by Ryan Wheat
Peanut Butter Lunches by Sammy Chez

LUNCHMEAT

BY B. LONEY

July 10, 1913

110 YEARS AGO, THE HOTTEST TEMPERATURE WAS RECORDED IN THE UNITED STATES.

Death Valley, which is already the hottest place in North America, hit a record high of 134°F in 1913. How does it get so hot here? The sun heats the bare ground of the valley, while the mountains surrounding it trap the air inside.

Despite its name, Death Valley is home to a lot of animals that have adapted to the area's high temperatures, including dozens of types of lizards. **This scene is a hot spot for lizards, too! Can you find all 26 of them?**

DEATH VALLEY is 282 feet below sea level, which also makes it the lowest point in the Western Hemisphere.

KIDS' SCIENCE QUESTIONS

NOT MANY PLANTS CAN GROW IN DEATH VALLEY, but those that do have adapted to low amounts of water and high amounts of heat.

What do you call a penguin in a desert?

Lost

How does a cactus live and grow without leaves?

Leaves would dry up quickly in the desert home of the cactus. So the green "machinery" that all plants use to make their food, which many plants have in their leaves, is in the cactus's skin.

153

TOUR DE FRANCE

This yearly bike race travels nearly 3,500 kilometers (or roughly 2,175 miles) through France. It takes about three weeks to complete. This year is the 120th anniversary of the first Tour de France, which took place in 1903.

Bicycles can take you all over the place. But a lot of bikes start off at the same spot: a bike shop! This bike shop is bustling with people, bikes, and hidden objects. **Can you find all 12 of the objects hidden throughout the shop?**

TONGUE TWISTER

magnet

hourglass

tent

sailboat

golf tee

golf club

hammer

can

peapod

pitcher

saltshaker

ring

July 20, 2023–August 20, 2023

FIFA WOMEN'S WORLD CUP

This year, qualifying soccer teams from around the world will compete in Australia and New Zealand to see who will win the World Cup.

Kick off your own soccer challenge by finding the right path to the goal in the maze below. The emojis will tell you which way to move.

The FIFA Women's World Cup has been held **EVERY FOUR YEARS** since the first tournament in 1991.

THE FIFA WOMEN'S WORLD CUP TROPHY is made with pure silver covered in 23-carat gold and white gold.

RIGHT — Move 1 space
DOWN — Move 1 space
UP — Move 1 space
LEFT — Move 1 space

PATH 1	PATH 2	PATH 3	PATH 4	PATH 5	PATH 6

EXIT

SOCCER TO 'EM

Test your soccer IQ with these quiz questions.

1. What are you required to wear to play organized soccer?
   a. Shorts
   b. Shinguards
   c. A smile

2. Who is the official that makes the calls in soccer?
   a. Umpire
   b. Referee
   c. Your principal

3. What position, on average, runs the most?
   a. Midfielder
   b. Forward
   c. Goalie

4. What is the maximum number of players a team can have on the field at a time?
   a. 11
   b. 3
   c. 25

5. How is a soccer game started?
   a. Throw-in
   b. Kickoff
   c. First pitch

6. The goalie is the only player who can touch the ball with what?
   a. Hands
   b. Head
   c. Armpit

7. Soccer balls come in different sizes. What size ball do professionals use?
   a. 3
   b. 5
   c. XL

July 12

PAPER BAG DAY

TAKE A FOX TO LUNCH!

Update your paper lunch bag with this cute fox.

1. To make the fox's ears, cut the corners of a **paper bag** as shown. Set the ears aside.

2. Fold down the top of the bag. **Tape** a **coffee filter** under the fold. Trim the coffee filter so it's the same width as the bag.

3. Tape the ears to the back of the bag.

4. Use **markers** to draw eyes, a nose, a mouth, and the inside of the ears.

July 31

UNCOMMON MUSICAL INSTRUMENT AWARENESS DAY

Check out how each of these one-of-a-kind instruments makes its unique sound.

The Great Stalacpipe Organ at Luray Caverns in Virginia is the world's largest musical instrument. It produces sound by gently tapping stalactites that hang from the ceiling of the caves.

The Sea Organ in Zadar, Croatia, is a series of 35 pipes of different sizes and lengths that are hidden in a series of stairs. The Adriatic Sea produces sound as the tide pushes water and air into the echoing chambers under the steps.

The Singing Ringing Tree in Burnley, England, is a swirling, 9.8-foot-tall sculpture made out of more than three hundred steel pipes. As the wind blows on the hill, the pipes make a beautiful and eerie sound.

NATIONAL MERRY-GO-ROUND DAY

The first carousels were simple machines boys used for training to become knights in Europe in the Middle Ages. In the 1800s, the carousel became popular again as a carnival ride.

While these kids go round and round, look for the eight objects hidden in the scene.

 boomerang

 envelope

banana

 teacup

 slice of pizza

 bowl

 carrot

artist's brush

157

July 19, 2023

NATIONAL HOT DOG DAY

What do you call a frozen frankfurter?

A chili dog!

Without showing this page to anyone, ask friends or family members for the words in parentheses. Then read the story out loud.

ANNOUNCER: Good afternoon! Welcome to the Hot-Dog Eating Contest, where the winner will

take home _____ extra-large _____! The defending champion is
(BIG NUMBER) (PLURAL NOUN)

_____. And the challenger is _____. All the other contestants
(FRIEND'S NAME) (DIFFERENT FRIEND)

ate too much _____ backstage and are too _____ to compete.
(KIND OF DESSERT) (ADJECTIVE)

And here they go! Most people add mustard or relish, but the champ is putting _____
(PLURAL NOUN)

on the hot dogs and eating them! If you think that's odd, the challenger is eating with a fork and

_____. Everyone knows you eat hot dogs with your _____!
(NOUN) (BODY PART)

Okay, time's up. We have a new champion! The challenger chowed down _____ hot
(BIG NUMBER)

dogs in three minutes. That's more than _____ eats! But wait—who's this? A delivery
(PET'S NAME)

person just arrived with _____ bags
(NUMBER)

of _____. I guess the new champ is
(FOOD)

still hungry!

In the United States, 818 hot dogs are eaten every second from Memorial Day to Labor Day.

The most popular hot-dog toppings are mustard, ketchup, onions, chili, and relish, in that order.

The southern part of the country eats more hot dogs in a year than any other region.

Americans eat about **20 billion** hot dogs a year. That's about 70 hot dogs per person.

158

July 31
NATIONAL AVOCADO DAY

Celebrate the day with these delicious avocado boats.

1. Ask an adult to help you cut 1 ripe **avocado** in half and remove the pit. Then scoop out the avocado into a bowl. Set the empty shells aside.

2. Combine ¼ cup finely chopped **celery**, 1 cup shredded or cubed cooked **chicken**, and 2 tablespoons **mayonnaise** in a bowl. Mix well.

3. Lightly mash the avocado with a potato masher or fork. Add it to the chicken mixture.

4. Fill each avocado "boat" with the mixture. Sprinkle **paprika** on top and dig in!

These four holidays give you a chance to celebrate even more delicious foods.

July 12	July 13	July 15	July 22

NATIONAL PECAN PIE DAY

The pecans float to the top of the pie by themselves while the pie is baking.

NATIONAL FRENCH FRY DAY

Belgium is the world's top french-fry eater. Belgians eat about 165 pounds of fries per person in a year.

NATIONAL GUMMY WORM DAY

Gummy worms were invented as a way to get kids' attention and gross out their parents.

NATIONAL MANGO DAY

Mangoes, cashews, and pistachios are all part of the Anacardiaceae family, which also includes poison ivy!

INDEPENDENCE

GET THE FACTS BEHIND THIS STAR-SPANGLED CELEBRATION.

EPIC FIREWORKS

There are over

16,000

fireworks displays around the country to celebrate the Fourth of July.

THE FIRST THIRTEEN

WHICH OF THESE WAS **NOT** ONE OF THE 13 ORIGINAL COLONIES?

- Delaware
- Georgia
- New York
- South Carolina
- New Hampshire
- Massachusetts
- North Carolina
- Rhode Island
- New Jersey
- Virginia
- Pennsylvania
- Maryland
- Vermont
- Connecticut

PATRIOTIC TOWN NAMES

EAGLE COLORADO

Patriot INDIANA

Equality ILLINOIS

Liberty Kentucky

FREEDOM CALIFORNIA

INDEPENDENCE MISSOURI

July 29

RAIN DAY

In the late 1800s in Waynesburg, Pennsylvania, a local farmer mentioned that it always seemed to rain on his birthday, July 29, which inspired his pharmacist to start an annual record of rainfall on that day. According to the official Rain Day Record Chart, it has rained in Waynesburg 115 times on July 29 between 1874 and 2019. Since 1979, the town of Waynesburg has celebrated Rain Day with a street fair, which includes an umbrella decorating contest!

Wayne Drop is the official Rain Day mascot!

KIDS' SCIENCE QUESTIONS

Why doesn't water that evaporates in your house form clouds and rain?

To form clouds and rain, water vapor (water that has evaporated into the air) needs both cool temperatures and a surface on which to condense (turn back into a liquid).

As warm, moist air rises outdoors, it carries water vapor high into the atmosphere, where there is less air pressure. The air expands, causing it to cool. Its water vapor condenses on atmospheric dust and may form a cloud.

Indoors, warm, moist air can't rise high because of ceilings. It can cool by meeting up with cold surfaces like windows. But any drops that form on airborne dust don't get large enough to fall as rain.

CREATE RAIN!

Pour a few inches of very warm **tap water** into a clear **drinking glass**.

Cover the glass with **plastic wrap**. Use a **rubber band** to hold it in place.

Set a few **ice cubes** on top. Over the next few minutes, watch as water vapor condenses beneath the plastic wrap. It may even "rain"—watch for drops!

WORLD EMOJI DAY

The term *emoji* comes from the Japanese words for *picture* (絵/e) and *character* (文字/moji). Circle sets of four emojis together that have two crying-laughing faces and two wacky faces. One side of each square must touch a side of another square in the same set. You are done when all the squares are circled.

July 1 is International Joke Day. What is your favorite joke?

What did the cow send in his text message?

An e-MOO-ji

How does a mermaid text her friend?

On her shell phone

In 2015, the *Face with Tears of Joy* was the Oxford Dictionaries Word of the Year.

July 28
NATIONAL WATERPARK DAY

Today is a *grrrr*-8 day to visit the water park! Figure out which path gets you from START to FINISH.

BONUS: See how many 8's you can find in the scene.

How many other words can you make out of the letters in **WATERPARK?** We found a fruit, a martial art, and a warm jacket.

BACKYARD WATERPARK

Even if you can't celebrate at a waterpark, have a splashing good time at home playing these water games.

With a parent's permission, set up plastic chairs in a circle around a sprinkler. Play **"musical" chairs** with water instead of music! Have someone in charge of turning the **sprinkler** on and off. Walk around the chairs when the water is on, and try to take a seat as soon as the water turns off.

Play **spray-bottle freeze tag**. To "freeze" the other players, *It* must squirt them using a small plastic spray bottle filled with water.

Instead of Duck, Duck, Goose, play **Duck, Duck, Drench**. Fill a cup with water. Walk around your friends in a circle. Choose your "goose," and dump the water on him or her.

July 1
CANADA DAY

This holiday celebrates the anniversary of July 1, 1867, on which the British government combined three North American colonies into one area called Canada. People celebrate with parades, barbecues, and fireworks.

Take a spin around the globe to see ho...

July 14
LA FÊTE NATIONALE

Known as Bastille Day outside of France, this celebration commemorates the beginning of the French Revolution. On July 14, 1789, an angry group of Parisians stormed a prison called the Bastille. The French Revolution sparked the abolishment of the French monarchy. French people spend the day with family and friends and watch fireworks at night.

Can you find at least 15 differences between these two pictures?

THE WORLD

July 26

📍 INDEPENDENCE DAY

On July 26, 1847, the Republic of Liberia declared independence, making it the first democratic republic in Africa. Liberia, which means *land of freedom*, was a colony first settled by freed American slaves in 1822. Each year, a National Orator is selected to give a speech.

Fill in the grid with these 14 popular Liberian ingredients and dishes.

BONUS: Read the highlighted letters in order, left to right, top to bottom, to find out the capital of Liberia.

CASSAVA
COCONUT
DUMBOY
FISH
FUFU
JOLLOF RICE
KANYAH
OKRA
PALAVA
PALM OIL
PEPPERS
PLANTAINS
POTATO GREENS
YAMS

July 28-29

📍 FIESTAS PATRIAS

Peru's biggest holiday spans two days. July 28 marks the date Peru declared its independence from Spain in 1821. And on July 29 people honor Peru's armed forces and police. Peruvians around the country celebrate with parades, concerts, food fairs, and fireworks.

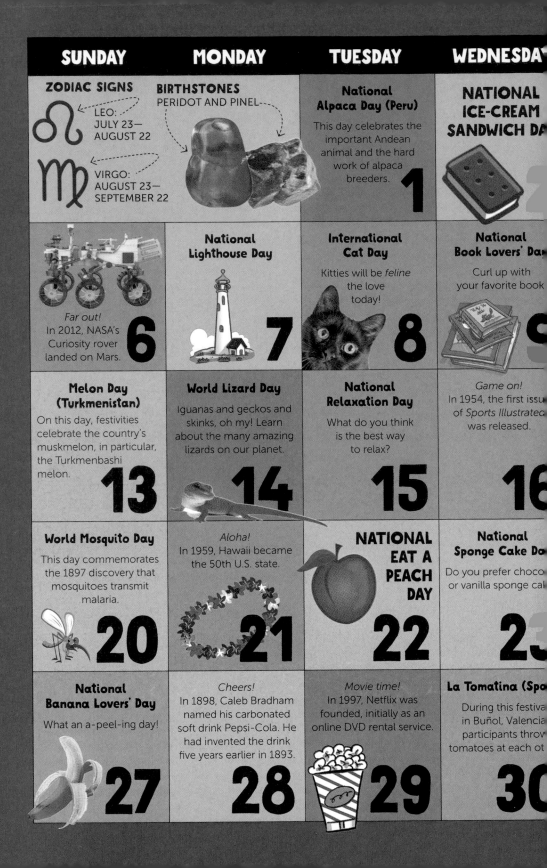

SUNDAY	MONDAY	TUESDAY	WEDNESDAY
ZODIAC SIGNS / LEO: JULY 23—AUGUST 22 / VIRGO: AUGUST 23—SEPTEMBER 22 — **BIRTHSTONES** PERIDOT AND PINEL		**National Alpaca Day (Peru)** This day celebrates the important Andean animal and the hard work of alpaca breeders. **1**	**NATIONAL ICE-CREAM SANDWICH DA** **2**
Far out! In 2012, NASA's Curiosity rover landed on Mars. **6**	**National Lighthouse Day** **7**	**International Cat Day** Kitties will be *feline* the love today! **8**	**National Book Lovers' Da** Curl up with your favorite book **9**
Melon Day (Turkmenistan) On this day, festivities celebrate the country's muskmelon, in particular, the Turkmenbashi melon. **13**	**World Lizard Day** Iguanas and geckos and skinks, oh my! Learn about the many amazing lizards on our planet. **14**	**National Relaxation Day** What do you think is the best way to relax? **15**	*Game on!* In 1954, the first issu of *Sports Illustrated* was released. **16**
World Mosquito Day This day commemorates the 1897 discovery that mosquitoes transmit malaria. **20**	*Aloha!* In 1959, Hawaii became the 50th U.S. state. **21**	**NATIONAL EAT A PEACH DAY** **22**	**National Sponge Cake Da** Do you prefer choco or vanilla sponge cal **23**
National Banana Lovers' Day What an a-peel-ing day! **27**	*Cheers!* In 1898, Caleb Bradham named his carbonated soft drink Pepsi-Cola. He had invented the drink five years earlier in 1893. **28**	*Movie time!* In 1997, Netflix was founded, initially as an online DVD rental service. **29**	**La Tomatina (Spo** During this festiva in Buñol, Valencia participants throw tomatoes at each ot **30**

THURSDAY	FRIDAY	SATURDAY

Go for the gold!
In 1936, Jesse Owens won his first of four gold medals at the Berlin Olympics.

3

Qixi Festival (China)

Also known as Chinese Valentine's Day, this festival celebrates the romantic legend of the cowherd and the weaver girl.

4

Abracadabra!
In 1926, Houdini spent 91 minutes underwater in a sealed tank before escaping.

5

You go, girl!
In 1993, Ruth Bader Ginsberg became the second woman to be sworn in as a Supreme Court justice.

10

National Play in the Sand Day

11

NATIONAL MIDDLE CHILD DAY

12

National Thrift Shop Day

Buying used clothes doesn't just save money—it's good for Earth, too!

17

Going up.
In 1868, helium was discovered by French astronomer Pierre Janssen.

18

National Potato Day

Mashed, fried, baked— potatoes are good no matter how you slice 'em!

19

Vesuvius erupts.
In 79 AD, Mount Vesuvius erupted, burying Pompeii in volcanic rock and ash. The city was untouched until it was excavated in the 18th century.

24

Kiss and Make Up Day

Arguments happen—but at the end of the day, it's important to forgive one another.

25

WOMEN'S EQUALITY DAY

This day celebrates the adoption of the Nineteenth Amendment in 1920, which gave women the right to vote.

26

National Trail Mix Day

Take a hike with a tasty treat!

31

FLOWERS
GLADIOLUS AND POPPY

AUGUST

NATIONAL CRAYON COLLECTION MONTH

Encourage friends, family, and restaurants to save their used crayons! Collect the crayons and donate them to classrooms in need of these colorful supplies.

Can you find the jigsaw pieces in this photo of crayons?

FAMILY FUN MONTH

What fun things will you do with your family this month? Get some ideas by unscrambling the activities below!

kihe ___ ___ ___ ___

somevi ___ ___ ___ ___ ___ ___

mage ignht ___ ___ ___ ___ ___ ___ ___

baek ___ ___ ___ ___

becaberu ___ ___ ___ ___ ___ ___ ___ ___

cmpa ___ ___ ___ ___

birofne ___ ___ ___ ___ ___ ___ ___

fhsi ___ ___ ___ ___

ikbe ___ ___ ___ ___

aftrc ___ ___ ___ ___ ___

NATIONAL EYE EXAM MONTH

Did you know that your eyes move about 100,000 times a day? Or that many experts think the eyes can detect millions of different colors? Human eyes are pretty special. And they need to be taken care of! A regular eye exam is a great way to make sure your eyes are healthy and working their best.

This eye doctor's office is bustling with kids and critters looking for some new glasses. What silly things can you see in the scene?

5 TIPS FOR HEALTHY EYES

Why did the dalmatian go to the eye doctor?

Because he was seeing spots.

1. Wear sunglasses when it's sunny outside.

2. Take a break every 20 minutes when you're staring at a screen to look 20 feet away for 20 seconds. (This is called the 20-20-20 rule!)

3. Get plenty of exercise. Healthy eyes start with a healthy body!

4. Speaking of healthy, be sure to eat plenty of fresh fruits and veggies.

5. If you notice any changes in your eyes, let an adult know and make an appointment to see the eye doctor.

August 15, 1843
180 YEARS AGO,
TIVOLI GARDENS OPENED, MAKING IT ONE OF THE OLDEST AMUSEMENT PARKS IN THE WORLD.

Georg Carstensen was the founder of the Gardens, which offered residents of Copenhagen, Denmark, a beautiful and fun place to visit. One of the first guests was Hans Christian Andersen, the author of "The Little Mermaid"! In 1914, Tivoli Gardens introduced its wooden roller coaster, which is now one of the oldest wooden roller coasters still operating in the world.

These dinosaurs may not have gotten to ride Tivoli's roller coaster, but they are having a great day on the Asteroid at Dinoland.

Can you find all eight objects hidden at this prehistoric amusement park?

lollipop

slice of pie

domino

ruler

feather duster

bell

celery

crescent moon

What do orthodontists do when they ride a roller coaster?

They brace themselves.

155 YEARS AGO,

ASTROPHYSICIST PIERRE JULES CÉSAR JANSSEN DISCOVERED THE ELEMENT HELIUM.

During a solar eclipse in India, Janssen used a tool called a spectroscope, which measures wavelengths of light. As he measured the wavelengths of light coming off the sun, he noticed one that was unfamiliar—no one had seen it yet on Earth. He didn't know at the time what it was, but we now know it was helium.

KIDS' SCIENCE QUESTIONS

What is helium?

Many people have wondered what helium is. It has no color and no odor, and when a balloon is filled with it, the balloon goes up instead of down!

Helium is a chemical element, one of the basic building blocks of matter. So we can't make helium at home by mixing other elements together. In our everyday experience, helium is a gas. The tiny particles that make it up are always moving around, bouncing off one another and off other objects. Helium is lighter than the other gases that make up the air around us, which is why a helium balloon rises into the air. When a balloon full of helium is held on a string, Earth's gravity pulls harder on the surrounding air than it does on the balloon. So that air is always slipping down under the balloon, pushing it upward.

SCIENCE FAIR

ANTI-GRAVITY DEVICE

JOE SEIDITA

Helium in Space

Helium is one of the building blocks of space. In fact, stars are born in clouds of dust and gas. One of the main gases is helium. This cloud is part of the Eagle Nebula.

The pillars are made mostly of invisible hydrogen and helium gas, plus some dark dust.

This pillar is so huge that light would take three years to go from the top to the bottom.

This star has just been born from a dense clump of gas and dust.

Scientists chose these false colors to show details in the gas. The true color here is reddish, not green.

2023
SUMMER
UNIVERSIADE

Every other year, a different country hosts over 10,000 university students from over 150 countries as they compete in a variety of sports.

This year, Russia will be hosting the games in Ekaterinburg. There are 15 sports that have to be played, and the host country may choose up to three additional sports to add to the roster.

The names of the 15 sports that must be played at each summer edition of the Universiade are hidden in the grid below. Look up, down, across, backward, and diagonally. Can you find them all?

WORD LIST

- ARCHERY
- ARTISTIC GYMNASTICS
- ATHLETICS
- BADMINTON
- BASKETBALL
- DIVING
- FENCING
- JUDO
- RHYTHMIC
  GYMNASTICS
- SWIMMING
- TABLE TENNIS
- TAEKWONDO
- TENNIS
- VOLLEYBALL

```
R A Y S I W U A G N F P K I A M B R
F H U O A B P I T A E K W O N D O E
G D Y M P D B N Z P W G O N E I B W
X N W T N A A B B D K T N R T V A A
W A W A H O D A W P A A L N B I N T
M R R R V M M P T I F B A E L N T E
P G F E N C I N G H A L Z B N G B R
I J O E B A N C H U Q E L D X R T P
Y B A B O K T N G A S T E N N I S O
R H A S M O O I B Y C E P P O X Q L
E Q O W P C N U A Q M N M A B G E O
H L N I N A E M C Y R N A L K O A H
C M R M W L B T M T I I A O F Z R N
R A A M O K T O P A W S G S E M S E
A R T I S T I C G Y M N A S T I C S
P O P N U A I C B A B G N W A I H R
V M R G W L B T M T I B R O U V C M
Z A T H L E T I C S W A G L D U L S
N X G V O L L E Y B A L L T S P E O
J U D O U A I C B A S K E T B A L L
```

Hurdles

Water Polo

Rugby

2023 SAILING WORLD CHAMPIONSHIPS

August 10–20, 2023

This year, the Sailing World Championships will be held in The Hague, Netherlands. The best sailors around the world compete in this tournament. The winners then get to compete in the next Summer Olympics (which will be in 2024 in Paris, France).

While these sailboats wait in the harbor, find the 19 objects hidden in the scene.

What do sailors play when they're bored?

Cards—because they always have a deck.

jellyfish

heart

drumstick

necktie

arrowhead

toothbrush

bat

cotton swab

bow

crown

pennant

sock

ice-cream cone

ghost

hairpin

golf tee

butter knife

fishhook

ruler

Where do ghosts like to go sailing?

Lake Eerie

Where do you take a sick sailboat?

To the nearest doc.

175

NATIONAL CLOWN WEEK!

August 1–7

Can you tell what's alike in each row of clowns, across, down, and diagonally?

"Bump a nose!" is how clowns wish each other good luck before a show.

CIRCUS LINGO

Step right up and try to match each of these slang terms for circus workers to their meaning.

1. candy butcher
2. funambulist
3. icarist
4. joey
5. mitt reader
6. roustabout
7. rubberman
8. slanger

A. acrobat who juggles another acrobat with their feet
B. balloon vendor
C. big cat trainer
D. circus laborer
E. clown
F. concession vendor
G. fortune teller
H. tightrope walker

NATIONAL TELL-A-JOKE DAY

These pups are learning how to tell great jokes. Can you help them figure out the punch lines? To solve these riddles, use the fractions of the words given below.

Why was the dog excited to go to school?

Last $\frac{1}{3}$ of BUS
First $\frac{1}{2}$ of MEOW
Last $\frac{1}{2}$ of PULL
Last $\frac{3}{5}$ of SWING
First $\frac{1}{4}$ of BALL
Last $\frac{1}{2}$ of TREE

The class was having a

☐☐☐☐☐☐☐☐
☐☐☐.

Why did the dog study before class?

First $\frac{1}{3}$ of PURPLE
Last $\frac{1}{4}$ of JUMP
First $\frac{2}{5}$ of QUEEN
Last $\frac{1}{3}$ of SKI
First $\frac{1}{5}$ of ZEBRA

In case the teacher gave a

☐☐☐ ☐☐☐☐

BONUS: How many bones can you find in this scene?

August 10 is National Spoil Your Dog Day. Give Fido some extra love!

August 5, 2023
CAMPFIRE DAY AND NIGHT

Solve the riddle, then celebrate Campfire Day and Night (the first Saturday in August) and Toasted Marshmallow Day (August 30) by finding 12 differences between the two pictures above.

I'm squishy and sweet and airy and light.
I'm brown when I'm roasted. Inside, I'm still white.
Need s'more hints? This might do the trick:
I'll be at the campfire stuck on your stick.

August 10
NATIONAL S'MORES DAY

Don't forget about National S'mores Day on August 10! Try these tasty twists on the classic treat!

Stuffed Apple

With a spoon, scoop out the core of a small **apple**. (Leave some apple at the bottom.) Combine **melted butter**, crushed **graham crackers**, **brown sugar**, **mini marshmallows**, **chocolate chips**, and **butterscotch chips**. Fill the center of the apple. Bake in a small baking dish until the apple is soft.

Banana Sandwich

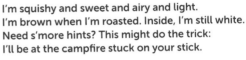

Graham cracker

Marshmallow creme

Chocolate syrup and peanut butter

Banana

August 31

EAT OUTSIDE DAY

Celebrate Eat Outside Day by finding things that rhyme with *grill* or *eat* in this scene.

BONUS! Find 9 grill spatulas in the scene.

The largest hamburger ever made weighed 2,566 lb 9 oz!

What's the best side of the house to put the grill on?

The outside

NATIONAL WATERMELON DAY

Find 8 pairs of matching watermelon slices.

WATERMELON PUNCH

In a blender, puree chunks of **watermelon**. Blend in some **honey**. Pour the puree into a punch bowl or a hollowed-out watermelon. (Make sure it's not wobbly!) Stir in cold **seltzer**. Garnish with **basil leaves**.

NAME THAT WATERMELON

More than 1,200 varieties of watermelon are grown in more than 96 countries around the world. Check out some of the fun names of each of the four main types.

Seedless Watermelons	**Picnic Watermelons**	**Icebox Watermelons**	**Yellow or Orange Watermelons**
Queen of Hearts	Charleston Gray	Sugar Baby	Desert King
King of Hearts	Jubilee	Tiger Baby	Tendergold
Millionaire	Crimson Sweet	Minilee	Honeyheart
Nova	Black Diamond	Rainbow Sherbet	Chiffon

A watermelon is both a fruit and a vegetable! It grows from a seed like a fruit, but it's part of the same family as squash.

Did you know that the whole fruit is edible? Rinds can be pickled, stir-fried, or stewed. In some places, the seeds are dried and roasted like pumpkin seeds.

WATERMELON FAN

When do you go on red and stop on green?

When you are eating watermelon.

1. Arrange three **large craft sticks** in a fan shape. **Glue** them together at the bottom. Let the glue dry.

2. Trace around the sticks on **red craft foam**. Cut a "rind" from **green** and **white craft foam**. Glue on the rind.

3. Cut a "bite" from the watermelon. Draw seeds with a **black marker**.

4. Glue the foam fan onto the craft sticks.

KIDS' SCIENCE QUESTIONS

How do seedless watermelons grow when the watermelons come from the seeds?

To understand how this is done, you first have to know some basic ideas about how a normal seed works. Each seed contains a complete set of coding—a blueprint—for making a new plant. That coding is in a set of long, chain-like molecules. All together, that set of molecules is called the plant's DNA.

When one watermelon flower is fertilized by pollen from a different watermelon plant, that flower makes new seeds. In each seed, half of the blueprint comes from one plant, and the other half comes from the other plant. That's what happens in most plants.

To make seedless watermelons, scientists use a trick. They use a special chemical to give each seed twice as much DNA as a normal seed has. These seeds can grow into watermelon vines and make watermelons that contain seeds.

But after one of these double-DNA seeds grows into a vine and that vine is fertilized by a normal plant, the new seeds will grow into an unusual vine. The vine is healthy, but because it has one and one-half sets of DNA, seeds will not form. So the vine gives seedless watermelons.

Scientists have grown watermelon vines that produce watermelons with no seeds.

Watermelons are 92% water! No wonder they're so refreshing.

181

HURRICANE

Hurricane season starts to peak in mid-August, although the official season for tropical cyclones and hurricanes in the Atlantic Basin is from June 1 to November 30. Hurricane Katrina hit the Gulf Coast on August 29, 2005, and Hurricane Irene struck the East Coast on August 27, 2011.

Be a storm tracker and search for the 21 hurricane names for 2023 hiding in this grid. Look for them up, down, across, backward, and diagonally. How many can you spot?

```
X  W  E  F  W  K  Y  S  J  G  L  B  N  I
Q  V  D  R  P  B  R  E  A  R  L  E  N  E
O  F  I  A  O  H  I  A  A  S  B  W  T  Z
P  W  U  N  T  C  I  N  K  A  T  I  A  H
H  L  G  K  C  O  I  L  U  I  X  Y  K  N
E  E  A  L  N  E  V  N  I  G  E  L  G  E
L  W  H  I  T  N  E  Y  D  P  X  X  I  B
I  S  K  N  M  L  S  T  C  Y  P  N  Y  O
A  D  L  O  R  A  H  A  T  H  I  E  J  N
Q  B  T  O  G  R  A  M  Z  G  J  N  O  N
O  S  I  O  C  N  I  M  R  F  E  E  S  I
B  N  I  D  R  A  M  Y  C  H  M  R  E  E
C  T  L  I  A  D  V  S  D  H  I  O  T  Y
I  E  R  H  E  L  M  I  N  L  L  P  N  D
Y  R  A  H  S  P  I  J  U  E  Y  R  A  O
A  B  E  G  R  I  N  A  A  E  V  I  D  N
```

2023 HURRICANE NAMES

ARLENE	GERT	MARGOT	TAMMY
BRET	HAROLD	NIGEL	VINCE
CINDY	IDALIA	OPHELIA	WHITNEY
DON	JOSE	PHILIPPE	
EMILY	KATIA	RINA	
FRANKLIN	LEE	SEAN	

The World Meteorological Organization has six lists of names that are used on a rotating basis. The list of names from 2023 will be used again in 2029.

SEASON

If a storm **is so deadly** that using the name again would be sensitive, that name is replaced.

This list of names is for the Atlantic Basin, which includes the **Atlantic Ocean**, the **Caribbean Sea**, and the **Gulf of Mexico**. There are different lists of names for storms in different parts of the world.

Wind speed is the difference between a hurricane and a tropical storm. Hurricane wind speeds are at least 74 miles per hour.

Hurricanes rotate around the eye in a counter-clockwise direction. The eyewall, created by the rotating storm clouds, is the most destructive part of a hurricane.

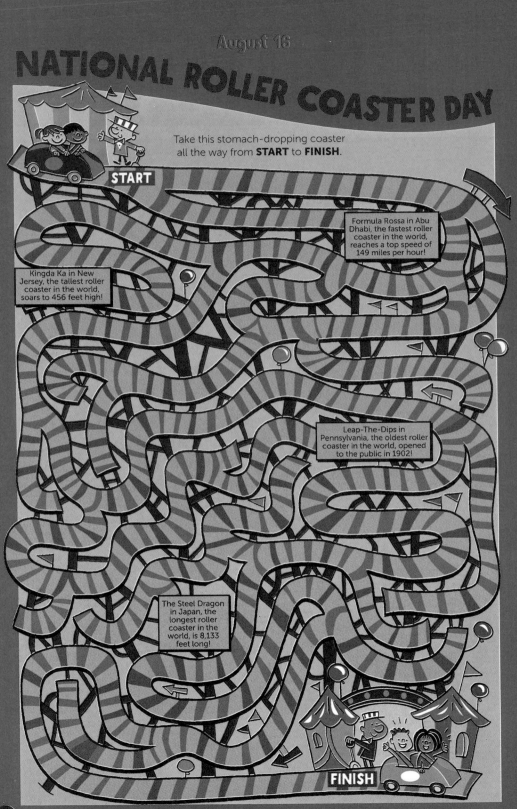

NATIONAL ROLLER COASTER DAY

August 16

Take this stomach-dropping coaster all the way from **START** to **FINISH**.

START

Formula Rossa in Abu Dhabi, the fastest roller coaster in the world, reaches a top speed of 149 miles per hour!

Kingda Ka in New Jersey, the tallest roller coaster in the world, soars to 456 feet high!

Leap-The-Dips in Pennsylvania, the oldest roller coaster in the world, opened to the public in 1902!

The Steel Dragon in Japan, the longest roller coaster in the world, is 8,133 feet long!

FINISH

August 30
NATIONAL BEACH DAY

Today is the day to slather on the sunscreen, put on your bathing suit, and hit the waves. Gullbert had a busy Beach Day. **Can you figure out the order in which these scenes occurred?**

A

B

C

D

E

F

G

H

DON'T LIVE NEAR A BEACH?
Here are some ways you can bring the beach to you.

1. Put on your bathing suit and sunglasses.
2. Lay a beach towel down in your living room or backyard.
3. Play relaxing sounds of the ocean waves on an electronic device.
4. Pour yourself a refreshing drink, like lemonade.
5. Relax while reading a book or make a sandcastle out of moldable sand.

185

Take a spin around the globe to see how

August 15

THE DAY THE LIGHT RETURNED

On August 15, South Koreans celebrate the National Liberation Day of Korea, or *Gwangbokjeol*, which literally means "the day the light returned." The holiday commemorates when Korea was liberated from Japanese occupation in 1945. Koreans take the day off from work and school to attend parades and celebrations. The national flag, called *Taegukgi*, is proudly displayed everywhere.

ROYAL EDINBURGH MILITARY TATTOO

Every August at Edinburgh Castle, more than 1,200 performers from around the world put on a spectacular show of music, dance, and military marches called a tattoo. Since the first Edinburgh Tattoo in 1950, more than 14 million people have attended. Each year, around 100 million people in 30 countries also watch on television.

Can you find 16 differences between these two pictures?

THE WORLD

people around the world celebrate in August.

August 20

⌖ HAPPY 1,023rd BIRTHDAY, HUNGARY!

Known as both Az államalapítás ünnepe (State Foundation Day) and Szent István ünnepe (Saint Stephen's Day), there are lots of reasons for celebration on August 20. Hungarians celebrate the foundation of the Kingdom of Hungary in the year 1000; the name day of the first king of Hungary, Stephen I; and the Day of the New Bread, which marks the traditional end of the grain harvest. Throughout the country on this national holiday, there are festivals, parades, and fireworks. The largest fireworks display is in the capital city, Budapest, over the Danube River in front of Parliament. Since 2007, there has also been a competition to find "The Birthday Cake of Hungary," with the winning cake announced (and eaten) on August 20.

A rakhi is a bracelet made of red and gold thread, like these here.

August 30, 2023

⌖ RAKSHA BANDHAN

Raksha Bandhan is an Indian festival that celebrates the loving and caring bond between sisters and brothers. This year, it falls on August 30. A sister ties a *rakhi* to her brother's wrist, and her brother responds with a gift. It is a special day when sisters and brothers think fondly of each other and pray for each others' blessings.

SUNDAY	MONDAY	TUESDAY	WEDNESDAY

BIRTHSTONE
SAPPHIRE

ZODIAC SIGNS
VIRGO: AUGUST 23–SEPTEMBER 22

LIBRA: SEPTEMBER 23–OCTOBER 22

FLOWERS
ASTER AND MORNING GLORY

U.S. BOWLING LEAGUE DAY

3

LABOR DAY

4

International Day of Charity
Look for ways to give in your community, whether it's a service, donations, or even just a smile.

5

Out to sea.
In 1620, the Pilgrims s[et] out on the *Mayflowe[r]* looking for a place t[o] live where they coul[d] have religious freedo[m]

6

St. George's Caye Day (Belize)
This holiday marks the defeat of the Spanish navy in 1798.

10

PATRIOT DAY

11

National Day of Encouragement
You can do it!

12

On your mark, get set, GO!
In 1970, the first New York City Marathon was held.

1[3]

The beginning of a legacy. On this day in 1849, Harriet Tubman escaped from slavery. She went on to help free dozens of enslaved people with the help of the Underground Railroad.

17

National Cheeseburger Day
You want fries with that?

18

:-)
In 1982, the first emoticon—a typed, sideways smiley face—was created.

19

National String Cheese Day
Grab one for a quick, tasty snack!

20

YOM KIPPUR
begins at sunset.

24

World Dream Day
What do you dream of? How can you make your dreams come true?

25

National Lumberjack Day
What's a lumberjack's favorite month? Sep-TIMBER!

26

NATIONAL SCARF DAY

27

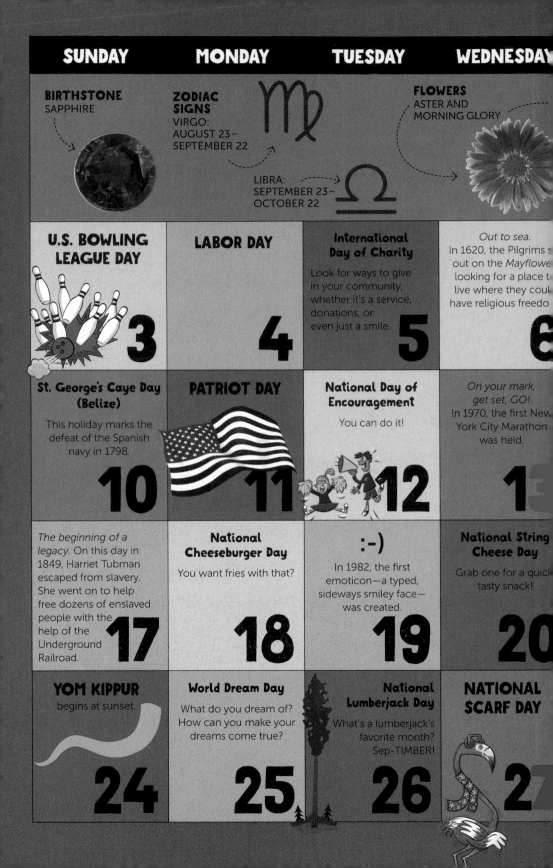

THURSDAY	FRIDAY	SATURDAY
	No Rhyme or Reason Day — This day celebrates words that don't rhyme and silly idioms. **1**	*This idea was right on the money.* In 1969, the first ATM in the U.S. opened. **2**
National Salami Day — It's a good day, any way you slice it. **7**	**International Literacy Day** — You read it here first! **8**	**NATIONAL TEDDY BEAR DAY** **9**
National Cream-Filled Doughnut Day — Doughnut make you smile? **14**	**ROSH HASHANAH** begins at sunset. **15**	**Malaysia Day (Malaysia)** — This patriotic holiday commemorates the formation of the Federation of Malaysia on this day in 1963. **16**
Miniature Golf Day — *FORE!* **21**	**National White Chocolate Day** — It may not technically be real chocolate, but this sweet treat sure is good! **22**	**FIRST DAY OF FALL** **23**
National Good Neighbor Day — Be a good neighbor today and every day. **28**	**SUKKOT** begins at sunrise.. **29**	**Independence Day (Botswana)** — Africa's oldest democracy, Botswana, became independent in 1966. **30**

SEPTEMBER

Franklin Chang-Díaz

NATIONAL HISPANIC HERITAGE MONTH

This month-long celebration (September 15–October 15) recognizes the contributions of Hispanic Americans and honors their history and culture. Match each pioneering Hispanic American with his or her historic achievement.

Sonia Sotomayor

1. Who was the first Hispanic American to serve in the U.S. Senate (1928)?

2. Who was the first Hispanic American MLB Hall of Fame inductee (1973)?

3. Who was the first Hispanic American to earn an EGOT, winning an Emmy, Grammy, Oscar, and Tony award (1977)?

4. Who was the first Hispanic American astronaut (1980)?

5. Who was the first Hispanic American doctor—and the first woman—to become U.S. surgeon general (1990)?

6. Who was the first Hispanic American activist inducted into the National Women's Hall of Fame (1993)?

7. Who was the first Hispanic American musician inducted into the Rock & Roll Hall of Fame (1998)?

8. Who was the first Hispanic American U.S. Supreme Court justice (2009)?

Octaviano Ambrosio Larrazolo

Rita Moreno

Dr. Antonia Novello

Carlos Santana

Roberto Clemente

Hispanic and **Latinx** don't mean the same thing. **Latinx** means that someone is from Latin America (nearly every country south of the U.S., including the Caribbean). **Hispanic** means from a Spanish-speaking country, and not all Latin American countries speak Spanish.

Dolores Huerta

NATIONAL CHICKEN MONTH

What time is it? Time to celebrate chickens! Say "Hooray!" for these important birds, then find the eight objects hidden in this chicken clock shop.

What do you get from a confused chicken?

Scrambled eggs.

Chickens are the closest living relative to the T. rex!

There are more chickens in the world than any other bird species.

What chicken makes jokes?

The comedie-hen

cookie

orange

ring

basketball

coin

ball of yarn

button

sun

BETTER BREAKFAST MONTH

SUNNYSIDEUP

Use the clues below to fill in the boxes of this spiral—but there's a twist! The last letter of each word is also the first letter of the next word. Use the linking letters to help you spin all the way to the center.

1. One way to serve fried eggs

11. People eat these by the stack

18. Fresh-_____ orange juice

25. Small, sweet fried cake, usually with a hole in the center

32. Machine used to heat slices of bread

38. Dried fruit topping for oatmeal

44. Popular flavor of jam

53. Color of butter

58. Type of dark-colored bread, heated up

67. This pouch sits in a mug of hot water to make a common breakfast drink

72. What you pour over biscuits

76. Yellow parts of eggs

80. What you pour over waffles

84. Containers of yogurt are made of this

90. _____ cheese is typically spread on a bagel

94. Liquid poured over cereal

97. Utensil used to spread butter or jelly

According to a 2018 survey, America's top 5 breakfast foods are eggs, sausage, bacon, pancakes, and toast. What's your favorite way to start the day?

HAPPY HEALTHY CAT MONTH

These kittens are having a ball! There are some differences between each picture.
Can you find them all?

Cats sleep an average of **15 to 20** hours a day.

Most cats are lactose intolerent. Check with your vet before giving your kitty milk!

PET-SITTER EDUCATION MONTH

Pet sitters don't have it easy! Nicole is watching four fussy cats who are waiting to be fed. They each get a different flavor of cat food: chicken, tuna, beef, or liver. Use the clues to figure out which flavor Nicole should give each cat.

 chicken

 tuna

 beef

 liver

Lucy will not eat chicken or beef.

Bailey will not eat tuna or liver.

Luna will not eat liver or beef.

Peanut will only eat chicken.

September 1 is Ginger Cat Appreciation Day.

Lucy

Peanut

Bailey

Luna

Ten cats were on a boat. One jumped off. How many were left?

None. They were all copycats.

September 5, 1698

325 YEARS AGO, RUSSIAN TSAR PETER THE GREAT STARTED TAXING MEN WHO HAD BEARDS.

No beard? No problem. But if you decided to rock the stubble three hundred years ago in Russia, you needed to pay up. When Peter returned to Russia after several years in Europe, he decided his country needed to adopt European fashion, which at the time meant a clean-shaven face. At first, it was mandatory to shave off beards, but the tsar eventually agreed to settle for a tax, which would let men keep their beards and put some money in the government's treasury.

Maintaining a beard or hairstyle can often involve too many cords. Darren, Karen, Rudy, and Judy have got their cords all mixed up! Follow the paths to help them figure out which outlet their styling tool is plugged into.

What does a hippo get if he stops shaving? A hippopata-mustache

Although the tax was wildly unpopular, it remained in effect until 1772, **47 YEARS AFTER PETER THE GREAT'S DEATH.**

ANCIENT BEARD TRENDS

Match the popular beard fashion with the appropriate civilization.

1. Kings and queens would tie a fake metal beard to their heads.

2. Men would curl their long beards with tongs.

3. This society preferred well-groomed, short beards. Eventually shaving your beard was the popular style.

4. Having a long beard was considered a sign of wisdom in this society.

5. For this society, beards were used to intimidate enemies.

A. Ancient India

B. Ancient Rome

C. Vikings

D. Ancient Egypt

E. Ancient Greece

King's victory against Riggs was a victory for all women athletes. It showed that women can play sports just as well as men.

An estimated 90 million viewers worldwide tuned in to watch the "Battle of the Sexes."

September 20, 1973
50 YEARS AGO,
BILLIE JEAN KING BEAT BOBBY RIGGS IN A TENNIS MATCH.

Bobby Riggs was a retired men's tennis player who had been number one during his career. He believed no woman could ever beat him, even at his age. Billie Jean King rose to the challenge, and in their infamous match titled "Battle of the Sexes," Billie Jean beat Bobby. Each tennis ball has an exact match. **Can you find all 20 pairs?**

King fought for equal pay for men and women in tennis before and after her match with Riggs. Thanks in large part to her efforts, the U.S. Open Tennis Championships in 1973 became the first major tournament to offer equal prize money to male and female winners.

TENNIS, ANYONE?
Chiara is practicing her serve, and tennis balls are everywhere! How many can you spot?

In 2009, King was recognized for her contributions by being awarded the Presidential Medal of Freedom, the nation's highest civilian honor.

In 2020, King became the first woman to have a major sports event named for her when the Fed Cup was renamed the Billie Jean Cup.

September 8–October 28, 2023

RUGBY WORLD CUP

Every four years, teams from around the world come together to compete in the Rugby World Cup. This year, the matches will be held in France. Below is a list of the 19 teams that will be competing against one another. **Use the number of letters in each team's name to help figure out where it belongs in the grid.** Hint: Only uppercase letters of team names go in the grid. Leave out the numbers.

LIKE SOCCER, rugby involves two teams trying to move a ball down a field and into the opponent's goal. **UNLIKE SOCCER,** players can carry the ball with their hands. Teammates can pass the ball to one another, but only sideways or backward— no forward passes allowed!

We don't know exactly how rugby began. But according to one legend, it got its start in **1823 AT THE RUGBY SCHOOL** (where the sport gets its name!). As the story goes, William Webb Ellis was playing soccer with classmates when he caught the ball in his hands. Instead of dropping the ball, he ran down the field holding onto it!

1. AFRICA 1	**8.** FIJI	
2. AMERICAS 1 and 2	**9.** FRANCE	
3. ARGENTINA	**10.** IRELAND	
4. ASIA/PACIFIC 1	**11.** ITALY	
5. AUSTRALIA	**12.** JAPAN	**15.** SCOTLAND
6. ENGLAND	**13.** NEW ZEALAND	**16.** SOUTH AFRICA
7. EUROPE 1 and 2	**14.** OCEANIA	**17.** WALES

September 3
U.S. BOWLING LEAGUE DAY

Whether you're in a bowling league or not, today is a great day to perfect your strike.
Can you find 16 objects hidden in this bowling alley?

Objects that may have been used for an early version of bowling were found in an ancient Egyptian grave dating back to 3200 BCE.

thimble

artist's brush

comb

crescent moon

crown

feather

harmonica

slice of watermelon

rolling pin

slice of pie

button

lollipop

needle

teacup

hockey stick

pencil

September 16
COLLECT ROCKS DAY

Rocks rock! And collecting rocks can be a lot of fun. There are so many different kinds to find on walks, at the beach, or even in your own backyard. Here's a craft you can do with some of the rocks you collect.

CREATE YOUR OWN CONSTELLATION

1. Wash and dry your **rocks**.

2. Use **white paint** to create stars. Let dry. Paint the stars with **glow-in-the-dark paint**. Let dry.

3. Optional: Use **black paint** in the area around the stars. Let dry.

4. Place your rocks in a sunny spot, inside or outside, such as a windowsill or backyard. Arrange the rocks to make your constellation. The stars will soak up the light during the day and glow at night.

September 17
INTERNATIONAL
COUNTRY MUSIC DAY

International Country Music Day is celebrated on September 17, the birthday of Hank Williams, one of the most influential singer-songwriters in 20th century America. Williams was rejected by the *Grand Ole Opry* show after his first audition in 1946, but he didn't give up and finally made his debut in 1949.

Take a trip to the Opry House in Nashville and find at least 15 differences between these two pictures.

The Grand Ole Opry is a live country music concert and radio show held a few times a week in Nashville, Tennessee. The show has been broadcast since 1925, making it one of the world's longest-running radio shows.

The best-selling country music artists of all time are Garth Brooks, George Strait, and Shania Twain.

The birthplace of country music is Bristol, Tennessee.

Nashville, Tennessee, is called the Music City because it's the home of the country music industry.

This photo of Hank Williams is a publicity photo from 1951. Radio stations used photos like this one to make listeners familiar with the voices they heard on the radio.

199

APPLE NACHOS

1. Place **apple slices** on a plate.
2. Drizzle **caramel and chocolate sauce** toppings over the apple slices.
3. Spoon **granola** over the slices.
4. Sprinkle on your favorite toppings, such as **chocolate chips, raisins,** or **sliced almonds.**

September 13

KIDS TAKE OVER THE KITCHEN DAY

Treat your family to these delicious desserts!

FRUIT KEBABS

1. Drain a can of **pineapple chunks**. Put the chunks into a bowl.
2. Wash some fresh **raspberries** and **blueberries**. Pat them dry.
3. Peel and slice a **kiwi**.
4. Peel an **orange** and a **grapefruit**. Cut them into bite-sized pieces.
5. Carefully poke **wooden skewers** through the fruit.
6. To eat the kebabs, remove the fruit with your fingers.

INTERNATIONAL CHOCOLATE DAY

How does your knowledge of this tasty treat stack up? Fill in each cocoa fact with the correct number.

1. It takes _____ cocoa beans to make one pound of chocolate.

2. Chocolate melts around _____ °F, just below the temperature of the human body. That's why it melts easily on your tongue.

3. A cacao tree doesn't produce its first beans for up to __ __ years.

4. Up to _____ people around the world depend on cocoa for a living.

5. There are approximately _____ cocoa farms in West Africa.

6. Côte d'Ivoire provides about _____ percent of the world's cocoa supply

7. Most dark chocolate bars contain at least _____ percent chocolate liquor

5 **50 million** **1.5 million** **35** **400** **40** **90**

September 16, 2023

Celebrate by making these three apple snacks.

INTERNATIONAL EAT AN APPLE DAY

About **2,500 types** of apples grow in the United States.

Apples are a member of the rose family.

APPLE SANDWICHES
Core and slice an apple. Use two slices for "bread." Possible fillings: cheese, peanut butter, or chocolate spread.

SWEET APPLE YOGURT
Chop up an apple. Put it in a bowl. Stir in honey and yogurt. Sprinkle cinnamon on top.

CARAMEL APPLE ON A STICK
Soften caramel dip in a microwave. Skewer an apple chunk and dip it in the caramel. Sprinkle it with chopped nuts, mini chocolate chips, or sprinkles. Let it set in the fridge.

Ask an adult to help with anything sharp or hot!

September 4, 2023

LABOR DAY

Labor Day honors the contributions of American workers. The first U.S. Labor Day was celebrated in 1882 as part of the labor union movement. Today, it's unofficially seen as the last weekend of summer. **"How's your job?"** Match each silly answer above to the worker.

A "shear" pleasure.

I'm drawn to it.

It's a piece of cake!

Out of this world!

I get a kick out of it!

Moving right along.

An apple a day couldn't keep me away!

DOCTOR

BAKER

SOCCER PLAYER

ASTRONAUT

ARTIST

HAIRDRESSER

TRAFFIC OFFICER

Think of other jobs, and create your own answers!

THE EIGHT-HOUR WORK DAY was established by the Adamson Act, which was passed on September 3, 1916. In the 19th century, Americans worked twelve hours a day, seven days a week!

At least **20,000 PEOPLE** showed support for unions by attending the first Labor Day parade in New York City in 1882.

Women ride on a float in the 1909 Labor Day parade in New York City.

WOMEN'S AUXILIARY TYPOGRAPHICAL UNION

Grover Cleveland signed an act in 1894 to make **LABOR DAY** a national holiday.

September 10, 2023

NATIONAL GRANDPARENTS DAY

SEPTEMBER 16 is National Stepfamily Day! Nearly 1.4 million households in the U.S. are made up of stepfamilies.

This holiday to honor grandparents is celebrated on the second Sunday in September. The 24 grandparent names below are hidden in this word search. Search up, down, across, backward, and diagonally to find them all. Only the words in CAPITAL LETTERS are hidden.

GRANDMOTHER WORD LIST
ABUELA (Spanish)
BABCIA (Polish)
BIBI (Swahili)
GRAMMY
GRANDMA
HALMONI (Korean)
LOLA (Filipino)
MAWMAW
NANA
NONNA (Italian)
OMA (German)
YIAYIA (Greek)

GRANDFATHER WORD LIST
ABUELO (Spanish)
BABU (Swahili)
DZIADZIU (Polish)
GRAMPS
GRANDPA
HALABEOJI (Korean)
LOLO (Filipino)
NONNO (Italian)
OPA (German)
PAPPOÚS (Greek)
PAWPAW
POP

The number of grandparents you have doubles with each generation: 4 grandparents, 8 great-grandparents, and 16 great-great-grandparents. How many grandparents do you have 10 generations back?

What do you call your grandparents?

```
M A Y S I W U A G N F P K I
F M U O A B P I O B V L N N
G D F M P D I N Z P W G O N
X N W S N A N B B D K G N R
W A W A X O P A W P A W N K
M R R R V P C P T I F I A E
P G B X L K Y Q O H A A Z B
I J O E B A L A H Ú Q B L D
U B A B O K Y N J A S U S O
Z H A L M O N I B F C E P P
T Q O T P C Y U A Q B L M A
O L N A N A E M C Y R A A L
V M R R W L B T M T I B R O
Z A A U O K T O P A W A G L
N X G G B M J V Z D R C V T
P O P O Ú A I C B A B G N W
```

5 WAYS TO HAVE FUN WITH YOUR GRANDPARENTS

1. Have a picnic together.

2. Build a zany sculpture.

3. Send each other postcards.

4. Play a board game or a video game.

5. Read stories aloud to each other.

HIGH HOLY DAYS

In Judaism, the High Holy Days are the holidays of Rosh Hashanah and Yom Kippur.

Rosh Hashanah marks the start of a new year in the Hebrew calendar. Jewish people often celebrate by eating apples and honey to symbolize a sweet new year. This year, Rosh Hashanah begins at sunset on **September 15** and ends at nightfall on **September 17**. It begins the ten days when Jews think about their actions from the previous year.

Yom Kippur means "Day of Atonement," and many Jews fast on this day and spend the day praying in a synagogue. This year, Yom Kippur begins at sunset on **September 24** and ends at nightfall on **September 25**.

SHOFAR

1. From **cardstock**, cut out two horns.

2. Glue the sides together to make a pocket. Use a **marker** to add decorations.

3. Punch two holes at the top. Tie on a **ribbon** hanger.

4. Write notes on **paper**. Place them inside the horn.

A *shofar* is a ram's horn that is blown like a trumpet on the Jewish High Holy Days. Most scholars and rabbis agree that it is meant as a wake-up call. The blast of the shofar reminds people to take time to think about what they can do to make the world a better place.

I'm sorry that I didn't listen.

I'm sorry that I was rude to my brother.

I'm sorry that I didn't listen.

I promise to be a better friend.

I promise to be patient.

APPLES-AND-HONEY PLATE

1. From **tissue paper**, cut out apples, leaves, and a beehive.

2. Use a **sealer** (such as Mod Podge) to glue the shapes to the back of a **clear plastic plate**. Use as many layers of tissue paper as needed to get the color you want.

3. Cover the shapes with two or three coats of sealer, letting it dry between coats.

Be sure to keep the sealer on the back of the plate, away from any food!

Pomegranate seeds symbolize *mitzvahs*, or good deeds, and are often eaten on Rosh Hashanah.

GOOD DEED POMEGRANATE

1. From **cardstock**, cut out a pomegranate-shaped card, two circles, and pomegranate seeds.

2. Glue the circles inside the card. Glue the seeds on the circles.

3. On each seed, write a good deed you plan to do in the coming year.

THE FIRST DAY OF FALL AUTUMN FALL

Wait a minute, is it *fall* or *autumn*? Why do the other three seasons only have one name? A long time ago, this season was called *harvest* because farmers gathered their crops between August and November for winter storage; however, as more and more people moved to cities in the 16th century, new names popped up.

Autumn comes from *autumnus*, a Latin word that means "drying-up season." Fall comes from *fiaell*, an Old English word that means "falls from a height," like the leaves that fall . . . in fall. Today, *autumn* is used more commonly in British English and *fall* is used more commonly in American English, but they're interchangeable.

So, whatever you call it, here are some ways to celebrate the season!

AUTUMN

Weaving Through Autumn Leaves

Help these kids find a clear path to the hot cider.

4 Ways to Have Fun with Autumn Leaves

1. Cut out a bird shape from **poster board**. Glue on colorful leaves as feathers.

2. Write a message on two small pieces of **brown paper**. Fill two buckets with leaves, and hide a message in each. Give the buckets to two friends. Whoever finds the message first wins!

3. Make a mobile! Use **string** to hang leaves from a **stick**.

4. Cut out the inside circle from a **paper plate**. Glue leaves around the outer rim to make a festive wreath.

FALL

Leafy Fall Maze

Help these kids find a clear path to their house.

4 Ways to Celebrate Fall

1. Make leaf-creature place mats! Use colorful **leaves**, clear **self-adhesive paper**, and **construction paper**.

2. Sip a warm autumn drink. Heat up some **apple juice**, stir it with a **cinnamon stick**, and toss in a few **cranberries**.

3. Pumpkin greetings! Instead of making a card, paint a small **pumpkin** for someone special.

4. In a nearby park, your backyard, or on a hike with your family, collect **leaves** and match them to the tree they fell from. For an added challenge, identify the tree.

NATIONAL IGUANA AWARENESS DAY

September 8

The green iguana is one of the world's best-known plant-eating reptiles. This lizard makes its home in the trees of the forests in Mexico, South America, and on some Caribbean islands.

A thin layer of skin covers the ears.

Males have taller spines than females do.

The *subtympanic* ("below the ear") plate is a big scale. Its use is unknown.

The whiplike tail can be used for balance and to defend against predators like hawks.

The dewlap is a flap of skin the lizard can open to look bigger when defending itself or its territory.

Its long toes and claws help it climb trees to eat leaves, flowers, and fruits and can also be used in defense.

SEA OTTER AWARENESS WEEK

September 24–30, 2023

The last full week in September recognizes the important role that sea otters play in the ecosystem where they live.

Where do otters go to watch movies?

What is an otter's favorite book series?

What did the otter say to the rock star?

An otter-torium

Harry Otter

"Can I have your otter-graph?"

Otters have the **thickest fur** of any mammal. They don't have blubber like other sea mammals, so the fur helps keep them warm.

Otters are one of the few mammals to use **tools.** They use rocks to break open clams and other shellfish.

September 22

NATIONAL ELEPHANT APPRECIATION DAY

An elephant's trunk is an amazing thing. It can be used as a snorkel, to store water, or even to shell a peanut!

To get the answer to the riddle below, first cross out all the pairs of matching letters. Then write the remaining letters in order in the space below the riddle.

QQ	BE	EE	NN	MM	OO	WW
LL	CA	SS	VV	YY	US	ZZ
ET	AA	RR	NN	HE	EE	YY
HH	XX	YL	DD	PP	UU	OV
GG	OO	ET	SS	CC	QQ	II
CC	RA	EE	MM	AA	TT	VE
LI	BB	KK	VV	ZZ	NG	TT

Why do elephants have trunks?

___ ___ ___ ___ ___ ___ ___

___ ___ ___ ___ ___ ___ ___

There are lots of holidays to celebrate animals in September. Here are just a few:

September 16, 2023

INTERNATIONAL RED PANDA DAY

Red pandas like to munch on bamboo, but they are not related to pandas. They are related to raccoons, weasels, and skunks.

September 23, 2023

INTERNATIONAL RABBIT DAY

Rabbits can turn their ears 180 degrees to listen for predators.

September 25

NATIONAL LOBSTER DAY

In the wild, most lobsters are greenish blue to blackish brown, but about one out of every two million lobsters is blue!

September 3
NATIONAL SKYSCRAPER DAY

Soar to the top with this skyscraper quiz.

1. Completed in 1885, the world's first skyscraper was the Home Insurance Building in Chicago, Illinois. How tall was it?
   a. 10 stories
   b. 20 stories
   c. 30 stories

2. Where is the Jeddah Tower, which started construction in 2013, located?
   a. Antarctica
   b. Batuu
   c. Saudi Arabia

3. When it was completed in 2010, the Burj Khalifa in Dubai, United Arab Emirates, was the world's tallest building. How many floors does it have?
   a. 16 floors with really high ceilings
   b. 163
   c. 1,630

4. Which New York City skyscraper was the tallest building in the world from 1931 to 1972?
   a. Chrysler Building
   b. Empire State Building
   c. Woolworth Building

5. The tallest building in the U.S. is the One World Trade Center in New York City. How tall is it?
   a. 1,001 feet
   b. 1,555 feet
   c. 1,776 feet

6. The Shanghai Tower in China has the world's tallest elevator, at 2,074 feet tall. How fast can it travel?
   a. 45.8 mph
   b. Mach 5
   c. Warp speed

September 8
NATIONAL AMPERSAND DAY

The ampersand symbol (&) means "and." September 8 was chosen for this celebration because 9/8 looks sort of like the ampersand symbol. Can you fill in the missing word in these famous pairs?

1. Peanut butter & _____

2. Thunder & _____

3. Shoes & _____

4. Bacon & _____

5. Rock & _____

6. Beauty & _____

7. Macaroni & _____

8. Arts & _____

9. Salt & _____

In the late 1800s, the ampersand was considered the **LAST LETTER OF THE ALPHABET**.

The ampersand symbol came from Latin, the language of ancient Rome. In Latin, the word *et* means "and." A writer joined the letters *et* into one symbol and created the &.

INTERNATIONAL SUDOKU DAY

September 9 is the perfect day to celebrate Sudoku. This logic number puzzle challenges puzzle lovers to fill a 9 x 9 grid with numbers from 1 to 9. The name is Japanese for "single number," but the first modern appearance of the puzzle, called "Number Place," was in an American magazine in 1979.

This Riddle Sudoku puzzle uses letters instead of numbers. Fill in the squares so that the six letters appear once in each row, column, and 2 x 3 box. Then read the yellow squares to find out the answer to the riddle.

Riddle: What did the nut say when it sneezed?

"___ ___ ___ ___ ___ ___ !"

Letters: **A C E H S W**

	W		S	A	
S			E		
H			W		
		A			
		W			S
E	S	C		H	

September 19

INTERNATIONAL TALK LIKE A PIRATE DAY

Ahoy, maties! *Aaaaarrr* you ready to get into the spirit of this silly holiday, which was created in 1995? Celebrate by helping these pirates find each sock's match on the ship. Then write the letter on each match to spell out the answer to the riddle.

What kind of socks does a pirate wear?

___ ___ ___ ___ ___ ___ ___ ___

Why couldn't the pirate play cards? Because he was sitting on the deck.

The lotus flower is a symbol of hope and purity.

Take a spin around the globe to see how

September 2

⦿ NATIONAL DAY

On September 2, 1945, Ho Chi Minh declared Vietnam's independence from France. Today, Vietnamese people commemorate this holiday by decorating streets and buildings with the country's flag to display patriotism.

Make a lotus, the national flower of Vietnam.

1. Cut a lily-pad shape from **green cardstock**.

2. For petals, cut out ten 4-inch raindrop shapes from **pink cardstock**. Cut a 1-inch slit in the rounded end of each petal to create two flaps. Glue one flap over the other so the petal creates a cupped shape. Repeat this with the remaining nine petals.

3. Glue the cupped ends of five petals in a circle on the lily pad. Glue a second circle inside the first with the remaining petals.

4. Cut two squares from **yellow cardstock**. Crumple one into a ball. Wrap the other around the ball. Flatten the wrapped ball and glue it to the center of the flower.

September 11

⦿ ENKUTATASH

These flowers are also known as adey abeba.

Happy Ethiopian New Year! Enkutatash marks the first day of the first month of the Ethiopian calendar. People celebrate Enkutatash by eating a traditional meal with their families and giving gifts to children. Children sing, dance, pick flowers, and paint pictures to give to their families and neighbors.

Children pick yellow daisies called meskel flowers, which only bloom during this season. Can you find the three puzzle pieces in this photo?

THE WORLD

September 18
FIESTAS PATRIAS

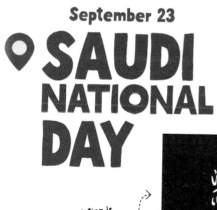

On this day in 1810, Chile decided to establish a Congress, a step which eventually led to the country becoming independent from Spain. Today, the September 18 anniversary is celebrated with "patriotic parties." Every town throws a large party with live music, dancing, and barbecues.

The national dance of Chile is called the *cueca*. During independence day celebrations, dancers will wear traditional clothing to perform the dance. Unscramble the names of five musical instruments that are traditionally used to accompany the cueca.

ARTIGU _____

PRAH _____

ANOPI _____

COCODRAIN _____

MEANITURBO_____

September 23
SAUDI NATIONAL DAY

On this day in 1932, two kingdoms were unified by King Abdulaziz ibn Saud, who changed the name to the Kingdom of Saudi Arabia to honor his family, the House of Saud. Today, people commemorate this occasion with all kinds of cultural events and celebrations. The people wear green, and everywhere they go, the country is decorated with Saudi Arabia's green flag.

Green represents Islam, as it is believed to be the prophet Muhammad's favorite color.

The Arabic inscription is the *shahāda*, the Islamic declaration of faith. The words are written in an artistic form of Islamic calligraphy called *Thuluth*.

The sword symbolizes how strictly the nation will uphold justice.

SUNDAY	MONDAY	TUESDAY	WEDNESDAY
National Hair Day What unique hairstyles can you come up with? **1**	**Gandhi Jayanti (India)** This national holiday honors Mahatma Gandhi's birthday with ceremonies and tributes. It is also the International Day of Nonviolence. **2**	**Soldiers' Day (Honduras)** This holiday takes place on the birthday of Francisco Morazán, a famous Honduran military leader. **3**	**National Taco Day** Taco 'bout awesome **4**
National Fluffernutter Day Peanut butter and marshmallow: sticky, but satisfying. **8**	**INDIGENOUS PEOPLES' DAY** **9**	**World Porridge Day** Watch out for Goldilocks! **10**	*One small step for woman . . .* In 1984, astronaut Kathryn Sullivan became the first American woman to perform a space walk. **1**
National _I Love Lucy_ Day The show premiered on CBS on this day in 1951. **15**	*Talk about a wordsmith. Today is the birthday of Noah Webster, the author of the first American dictionary.* A-Z DICTIONARY **16**	**Dessalines Day (Haiti)** This national holiday celebrates the founding father of Haiti, Jean-Jacques Dessalines, who was killed on this day in 1806. **17**	**Alaska Day** In 1867, the U.S. purchased Alaska, our biggest state. **18**
International Caps Lock Day IT'S LIKE YELLING BUT ON PAPER. **22**	**National Boston Cream Pie Day** **23**	**United Nations Day** The United Nations was formed on this day in 1945. World War II had just ended, and 51 countries joined together to try to maintain peace around the world. **24**	**WORLD PASTA DAY** **25**
International Internet Day How has the internet made your life easier? **29**	**National Checklist Day** ✔ Pencil ✔ Paper ✔ List **30**	**HALLOWEEN** TRICK OR TREAT **31**	**BIRTHSTONES** OPAL TOURMALINE

THURSDAY	FRIDAY	SATURDAY
NATIONAL DO SOMETHING NICE DAY **5**	**National Noodle Day** Spaghetti, pho, pad thai, udon—slurp up a noodle to celebrate today! **6**	**NATIONAL LED LIGHT DAY** **7**
Table for six billion? On this day in 1999, the six billionth living human was born. **12**	**NATIONAL M&M DAY** **13**	*Elementary, my dear Watson. The first installment of The Adventures of Sherlock Holmes was published in 1892.* **14**
NATIONAL NEW FRIENDS DAY Make new friends, but keep the old! **19**	**NATIONAL SUSPENDERS DAY** **20**	*Let there be light! In 1879, Thomas Edison's light bulb stayed lit for thirteen and a half hours, becoming the first light bulb to work for longer than a few minutes.* **21**
National Mule Day A mule is a cross between a male donkey and a female horse. **26**	*City of Brotherly Love. In 1682, Philadelphia was founded.* **27**	**National First Responders Day** Celebrate the helpers who take immediate action in emergency situations. **28**

ZODIAC SIGNS
LIBRA: SEPTEMBER 23– OCTOBER 22

SCORPIO: OCTOBER 23– NOVEMBER 21

FLOWERS
MARIGOLD

COSMOS

OCTOBER

EAT BETTER, EAT TOGETHER MONTH

To celebrate this month, make a goal to eat with your family every night. Get involved in helping pick a healthy menu filled with protein, grains, and fruit or veggies!

There are eight objects hidden in this dinnertime scene. Can you find them all?

house

comb

toothbrush

flute

boomerang

ring

lollipop

fish

NATIONAL BULLYING PREVENTION MONTH

If you've ever wondered if you have been a bully, this quiz could help you find out.

The sad truth is, bullying is pretty common. Without realizing it, even you could have been a bully to someone in your life. This month, make an extra effort to be kind to everyone you meet. The bullying can stop with you!

1. **You hear your best friend teasing a kid about being overweight. You:**

   a. Laugh. Your friend said it in a funny way.

   b. Leave. You don't want any part of your friend's behavior.

   c. Quietly urge your friend to leave the kid alone.

2. **A really embarrassing picture of a kid you know is being sent around. You:**

   a. Show it to everyone around you and then forward it to someone else.

   b. Refuse to accept it, or if it's electronic, delete it from your phone or email.

   c. Tell an adult you trust and ask him or her what to do.

3. **When your teacher tells you to form groups, you notice that the same kids are excluded every time. This time, you:**

   a. Hurry to form your group so that you won't get stuck with those kids.

   b. Don't worry about those kids. Someone else will choose them.

   c. Invite them into your group. No one wants to be left out.

4. **A popular group of kids you really want to be friends with asks you to help play a mean trick on someone. You:**

   a. Play along. They are going to do it with or without you, and this might make you friends with the popular kids.

   b. Pretend you are not going to be in school the day of the trick so you can't be part of it.

   c. Tell them you think it sounds mean and they shouldn't do it.

5. **You see your friend pushing around a kid at recess. You:**

   a. Watch. The kid probably had it coming, and no one else who's watching is stopping the fight.

   b. Leave. It isn't your fight.

   c. Get a teacher. Your friend may not like it, but at least no one will get hurt.

Results

If you answered mostly a:
Careful! You could be a bit of a bully. Before you act, think about how your actions might make others feel.

If you answered mostly b:
You don't bully others, but you don't stick up for kids who are being bullied, either. Ask yourself, "How can I help?"

If you answered mostly c:
You stick up for kids who are being bullied. Good for you! Soon, others may follow your lead.

GLOBAL DIVERSITY
AWARENESS MONTH

The world is full of many different cultures, and this month we get to celebrate them! You probably have friends who have different traditions than you. Many of these traditions have come from other cultures.

The diversity we can find in the United States is one of the things that make it such a great country. We celebrate our differences and learn from each other.

What goes around the world but doesn't move?

The equator

Birthday Traditions Around the World

On birthdays in MEXICO, it's traditional for someone to shove the birthday boy or girl's face into their cake after they take their first bite.

AUSTRALIANS celebrate their birthday by eating fairy bread— buttered bread with rainbow sprinkles.

In THE NETHERLANDS, everyone in the family gets birthday wishes, not just the birthday person.

JAMAICAN birthday boys or girls get flour thrown at them!

In VIETNAM, everyone celebrates their birthday on the same day of the year, called Tet, which is also the beginning of the new year. Children get red envelopes filled with money as presents.

Can you match the cultural tradition with the country that practices it?

China   Greece   Norway

Iceland   Japan

1. In the most populated country in Asia, it isn't rude to slurp noodles—it just means you're enjoying the food!

2. On Christmas Eve in this country, everyone gives books as gifts, followed by an evening of reading together.

3. In homes in this large island country, you always remove your shoes before entering.

4. Even when eating a sandwich, the people in this country are big on using silverware. Table manners are very important to them.

5. Instead of putting their baby teeth under a pillow, kids in this European country throw their teeth onto their roofs.

NATIONAL DESSERT MONTH

Celebrate by making a delicious ice-cream sandwich.

1. Soften a pint of **ice cream** in the refrigerator for a few hours.

2. If you're using add-ins, spoon some of the ice cream into a bowl and mix them in. (Try **mini chocolate chips**, **coconut flakes**, or **berry jam**!)

3. Spoon the mixture into small **paper cups**. Cover each cup with **aluminum foil**. Freeze until the ice cream is solid.

4. On a plate, pair up small, flat **cookies** that are about as wide as your paper cups.

5. Working quickly so the ice cream doesn't melt, peel the paper from one cup. Cut the ice cream into slices, using a **butter knife** dipped in warm water (or using **dental floss** as a "saw"). Place each slice on a cookie. Top it with another cookie.

6. Put each little sandwich in the freezer to harden.

7. Repeat with the other cups and cookies. Then serve.

Try This!
Use different kinds of cookies, wafers, or brownies.

Try This!
Roll the sides of the finished sandwiches in a topping before step 6.

Try This!
If cookies break or things get messy, plop it all into a bowl for a sundae. **Yum!**

TOP 10 MOST POPULAR DESSERTS

1. Fudge
2. Chocolate Cake
3. Chocolate Chip Cookies
4. Brownies
5. Ice Cream
6. Apple Pie
7. Carrot Cake
8. Jell-O
9. Cupcakes
10. Cheesecake

October 7–15, 2023
ALBUQUERQUE INTERNATIONAL
BALLOON FIESTA

For nine days every October, Albuquerque, New Mexico, holds its International Balloon Fiesta. Balloonists from all over the world come to ride, race, and revel in the hundreds of hot-air balloons in attendance. **Find at least 12 differences between the two pictures.**

October 29, 1998
25 YEARS AGO, ASTRONAUT JOHN GLENN RETURNED TO SPACE ON THE SHUTTLE *DISCOVERY*.

At age 77, Glenn became the oldest man to journey off planet, 36 years after his first trip in 1962. His 1998 mission was nine days long. The crew orbited Earth 134 times, traveling 3.6 million miles in all.

Before this space shuttle takes off, try to find all 10 hidden objects.

balloon

slice of pizza

egg

BEFORE THIS TIME, no one of Glenn's age had left Earth's atmosphere. So Glenn's main mission was to see how being in space affects an older body.

On October 15, 2021, actor William Shatner broke John Glenn's record for oldest person in space. Shatner was 90 years old when he made his brief journey off Earth.

Why did the astronaut smile during takeoff?

It was a blast.

pencil

caterpillar

needle

mushroom

iron

tugboat

crayon

TONGUE TWISTERS
REESE'S ROCKET REALLY ROCKS!
RITA READIED THE WRONG ROCKET.
LANA AND LUNA HAD LUNCH BEFORE LAUNCH.

WORLD SERIES

The annual championship series of North American Major League Baseball has been played since 1903. The American League champion team faces off against the National League champion team in a best-of-seven-games series. But why is it called the *World* Series if only North American teams are eligible to play? One legend is that the *New York World* newspaper was the series's original sponsor; however, that's incorrect. When the World Series was first created at the turn of the century, baseball was the quintessential all-American game, and it wasn't played in many other countries around the world. So the organizers claimed that their championship series was showcasing the best baseball players in the world, as a way to draw a bigger crowd. And the name stuck, even as baseball has gained popularity in many countries around the globe.

October 5, 1921

One hundred and two years ago, the first radio broadcast of a World Series game took place as the New York Giants played against the New York Yankees.

A Yankees player, a Giants player, and umpires at the 1921 World Series

This is what a home radio looked like in the 1920s!

RECORD SETTERS

Which player holds each of these career records?

5,714 STRIKEOUTS
Nolan Ryan
or Randy Johnson?

4,256 HITS
Ty Cobb
or Pete Rose?

511 WINS
Cy Young
or Sandy Koufax?

1,406 STOLEN BASES
Willie Mays
or Rickey Henderson?

14 WORLD SERIES APPEARANCES
Yogi Berra
or Babe Ruth?

How do baseball players stay cool?

By sitting next to the fans.

Why are baseball players so rich?

Because they play on diamonds.

How is a baseball team similar to a pancake?

They both need a good batter.

CHAMPIONSHIP

IF AT FIRST . . .

How well do you know your measurements? Answer each "If" statement below to get a letter and find where it goes in the riddle's answer.

A. If a cup is larger than a pint, the third letter is a **U**. If not, it is an **O**.

B. If there are 100 centimeters in a meter, the first and tenth letters are **A**. If not, they are **I**.

C. If a liter is smaller than a gallon, the last letter is an **R**. If not, it is a **T**.

D. If there are three teaspoons in a tablespoon, the sixth letter is an **L**. If not, it is a **D**.

E. If there are 5,000 pounds in a ton, the seventh, ninth, and twelfth letters are **C**. If not, they are **E**.

F. If there are 1,000 grams in a kilogram, the fourth letter is a **U**. If not, it is a **V**.

G. If there are seven feet in two yards, the eighth letter is an **A**. If not, it is an **H**.

H. If a mile is longer than a kilometer, the fifth letter is a **B**. If not, it is a **T**.

I. If 1,000 millimeters equals 1 centimeter, the second and eleventh letters are **B**. If not, they are **D**.

What do you get when you cross a monster and a baseball game?

1	2	3	4	5	6	7	8	9	10	11	12	13

October 4, 2023

RANDOM ACTS OF POETRY DAY

What kind of tree has poems on it?

A poetry

4 Random Ways to Celebrate Poetry

1. Make up a tune and turn your favorite poem into a song. Perform it for your family.

2. Write a poem from an interesting point of view. For example, imagine what a fork would say about being in the dishwasher.

3. Research some poets and read their poems. Try to memorize a poem you like.

4. Challenge yourself to write a short poem and share it with a friend.

What hand is best to write poetry with?

Neither—you should use a pencil!

October 7, 2023

WORLD CARD MAKING DAY

Celebrate the day by making these Halloween-inspired cards to give to a friend!

"Eye" Hope You Have a "Ball" This Halloween!

Spooky Eyeball Card

1. Fold a piece of **cardstock** in half.

2. On the front, use a **white paint pen** to write: *"Eye" hope you have a "ball" this Halloween!*

3. For eyes, glue **cotton balls** onto the card. Cut out irises from cardstock and draw pupils on them with a black **marker**. Glue the irises to the cotton balls.

4. Write a message inside.

Drizzle Art Card

1. Drizzle **gel glue** in a fun design onto **craft foam**. Let the glue dry overnight.

2. Paint over the craft foam and dried glue using no more than two coats of **acrylic paint**. Let it dry.

3. Carefully peel off the glue. Glue the drizzle art to a folded piece of **cardstock** to make a card.

70% of people include their pet's name when signing greeting cards.

October 16
DICTIONARY DAY

There are tons of fun words hidden in the dictionary. Take a moment to find a new word to add to your vocabulary. Here are some of our favorites. **What are your favorite words?**

A dictionary's pages contain many words, but so do its letters! Using only letters in the word DICTIONARY, spell:

1. A child's plaything

——— ——— ———

2. An insect in a colony

——— ——— ———

3. A vegetable on a cob

——— ——— ———

4. Dry mud

——— ——— ———

5. Falling drops of water

——— ——— ———

6. Railroad cars and an engine

——— ——— ———

7. A milk container

——— ——— ———

gewgaw: a trinket

splendiferous: magnificent

collywobbles: a stomachache or feeling of nervousness

bumfuzzle: to confuse

widdershins: counterclockwise

flibbertigibbet: someone who is silly and talks a lot

xertz: to greedily eat or drink

The *Oxford English Dictionary* is one of the most widely used dictionaries in the English language. The first edition took 50 years to complete and was finished in 1928. It included more than 400,000 words and phrases from the 12th century to the present!

October 22
NATIONAL COLOR DAY

Each group of 3 words describes a color. Use your color IQ to figure out each one.

Where do crayons go on vacation? Colorado

1. Crimson   Ruby   Scarlet
2. Azure   Cobalt   Teal
3. Auburn   Mahogany   Sepia
4. Amber   Citron   Canary
5. Sage   Chartreuse Jade
6. Plum   Mauve   Lavender
7. Tangerine   Marigold   Persimmon
8. Jet   Charcoal   Onyx

October 22 is also **National Smart Is Cool Day.** Get together with your friends and share your favorite trivia!

WORLD FOOD DAY

KIDS' SCIENCE QUESTIONS

Why do some kids like foods that other kids don't?

The foods people like best are often the ones they're used to eating or that they think of positively. A good or bad experience can make a person like or dislike a certain flavor or even a food's texture or appearance. You'd probably rather eat a food you always eat at parties than a food you remember eating just before getting sick!

People can also inherit traits that make them more likely to enjoy or dislike certain foods. For example, if you inherited an ability to detect very small differences in flavors, you might think a food is way too spicy while other kids think it's just right.

But good news! Scientists say that we can learn to like foods. So even if you give a thumbs-down to a food today, in time you might give it a thumbs-up.

Ask for an adult's help with anything hot.

October 26

NATIONAL PUMPKIN DAY

PUMPKIN BREAD

1. Have an adult preheat the oven to 350°F.
2. Spray two loaf pans with **cooking spray**.
3. In a medium bowl, mix 3 cups **all-purpose flour**, 1 teaspoon **cinnamon**, 1 teaspoon **nutmeg**, 1 teaspoon **salt**, and 1 teaspoon **baking soda**.
4. In a large bowl, whisk 4 large **eggs**. Add 1½ cups **sugar**, 1 15-ounce can **pumpkin**, ½ cup **vegetable oil**, ½ cup **applesauce**, 1 teaspoon **vanilla extract**, and ½ cup **chocolate chips**.
5. Mix wet and dry ingredients in the large bowl. Pour the batter into the pans.
6. Bake 50–55 minutes.

WORLD PASTA DAY

Pasta has been eaten for thousands of years. In that time, over 300 different types of pasta have been created in Italy alone. Twenty-six popular types of pasta are listed below. **Can you find where each name fits in the grid? Use the number of letters in each word to figure out where each one belongs.**

WORD LIST

4 letters
ORZO
ZITI
5 letters
FIORI
PENNE
6 letters
ROTINI
7 letters
FUSILLI
GEMELLI
GNOCCHI
LASAGNE
PASTINA
RAVIOLI
ROTELLE
8 letters
COUSCOUS
FARFALLE
LINGUINE
RIGATONI

9 letters
CAPELLINI
MANICOTTI
RADIATORE
SPAGHETTI
10 letters
CANNELLONI
FETTUCCINE
TORTELLINI
VERMICELLI
11 letters
ORECCHIETTE
TAGLIATELLE

R A V I O L I

This day was established by the **WORLD PASTA CONGRESS—** a group of pasta makers from around the world.

PASTA PAIRING

Many countries have their own version of this popular food. Can you match the country with its pasta?

1.	GERMANY	A.	SORRENTINOS
2.	GREECE	B.	PIEROGI
3.	POLAND	C.	PTITIM
4.	JAPAN	D.	SPAGHETTI AND MEATBALLS
5.	MOROCCO	E.	COUSCOUS
6.	ARGENTINA	F.	SPAETZLE
7.	ISRAEL	G.	ORZO
8.	UNITED STATES	H.	UDON

October 6 is **NATIONAL NOODLE DAY** and October 17 is **NATIONAL PASTA DAY**. October has plenty of opportunities to indulge in your favorite pasta dish!

October 31
HALLOWEEN

Check out these frightening and fascinating facts!

THE SCOOP ON PUMPKINS

The heaviest pumpkin on record weighed **2,625 pounds.**

That's about as much as an adult giraffe!

A pumpkin that big could make about **602 pumpkin pies.**

SWEET STATS

Americans' favorite Halloween treats:

Chocolate
68%

Candy Corn
10%

Chewy Candy
7%

WHAT A SCREAM!

The loudest scream ever recorded reached **129 DECIBELS (dB).** That's louder than a chainsaw.

100 dB
108–114 dB
120 dB
129 dB

BY THE NUMBERS

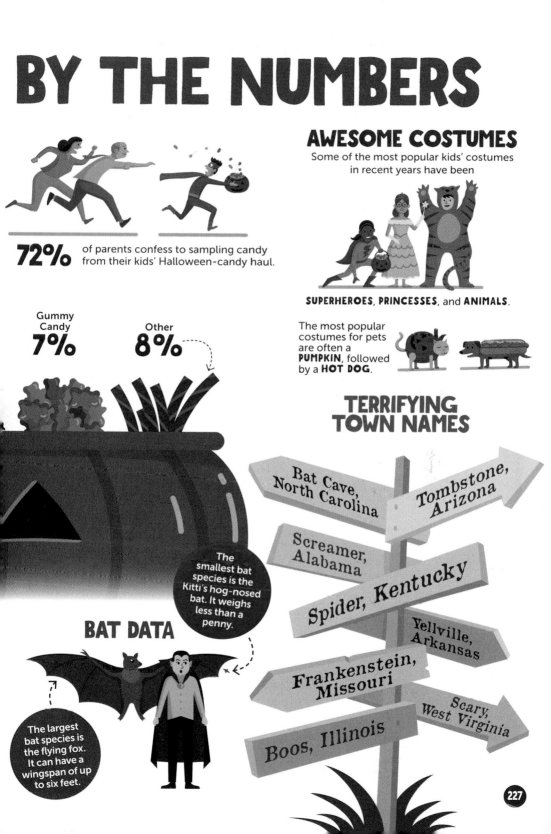

72% of parents confess to sampling candy from their kids' Halloween-candy haul.

AWESOME COSTUMES
Some of the most popular kids' costumes in recent years have been

SUPERHEROES, PRINCESSES, and **ANIMALS.**

Gummy Candy
7%

Other
8%

The most popular costumes for pets are often a **PUMPKIN,** followed by a **HOT DOG.**

TERRIFYING TOWN NAMES

Bat Cave, North Carolina

Tombstone, Arizona

Screamer, Alabama

Spider, Kentucky

Yellville, Arkansas

Frankenstein, Missouri

Scary, West Virginia

Boos, Illinois

The smallest bat species is the Kitti's hog-nosed bat. It weighs less than a penny.

BAT DATA

The largest bat species is the flying fox. It can have a wingspan of up to six feet.

October 1

INTERNATIONAL RACCOON APPRECIATION DAY

A raccoon's paws really come in handy. In fact, raccoons use the sense of touch in their paws more than their other senses. If you've ever seen a raccoon "washing" its food, it's actually doing something called dousing. Getting their paws wet heightens raccoons' sense of touch, so they're able to feel what they are holding better.

This raccoon and his woodland friends are having a blast trick-or-treating. How are these pictures the same? How are they different?

October 8

WORLD OCTOPUS DAY

OCTOPUSES HAVE THREE HEARTS.

Octopuses are talented, eight-limbed creatures. Among their many skills is their ability to change colors. This talent helps them camouflage to stay safe from predators or to hide while hunting for food. Changing colors is also how they communicate with other octopuses! If humans spoke in colors, what color do you think "hello" would be?

Having eight arms in the kitchen would definitely be helpful! **Hunt for the six objects in this scene while Chef Cephalopod prepares dinner.**

oar   oak leaf   octagon   orange   owl   ornament

October 20
INTERNATIONAL SLOTH DAY

The sloths are all celebrating International Sloth Day at Sloth-Land Adventure Park! Snoozanne wants to see a concert, Snorbert can't wait to go on a tube tour, and Dozallta is eager to try the ropes course. But all three activities have just started! What time is it?

Three-toed sloths' fur is home to moths and algae. The moths help the algae grow, and the algae is a form of food and camouflage for the sloths.

Sloths live for a long time—on average about 20 years. The oldest sloth grew up in Australia's Adelaide Zoo and lived to be **43 years old!**

ROCK-A-BYE CONCERTS
Every 3 hours from 12:00 P.M. to 9:00 P.M.

LAZY RIVER TUBE TOURS
Every 1½ hours from 12:00 P.M. to 9:00 P.M.

TREETOP ROPES COURSE
Every 2 hours from 2:00 P.M. to 8:00 P.M.

October 29
NATIONAL SEA SLUG DAY

Sea slugs roam the ocean floors and coral reefs. They are known as *nudibranchs* (NEW-duh-branks), which means "naked gill." This snail-without-a-shell looks as if it would be easy prey, but even without a shell, nudibranchs have ways to avoid predators.

Rhinophores (RYE-no-fours) detect odors, helping the nudibranch find prey and avoid predators.

These bright colors may warn a predator who takes a toxic taste to stay away next time!

This nudibranch's "naked gills" are on its back.

With a wavelike motion of its long, muscular foot, the nudibranch can crawl with the current. Some species even swim.

It can safely eat toxic prey like anemones and sponges, absorbing the toxins to use for its own defense.

What's a slug's favorite dessert?

Key slime pie.

October 4 is World Animal Day! With over 1.2 million species discovered so far, there is a lot to celebrate today.

229

October 13, 2023

ADA LOVELACE DAY

This holiday celebrates the achievements of women in STEM (science, technology, engineering, and math). It is named for Ada Lovelace, who has been called the world's first computer programmer because of her work translating and commentating on Charles Babbage's Analytical Engine. She realized that computers had potential beyond mathematics.

Using the clues below, can you figure out which woman in STEM each kid is learning about and how they're presenting their project?

	Dorothy Hodgkin	Hedy Lamarr	Edith Clarke	Katherine Johnson	Book Report	Diorama	Poster	Scale Model
Ada								
Eli								
Marie								
Charles								

1. One of the kids picked a woman whose first name starts with the same letter as his name and who was the first woman to earn an electrical engineering degree from MIT.

2. Marie checked out a biography to write about the 1964 Nobel Prize in Chemistry winner.

3. Ada drew a movie poster to show the inventions of the actress and inventor she selected.

4. Everyone loved the space capsule model Charles did about his subject, whose mathematical calculations for NASA helped send astronauts to the moon.

October 31

NATIONAL MAGIC DAY

Can you help Tricky Trixie find her way to her magic show? The symbols will tell you which way to move.

Move 1 space down

Move 1 space up

Move 1 space right

Move 1 space left

Path 1	Path 2	Path 3	Path 4	Path 5	Path 6

What do you call an owl magician?

Whoo-dini

Take a spin around the globe to see how

October 10

NATIONAL DAY

National Day in Taiwan, also known as Double Ten Day, celebrates the 1911 Wuchang Uprising, which ultimately led to the collapse of the Qing Dynasty. There is a large parade held at the Presidential Office Building and a huge fireworks display held in the evening.

The Presidential Office Building in Taipei, one of Taiwan's most famous buildings, has more than 300 rooms.

October 18

INDEPENDENCE DAY

The blue stripe and the crescent represent Azerbaijan's Turkic origins.

32 years ago, in 1991, Azerbaijan adopted a constitutional act that restored its independence from the Soviet Union. The vote to support the act was unanimous among the citizens of Azerbaijan.

Like most flags, this one is full of symbolism.

There are over **400 VOLCANOES** in Azerbaijan, but they don't shoot lava—they shoot mud and sometimes oil. When they aren't making a muddy mess, they let out sulfur gases, making the area smell a lot like eggs.

The red portion symbolizes developing democracy.

The green is a nod to Islam, the most practiced religion in Azerbaijan.

The eight-point star is a reference to how Azerbaijan was written in the old alphabet, with eight letters.

THE WORLD

The Austrian Parliament building in Vienna was built between 1874 and 1883. The main statue in the fountain in front of the building is Athena, the Greek goddess of wisdom.

October 26
NATIONAL DAY

This day is a celebration of the Austrian Parliament passing a law in 1955 that Austria would remain a neutral country.

At the time, it was occupied by four countries (the Soviet Union, the United States, Great Britain, and France), post–World War II. By declaring neutrality, the law ended the occupation and allowed Austria to be its own country again. On this day, in addition to several rituals performed by the government, federal museums open their doors for free to Austrian citizens.

October 29
REPUBLIC DAY

This is a day to celebrate in Turkey, as people remember Turkey's victory in the War of Independence in 1923. There are fireworks, art events, concerts, and celebrations throughout the country. Can you find where the three jigsaw pieces fit into this photo of a Republic Day celebration?

233

SUNDAY	MONDAY	TUESDAY	WEDNESDAY

FLOWER
CHRYSANTHEMUM

ZODIAC SIGNS
SCORPIO:
OCTOBER 23–
NOVEMBER 21

SAGITTARIUS:
NOVEMBER 22–
DECEMBER 21

National Author's Day
Who's your favorite author? Is there an author whose books you've wanted to read?

Bye-bye, Daylight Saving Time! Did you turn back your clock one hour?
*You're off the hook again, Arizona and Hawaii.
5

National Nachos Day
Grab your chips and pile on the toppings. Today is a great day for nachos.
6

ELECTION DAY
VOTED
7

Cook Something Bold and Pungent Day
Fill your home with smells of spicy pepper, garlic, onions, or whatever flavors say *BAM!*
8

DIWALI
12

WORLD KINDNESS DAY
You're welcome!
13

In 1989, George H. W. Bush made pardoning a live Thanksgiving turkey a national tradition.
14

America Recycles Day
Take the pledge to "Keep America Beautiful"!
15

In 1997, Bobbi McCaughey became the first woman to successfully give birth to septuplets (seven babies). Today, they are 26 years old!
19

NATIONAL PEANUT BUTTER FUDGE DAY
Take a bite of this sweet treat!
20

World Hello Day
Guten Tag! Hola! Konnichiwa!
Aim to greet 10 new people today.
21

Go for a Ride Day
Hop on your bike or board, and get out of the house!
22

National Cake Day
This day takes the cake!
26

So many floats! In 1924, Macy's department store sponsored its first Thanksgiving Day Parade. Although held on Thanksgiving, it was actually a Christmas parade.
27

National French Toast Day
In France, French toast is called *pain perdu*, or "lost bread."
28

One giant footstep! In 2004, movie monster Godzilla was given a star on the Hollywood Walk of Fame.
29

THURSDAY	FRIDAY	SATURDAY
NATIONAL DEVILED EGG DAY **2**	**WORLD JELLYFISH DAY** **3**	*Westward, ho!* The first wagon train arrived in California 181 years ago. The group had left Independence, Missouri, on May 1, 1841. **4**
Independence Day (Cambodia) This holiday celebrates independence from France in 1953 with speeches and a torch-lighting ceremony. **9**	*What a wall!* In 1970, China opened up the Great Wall of China to tourists from around the world for the first time. **10**	**VETERANS DAY** **11**
HAVE A PARTY WITH YOUR BEAR DAY **16**	*Click this!* In 1970, Douglas Engelbart was granted a patent for the "X-Y Position Indicator for a Display System," what we now call a computer mouse. **17**	**National Apple Cider Day** A delicious fall drink! **18**
THANKSGIVING DAY **23**	**Celebrate Your Unique Talent Day** **24**	**National Parfait Day** Layers of yogurt, fruit, and granola—sounds pretty perfect! **25**
Saint Andrew's Day (Scotland) Scots honor the patron saint of Scotland with festivals and celebrations full of music, dance, and food. **30**	**BIRTHSTONES** TOPAZ -->	CITRINE

NOVEMBER

NATIONAL NATIVE AMERICAN HERITAGE MONTH

November celebrates the diverse and rich culture, history, and traditions of Native peoples. It's also a time to raise awareness about the struggles Native people have faced in the past as well as in the present.

There are 573 federally recognized Native American Nations in the United States. Two hundred and twenty-nine of these are in Alaska.

More than 5.2 million Americans, or 1.7 percent of the U.S. population, are of Native heritage.

The sport of lacrosse comes from stickball games the Native Americans played as early as the 12th century. It could be a violent sport, which gave the game the reputation of being good for combat training.

A Navajo girl in a traditional handwoven blanket looks out over Monument Valley.

The names of the 10 largest Native American tribes are listed here in alphabetical order. Use the number of letters in each word as a clue to where it might fit in the grid.

APACHE
BLACKFEET
CHEROKEE
CHICKASAW
CHOCTAW
HAUDENOSAUNEE
MUSCOGEE
NAVAJO
OJIBWE
PUEBLO

Ask a teacher or librarian to help you learn about the Native history of your area.

NATIONAL MODEL RAILROAD MONTH

Passenger railroads started in the 1820s, and toy trains made of wood and metal arrived in the 1860s. Today, kids and adults enjoy model railroading.

Fill in the letters in the picture code to answer the riddle.

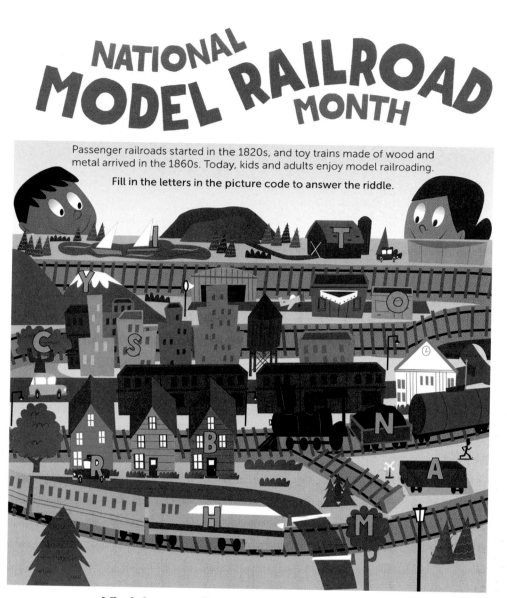

What do you call a locomotive that sneezes?

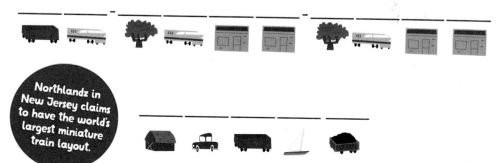

Northlandz in New Jersey claims to have the world's largest miniature train layout.

FAMILY STORIES MONTH

Everyone has a story. Ask your parents, grandparents, or other family members for theirs! Share yours, too.

What's silly in this family photo? Take turns telling a silly (but true!) story about your family.

STORY STARTS

Genealogy is the study of family history and ancestry. Be your family's genealogist! Write down or record your relatives' stories. You might ask these questions:

- What is your earliest memory?
- What was your favorite game growing up?
- Who was your best friend when you were my age?
- What was your first job?
- What was your favorite song, TV show, or movie?
- Where was your favorite place to visit?

> Look around your house. An old photo album, school diploma, or favorite knickknack may spark a family member's story.

KIDS' SCIENCE QUESTIONS

Why can't you remember anything from when you were a baby?

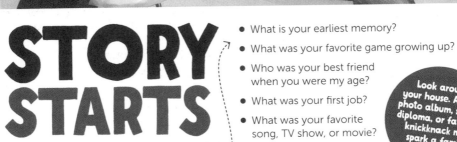

> Short-term memories last for seconds to hours. Long-term memories last for years.

Babies do form memories as building blocks for their development. Babies remember faces, copy what they see, and learn how to talk. Later on, using words to store memories helps them to recall specific events. We may not remember events from when we were babies because we didn't have the words to attach to the memories. Thank goodness for baby photos and videos!

NATIONAL NOVEL WRITING MONTH

November is also Picture Book Month.

NOVEMBER 15 is I Love to Write Day.

Every November, aspiring authors attempt to write a novel in just 30 days. Challenge yourself to write this month, even if you're not writing a novel. Here are some writing activities you can use to hone your skills.

CHARACTER PLAY

With a partner, decide on two characters from books, movies, your imagination, or the real world that could have a conversation—maybe Harry Potter and Peter Pan, Goldilocks and Baby Bear, or a lion and a hippo who both want to drink from the same watering hole.

One of you starts the conversation on paper, writing a sentence as one of the characters. The other person writes a response as the second character. Keep going back and forth until you have written for about 10 minutes. Then read your script out loud, with each person reading their character's part.

OOPS!

We all make mistakes. Luckily, most mistakes aren't serious, and sometimes they're funny when they're in the past. Write about one of your funny mistakes.

PERFECT PROFESSIONS

When writers come up with names for their characters, there are often specific reasons for them. Maybe the name sets a mood, says something about the character, or is just funny. Here are some character names that fit their professions. Can you come up with more?

CONTRACTOR: I. M. BUILDER

DINER CHEF: PATTY COOK

SWIMMER: WILL FLOAT

AUTHOR: PAGE TURNER

CHAUFFEUR: MERCEDES D. DRIVER

VALET: PARKER CARR

TRACK AND FIELD COACH: MILES LONG

BANKER: RICH N. CASH

BODYGUARD: JUSTIN CASE

Sue Justice

Lawyer

Hunter N. Skye

Astronomer

Barry D. Treasure

Pirate

November 1, 1848
175 YEARS AGO, THE FIRST WOMEN'S MEDICAL SCHOOL OPENED.

Boston Female Medical School was founded in Boston, Massachusetts, by Samuel Gregory. There were only twelve students in the first graduating class. Before this school opened, it was difficult for women to get medical degrees. The Boston Female Medical School became one more small step toward welcoming women into the medical field.

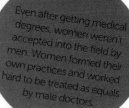

Even after getting medical degrees, women weren't accepted into the field by men. Women formed their own practices and worked hard to be treated as equals by male doctors.

There are 14 items hidden in the scene. Can you find them all?

clothespin

funnel

thimble

button

cracker

lollipop

ruler

wristwatch

mallet

compass

domino

feather

pennant

toothpaste

November 30, 1858
165 YEARS AGO, THE MASON JAR WAS INVENTED.

John Landis Mason invented the Mason jar to create a more effective way to store food. His airtight jars helped food stay fresher for longer, which cut down on foodborne illnesses.

Pickling food helps it last longer. Pickled vegetables can last **UP TO TWO MONTHS** in the fridge when stored in an airtight container like a Mason jar.

MAKE YOUR OWN PICKLED VEGGIES

Ask for an adult's help with anything sharp or hot.

1. With help from an adult, peel 2 large, seedless **cucumbers**. Trim the ends, halve lengthwise, and cut crosswise into ¼-inch-thick slices. Peel a **carrot** and cut into ¼-inch slices.

2. Put the cucumbers and carrot in a **1-quart Mason jar** or other acid-proof container with a tight-fitting lid.

3. To make the brine, put ¾ cup **rice vinegar**, ¾ cup **hot water**, 6 tablespoons **sugar**, and ½ teaspoon **salt** in a heat-proof bowl.

4. Stir the brine until the sugar and salt dissolve. Let it cool for 15 minutes. Then pour it into the jar. Chill the veggies in the refrigerator for at least three hours.

RICE VINEG

SUGAR

S

MASON JAR CANDLE HOLDERS

Mason jars aren't just good for storing food. Many people use them to make crafts, like this candle holder.

1. Cut or tear **tissue paper** into small pieces.

2. Coat a small section of a **Mason jar** with **glue**. Cover with tissue paper.

3. Repeat until you've covered the outside of the jar.

4. Place a **battery-powered candle** in your candle holder and watch it glow.

NATIONAL TAKE A HIKE DAY

About **35 million** Americans go day hiking.

The Appalachian Trail is the longest hiking-only footpath in the world. It covers about **2,190 miles** from Maine to Georgia, passing through **14 states.** Each year, more than 3 million people walk a bit of it and about 3,000 try to hike it from beginning to end, which takes five to seven months.

As Mike hiked with his family, he wrote about their day. Later, he noticed that each sentence contained an item they took on the hike! Can you find a hiking item hidden in each of the sentences below? Hint: All the items are in the scene.

EXAMPLE: Like all good hikers, we left the trail unchanged. (lunch)

1. Emma planned the route.

2. We stopped to sketch at the bridge.

3. Two squirrels came racing along a log!

4. The whole crew ate raisins for energy.

5. We came upon chopped trees near a beaver dam.

6. Our pace had to slow at challenging, rocky parts of the trail.

BONUS! How many squirrels can you find in the scene?

COMPASS CODE

To answer the riddle below, **start at the North (N) circle**. Then move in the directions listed and write the letters you find in the correct spaces.

Where's the best place to eat while hiking?

Where there's ___ ___ ___ ___ ___ ___ ___ ___

___ ___ ___ ___ ___ ___ ___ ___

1. S 1 ___
2. SE 2 ___
3. W 3 ___
4. NW 1 ___
5. S 3 ___
6. NE 3 ___
7. W 1 ___
8. S 2 ___
9. N 1 ___
10. SE 2 ___
11. W 3 ___
12. N 1 ___
13. E 2 ___
14. NW 2 ___

NATIONAL SQUARE DANCE DAY

Swing your partner—do-si-do! In this folk dance, four couples face each other to form a square and follow the steps sung or called out by a "caller."

There are at least 10 differences in these pictures. How many can you find?

BOW TO YOUR PARTNER!

Here's how to do some of the most common square-dance moves.

Allemande Left: Turn to the dancer next to you who is not your partner (also called your *corner*). Then join left hands or link elbows, and circle around until you are back next to your partner.

Do-Si-Do: Face your partner. Step past each other, passing right shoulders. Without turning, step around, back to back, passing left shoulders, until you are in front of your partner again.

Right and Left Grand: Face your partner, join right hands, and walk past each other. Then join left hands with the next person stepping toward you. Circle around, switching hands, until you come back to your partner.

Promenade: Stand side by side with your partner and join hands, right with right, left with left. Walk together counterclockwise in a circle until you reach your starting position.

Swing Your Partner: Link right elbows and step in a clockwise circle, staying in the same spot in the square.

The largest square dance, with **1,632 PARTICIPANTS,** took place at the 66th National Square Dance Convention in 2017.

FROM ALABAMA TO WASHINGTON, as many as 31 states have listed the square dance as their "state dance" or "state folk dance."

NATIONAL COOK FOR YOUR PETS DAY

Make a special meal for your furry or feathered or scaly friend. You won't even need a stove to "cook up" these treats!

Ask an adult for help with anything sharp. Check with your vet before feeding new foods to your pet.

PUP CAKE

1. Mix together 2 tablespoons **dry dog food**, 1 tablespoon **peanut butter**, and 1 tablespoon **mashed banana**.
2. Press the mixture into a muffin-tin cup. Carefully tap the treat out and place it on a dog dish.
3. Add **banana slices**. Top with a **dog treat**.

CAT SNACK

1. Mix together 2 tablespoons **tuna**, 1 tablespoon **shredded cheese**, and 1 teaspoon **oatmeal**.
2. Press the mixture into a muffin-tin cup. Carefully tap the treat out and place it on a cat dish.
3. Top with small **cat treats**.

TOWERING TREAT

1. For other animals, slice up their favorite **fruits** and **vegetables**.
2. Stack the pieces in layers.
3. Top with their favorite **treat**.

NATIONAL CIDER DAY

HOT SPICED CIDER

1. Pour 1 gallon **cider** into a large slow cooker. Stir in 3 tablespoons **honey** and ¼ teaspoon ground **ginger**.
2. Add 12 whole **cloves**, 1 **cinnamon stick**, and ⅓ of an **orange**, sliced.
3. Place the lid on the slow cooker. Heat on HIGH for 2 hours.
4. Ask an adult to use a spoon to remove the cloves, cinnamon stick, and orange slices.
5. Ladle the cider into mugs. Top with **whipped cream**.

Ask for an adult's help with anything sharp or hot.

NATIONAL FRENCH TOAST DAY

OVERNIGHT FRENCH TOAST

1. Cut a 16-ounce loaf of French bread into 1-inch slices.
2. Place 5 eggs, 1½ cups milk, ½ cup half-and-half, ⅓ cup maple syrup, and ½ teaspoon salt into a large bowl. Whisk the mixture until blended.
3. Place the sliced bread into a baking dish. Pour the mixture over the bread and press the slices into it. Cover the dish with foil and refrigerate overnight.
4. Remove the dish from the refrigerator at least one hour before baking.
5. Ask an adult to preheat the oven to 375°F. Bake the French toast for 35 minutes or until golden brown.
6. For the topping, combine 2 tablespoons melted butter and 2 tablespoons maple syrup. Pour it over the French toast before serving.

SAXOPHONE DAY

There's music in the air! Use the list of instruments to solve these music jokes. Each coded space has two numbers. The first number tells you which instrument to look at. The second number tells you which letter in that instrument to use.

Tongue Twister:
Six sassy saxophones sit.

Instrument List

1. DRUM
2. FLUTE
3. VIOLIN
4. TRUMPET
5. CLARINET
6. COWBELL
7. KEYBOARD
8. TROMBONE
9. SAXOPHONE

What kind of music do they play at Stonehenge?

H __ __ __ __ __ __ __ __ __ __
9-6 5-3 1-2 7-8   4-2 3-3 5-1 7-1

How can your hair make music?

__ __ __ __ __ __   __ __   __ __ __ __ __ __ __ __ __
6-3 5-5 2-4 9-6   7-6   9-6 2-5 5-3 1-1 6-4 9-2 3-6 7-8

Who leads the bird band?

__ __ __ __ __-__ __ __ __ __ __-__ __ __ __ __
4-1 9-6 7-2   5-1 6-2 8-7   1-1 4-3 6-1 7-1   2-4 9-4 8-2

How do you make a bandstand?

__ __ __ __ __ __ __ __ __ __ __ __ __ __ __ __
8-1 5-3 7-1 8-8   7-6 6-3 9-2 7-3   4-1 9-6 2-5 3-2 8-2

__ __ __ __ __ __ __
6-1 9-6 5-3 3-5 8-2 9-1

STEP TO THE MUSIC

Who took the same number of steps to their music stands? Who took the fewest?

Although the saxophone is usually made of brass, it is considered a wind instrument.

Tim
Andy
Rachel
Caitlin

Use a couch or desk as a stage, or make your own! --->

SESAME STREET DAY

Make your own puppets to celebrate our puppet friends from Sesame Street.

1. For a face, cut out a circle from cardstock. Glue on yarn for fur, pompom eyes with felt pupils, a balloon nose, and a rickrack mouth. Glue the face to the toe of an old sock.

2. For armholes, cut a slit in each side of the sock below the head. Put an old glove inside the sock, with the thumb and pinky finger sticking out of the slits.

3. For claws, glue rickrack to the end of each arm.

4. For a tail, pinch a bit of fabric on the back of the puppet. Poke a fuzzy stick through the fabric and twist it in place. Bend or curl the tail.

5. Make a few puppets, and put on a show!

November 11

NATIONAL ORIGAMI DAY

Origami comes from the Japanese words oru (to fold) and kami (paper).

Origami is the art form of folding paper into different shapes. Origami Day began in Japan, where the folded-paper crane has become a symbol of peace.

MAKE AN ORIGAMI DRINKING CUP

1. Fold the paper in half diagonally (corner to corner).

2. Fold the left corner over the right side.

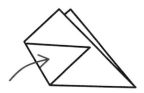

3. Fold the right corner over to the left side.

4. Fold the top front flap down.

5. Flip the cup over. Fold the other top flap down.

6. Open your cup, fill it up, and take a sip!

THANKSGIVING

THANKFUL TURKEY

Cut a head, body, wings, and feet from poster board. Decorate them with cardstock, yarn, and markers.

Buddy, my hamster

hugs!

Ice Cream

wednesdays with Grandma

my Teacher

flute lessons

Birthday parties

My CAT

I AM THANKFUL FOR . . .

Cut feathers from cardstock. Write something you're thankful for on each feather. Glue or tape them onto the turkey.

Adult turkeys have **5,000–6,000** feathers, including 18 large quill feathers on their tails.

Save some feathers and have your Thanksgiving guests write what they're thankful for!

WHICH THANKSGIVING FOOD ARE YOU?

1. To cheer up a friend, you . . .
   a. Play their favorite game
   b. Talk about what's wrong
   c. Make them a card full of jokes

2. Your ideal birthday is . . .
   a. Playing laser tag
   b. Going to the movies
   c. Visiting an animal shelter

3. Which do you do for fun?
   a. Try out a new activity
   b. Read
   c. Invite friends over to play

4. What is your favorite part of the school day?
   a. Recess
   b. Art class
   c. Talking with friends at lunch

5. Which do you love most about Thanksgiving?
   a. Goofing around with family
   b. Remembering what you're thankful for
   c. Helping to prepare the Thanksgiving feast

MOSTLY A's: You are turkey. You are an outgoing person who likes to be in the middle of the action.
MOSTLY B's: You are mashed potatoes. Friends and family are drawn to your quiet, warm personality.
MOSTLY C's: You are pumpkin pie. You go out of your way to do or say sweet things to brighten someone's day.

TURKEY TROT

Help Tara get to the oven to take the turkey out.

START

FINISH

MAKE A MATCH

Find five pairs of matching turkeys.

FAVORITE FOODS

Unscramble these top 10 favorite Thanksgiving foods. Which dish is your favorite?

1. IPE
2. GUFFNITS
3. VAGYR
4. EWEST APESTOTO
5. MAH
6. ASHDEM ETTAOOPS
7. CAM NAD ESHEEC
8. ENGER ANEB ACRESOLES
9. NCOR DEBRA
10. KURTYE

The Wampanoag, or Wôpanâak, have lived in what is now New England for about twelve thousand years. Their ancestors met the Pilgrims in 1620. One year later, they and the settlers participated in several days of feasting and games that we now call the first Thanksgiving.

249

November 1

NATIONAL VINEGAR DAY

Vinegar is versatile. It can be used for cooking, baking, cleaning—even science experiments! Watch what happens when you mix vinegar with baking soda in the following experiment.

1. Set a **muffin tin** on a **baking sheet**. Add ¼ cup **baking soda** to each muffin cup.
2. Put 10–15 drops of **food coloring** into each cup, one color per cup.
3. Quickly pour **vinegar** into each muffin cup. Watch what happens!

WHAT CAUSES THIS REACTION?

When baking soda and vinegar mix, they create a gas that makes the mixture foam up with lots of little bubbles.

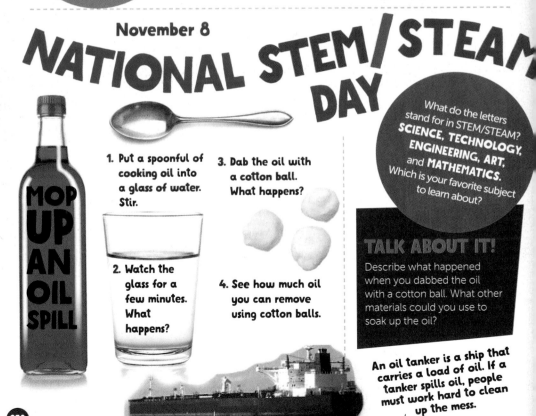

November 8

NATIONAL STEM/STEAM DAY

1. Put a spoonful of cooking oil into a glass of water. Stir.

2. Watch the glass for a few minutes. What happens?

3. Dab the oil with a cotton ball. What happens?

4. See how much oil you can remove using cotton balls.

MOP UP AN OIL SPILL

What do the letters stand for in STEM/STEAM? **SCIENCE, TECHNOLOGY, ENGINEERING, ART,** and **MATHEMATICS.** Which is your favorite subject to learn about?

TALK ABOUT IT!

Describe what happened when you dabbed the oil with a cotton ball. What other materials could you use to soak up the oil?

An oil tanker is a ship that carries a load of oil. If a tanker spills oil, people must work hard to clean up the mess.

250

November 8
WORLD RADIOGRAPHY DAY

Also known as the International Day of Radiology and National X-Ray Day, this date marks the discovery of the X-ray by Wilhelm Roentgen in 1895.

Follow the correct maze path from START to FINISH. Write down the letters you pick up along the way. Then unscramble them to learn what caused Xavier's tummyache.

START

FINISH

LETTERS: _ _ _ _ _ _ _ _ _ _ _ _ _

ANSWER: _____

BONE UP!

In what part of your body can you find these bones? **Hint:** One letter from each word, in order, spells out the answer.

ULNA

RADIUS

HUMERUS

What has fingers but no bones?

A glove

How do you say "Good day" to a French skeleton?

"Bone-jour!"

November 12, 2023
INTERNATIONAL
TONGUE TWISTER DAY

Say "It's the second Sunday of the eleventh month" five times fast. That's International Tongue Twister Day. These word workouts have been used to help learn a new language, overcome speech problems, and cure hiccups.

TOUGHEST TWISTERS

Pad kid poured curd pulled cod. This twister was created in a study by speech researchers at the Massachusetts Institute of Technology in 2013. The MIT team said those who tried to say the phrase either could not repeat it or stopped talking altogether.

The sixth sick sheikh's sixth sheep's sick.
This was the most difficult tongue twister in the English language as of 1974, the last time the category was listed in *Guinness World Records*.

Iqaqa laziqikaqika kwaze kwaqhawaka uqhoqhoqha.
In 1974, *Guinness World Records* also included this as the most difficult tongue twister in the world. It's in the Xhosa language of South Africa and has three clicking sounds in the last word. It means "The skunk rolled down and ruptured its larynx."

TWISTED HISTORY

Peter Piper picked a peck of pickled peppers. This first appeared in 1813 in John Harris's *Peter Piper's Practical Principles of Plain and Perfect Pronunciation.* Some say this phrase refers to a French spice grower named Pierre Poivre, who wrote about his travels in 1769. His name translates to *Peter Pepper*, but *piper* is also a Latin and an Old English word for *pepper*.

November 16
NATIONAL BUTTON DAY

People have been collecting antique and decorative buttons since at least 1938. The National Button Society was founded on this date!
This fasten-ating jar holds more than just buttons. Find: 1 letter *B*, 2 dog bones, 3 rubber balls, 4 pennies, and 5 wrapped candies.

The word button is from the French word **BOUTON,** meaning "bud" or "knob."

The oldest button, carved from a shell, was found in what is now Pakistan. It is about **5,000 YEARS OLD.** But these early buttons were used as decorations on clothing, not as fasteners.

In the 14th century, wearing many buttons—especially those made of gold, silver, or ivory—showed how wealthy you were.

November 13
WORLD KINDNESS DAY

Spread kindness to someone who could use a pick-me-up. Give them a jar of sunshine!

1. Fill a clean **jar** with happy messages or quotes written on **yellow paper**. Add other small **yellow objects**.

2. For labels, decorate two pieces of yellow paper. **Tape** one piece to the jar and another to the lid.

November 19
NATIONAL CAMP DAY

Head out into the wilderness and pitch your tent. Today is National Camp Day! **Can you find all eight objects hidden at this campsite?**

baseball bat

heart

paper clip

piece of popcorn

envelope

glove

tennis ball

fishhook

Calacas (skeletons) and calaveras (colorful skulls) appear in parades, as costumes or masks, and even as chocolate or cookie shapes.

Take a spin around the globe to see how peopl

November 1–2

◉ DÍA DE LOS MUERTOS

Mexicans in Mexico and in other countries celebrate the Day of the Dead (Día de los Muertos) as a time to remember family members who have passed away and to encourage their spirits to return for a visit. Many people make the celebration into a party. They have special foods, music, games, stories, and dances.

Look for these objects hidden in the picture: butterfly, candy, clock, ghost, fan, fish, footprint, loaf of bread, pumpkin, and watermelon.

November 4

◉ FLAG DAY

Panama declared independence from Columbia on November 3, 1925. The flag designed by the family of the country's first president, Manuel Amador, was officially adopted the next day.

The flag represents Panama's political parties and values of the time.

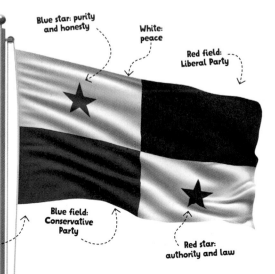

Blue star: purity and honesty

White: peace

Red field: Liberal Party

Blue field: Conservative Party

Red star: authority and law

THE WORLD

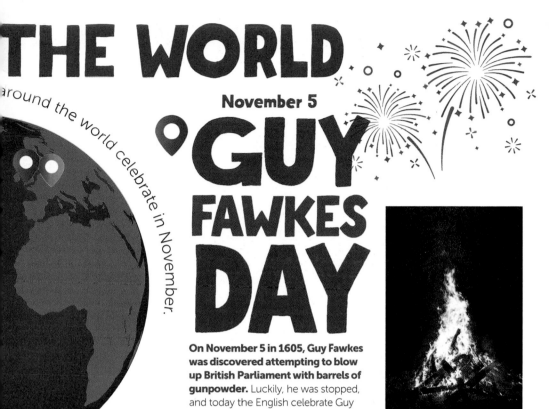

around the world celebrate in November.

November 5

GUY FAWKES DAY

On November 5 in 1605, Guy Fawkes was discovered attempting to blow up British Parliament with barrels of gunpowder. Luckily, he was stopped, and today the English celebrate Guy Fawkes Day with fireworks and bonfires.

November 11

SAINT MARTIN'S DAY

In Germany, this holiday honors St. Martin of Tours, a Roman soldier who was made a bishop and later a saint by the Catholic Church. A kind man, he was said to have cut his cloak in half with his sword to share with a beggar during a snowstorm. Processions are often led by a man on horseback dressed as St. Martin in his long red cloak. School kids hold paper lanterns as he passes. **Can you find the three puzzle pieces in this photo?**

SUNDAY	MONDAY	TUESDAY	WEDNESDA...

BIRTHSTONES
TANZANITE, TURQUOISE, AND ZIRCON

ZODIAC SIGNS
SAGITTARIUS: NOVEMBER 22–DECEMBER 21

CAPRICORN: DECEMBER 22–JANUARY 19

FLOWERS
NARCISSUS HOLLY

Game on.
In 1994, Sony PlayStation was released in Japan at a price of ¥39,800 (about $366). It sold 100,000 consoles on the first day!

3

INTERNATIONAL CHEETAH DAY

4

INTERNATIONAL VOLUNTEER DAY

5

Its fleece was white a... snow. In 1877, Thoma... Edison made the first recording of the hum... voice, a recitation of "Mary Had a Little Lamb."

6

Honoring greatness.
In 1901, the first Nobel Peace Prize was awarded. One of the recipients was Henry Dunant, who founded the Red Cross.

10

NATIONAL APP DAY

It seems like there is an app for anything you might need. What is your favorite app?

11

NATIONAL GINGERBREAD HOUSE DAY

Home sweet home.

12

Saint Lucia's Da... (Scandinavia)

Wearing a crown of candles, the oldest daughter sings a song t... wake her family, bringir... them saffron buns and gingerbread cookies.

13

National Maple Syrup Day

Pour some on a stack of waffles and dig in!

17

Answer the Telephone Like Buddy the Elf Day

18

Don't be a Scrooge!
In 1843, *A Christmas Carol* by Charles Dickens was published.

19

Go Caroling Da...

Warm up your voic... with vocal exercise...

20

24

National Eggnog Day

New Year's Eve

31

CHRISTMAS

25

KWANZAA BEGINS

26

Make Cut-Out Snowflakes Day

Create your own winter wonderland.

2...

THURSDAY	FRIDAY	SATURDAY

THURSDAY

FRIDAY

"I was . . . tired of giving in." In 1955, Rosa Parks refused to give up her seat for a white patron on a bus in Montgomery, Alabama, which helped start the civil rights movement. **1**

SATURDAY

National Fritters Day

Do you prefer sweet or savory? **2**

HANUKKAH begins at sunset. **7**

Pretend to be a Time Traveler Day

To what time will you travel? **8**

A Charlie Brown Christmas debuted on CBS in 1965. **9**

National Roast Chestnuts Day **14**

NATIONAL UGLY CHRISTMAS SWEATER DAY **15**

National Chocolate-Covered Anything Day **16**

FIRST DAY OF WINTER **21**

A bright idea. In 1882, Edward H. Johnson created the first string of electric Christmas lights. **22**

Farmer's Day (India)

This holiday that celebrates farmers takes place on the birthday of Chaudhary Charan Singh, the fifth prime minister of India. **23**

NATIONAL DOWNLOAD DAY

Seventy-three percent of Americans download apps on this day! **28**

It's fun to stay at the YMCA! In 1851, the first American YMCA opened in Boston. **29**

We're not alone . . . On this day in 1924, the Hubble telescope helped prove there are other galaxies outside of the Milky Way. **30**

DECEMBER

"HI, NEIGHBOR" MONTH

Get to know your neighbors better this holiday season—it all starts with a smile and a hello! Here are a few other ideas of how you can spread holiday joy.

1. Make a card and write a nice note inside.
2. Bake cookies to share.
3. With permission, shovel snow from a neighbor's sidewalk or driveway.
4. Make a homemade gift to give.
5. Collect food for your local food bank.
6. Tell your neighbors what you admire most about them.

TREE TREATS

Give a "heartwarming" gift.

1. Wash a **plastic ornament** inside and out. Decorate it with **puffy paint**. Let it dry.

2. Make a funnel by rolling and taping a half circle cut from **paper**.

3. Remove the top of the plastic ornament. Use the funnel to fill the ornament with **hot-cocoa powder**, **tea leaves**, or **coffee beans**.

4. Add a **ribbon** hanger and a **cardstock** tag with drink-making instructions.

December 3 is National Make a Gift Day!

NATIONAL ROOT VEGETABLE MONTH

This month celebrates all the root vegetables that make our meals wonderful. Root vegetables grow underground at the base of a plant. They're full of vitamins and minerals. They're also packed with flavor. That makes it easy to root for these veggies!

There are 16 root veggies hidden in the grid below. Look for them up, down, across, backward, and diagonally. Which is your favorite to eat?

WORD LIST

BEET
CARROT
DAIKON
GARLIC
GINGER
JICAMA
ONION
PARSNIP
POTATO
RADISH
RUTABAGA
SWEET POTATO
TARO
TURNIP
YAM
YUCA

```
J C M I E O R A N V N Q P M C
B I E P T N X G N O O V A I Q
U O C E L I O A O H K X L Y J
N J A A Z O Q B Z Y I R A L P
X W R P M N G A O O A M T J O
S A R A N A P T H G D P U C K
M L O V I A I U H M J Z R P H
T M T A R M L R H T Y H N U P
K Q T S S R P S U S A V I S Y
V Z N O H W T E E B I R P B L
Q I Z W R G I N G E R D O M K
P A C U Y Q P O T A T O A B F
O T A T O P T E E W S K M R I
H S D E C T L C U C G T D Y M
O U Y I P F S Z Z P K U O G D
```

HIDDEN VEGGIES

A root vegetable is hidden in the letters of each sentence. Find Y-A-M in the first sentence. **Then find a different veggie in each of the others.**

1. Please try a marshmallow.

2. That bee tried to sting me!

3. I bought a teapot at Oscar's sale.

4. "He'll return," I promised.

5. Sandra dishes out the best pie in town.

6. In the showroom, a car rotated on a platform.

7. Mr. Caspar snips hedges into shapes.

Why did the vegetable band break up?

It didn't have a beet.

What do you get when a football team practices in your garden?

Mashed potatoes

What is small, red, and whispers?

A hoarse radish

259

LEARN A FOREIGN LANGUAGE MONTH

There are **7,139** known languages spoken throughout the world.

To celebrate this month, try your hand at a new language! There are a variety of apps, books, and websites that can help you learn another language. Ask a parent or librarian to help you find the best resource for you to use.

There are many ways to say "hello." Can you match each greeting with the correct language?

1. Hola (OH-lah)	JAPANESE
2. Konnichiwa (co-nee-chee-wah)	CHINESE
3. Hallo (HA-lo)	SPANISH
4. Privet (PREE-viet)	GERMAN
5. Bonjour (bohn-ZHOOR)	RUSSIAN
6. Ciao (chOW)	SWAHILI
7. Jambo (JAM-bo)	FRENCH
8. Ni hao (Nee HaOW)	ITALIAN

Zimbabwe holds the record for the most official languages spoken in one country with a whopping 16 different languages!

UNIVERSAL HUMAN RIGHTS MONTH

Eleanor Roosevelt was the chair of the Human Rights Commission.

On December 10, 1948, the United Nations published a document called the *Universal Declaration of Human Rights*, which states that fundamental human rights must be universally protected. People from all over the world from a variety of backgrounds helped draft the declaration, which was the first of its kind in the history of human rights.

READ A NEW BOOK MONTH

There are six words hidden in this scene. As everyone reads a new book, can you find the words BOOK, NOVEL, PAGE, READ, STORY, and WORDS?

BOOK SWAP!

One way to find a new book to read is to have a book swap. With a group of friends, exchange your favorite books. After you've read them all, give them awards such as "Coolest Adventure" or "Favorite Main Character."

You won't find these silly books in your local library. They're books never written! Try coming up with your own silly titles.

Zoology by Annie Mals

What to Take on an Airplane by Carrie On

Living with Dinosaurs by Terry Dactel

Help the Environment by Reese Ikel

How to Write a Book by Paige Turner

December 5, 1848

175 YEARS AGO, PRESIDENT JAMES K. POLK VERIFIED THERE WAS GOLD IN CALIFORNIA.

Gold was discovered in Sutter's Mill, near San Francisco, California, in January 1848. While many began to migrate west with dreams of becoming rich overnight, even more Americans thought the news of gold was a scam. Colonel Richard B. Mason sent a report on the amount of gold miners were finding, along with a tin of gold, to President Polk in Washington, D.C. Polk announced at his State of the Union address on December 5 that there was in fact gold in California—and a lot of it. That was all the public needed to hear. The Gold Rush began.

These miners struck gold! While they celebrate their success, can you find the 15 objects hidden in the scene?

Over the course of the Gold Rush, miners found about 750,000 POUNDS, or about $2 billion worth, of gold.

The year 1949 brought a surge of new residents to the California Territory. These gold-seekers were nicknamed **THE FORTY-NINERS**. By the end of the year, almost 100,000 people had moved to California.

pencil

horn

table-tennis paddle

toothbrush

sock

snake

duck

slice of cake

tube of toothpaste

hammer

golf club

banana

nail

artist's brush

screwdriver

December 12, 1913

110 YEARS AGO, THE STOLEN *MONA LISA* WAS RECOVERED.

On August 21, 1911, a group of men posing as janitors infiltrated the Louvre (pronounced "LOOV") in Paris, France. They successfully stole Leonardo da Vinci's painting, the *Mona Lisa*. One of these robbers, Vincenzo Peruggia, was keeping the *Mona Lisa* in his hotel room in Florence, Italy, when he was caught by police two years later. Today, this iconic painting is once again on display in the Louvre, but it is protected by bulletproof glass to prevent it from being stolen again.

Find the hidden objects in the Louvre's courtyard and learn how to say them in French, too.

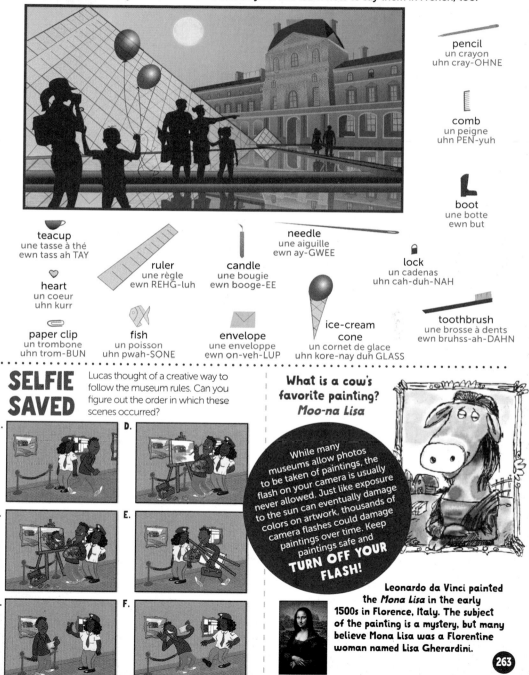

pencil
un crayon
uhn cray-OHNE

comb
un peigne
uhn PEN-yuh

boot
une botte
ewn but

teacup
une tasse à thé
ewn tass ah TAY

ruler
une règle
ewn REHG-luh

needle
une aiguille
ewn ay-GWEE

candle
une bougie
ewn booge-EE

lock
un cadenas
uhn cah-duh-NAH

heart
un coeur
uhn kurr

paper clip
un trombone
uhn trom-BUN

fish
un poisson
uhn pwah-SONE

envelope
une enveloppe
ewn on-veh-LUP

ice-cream cone
un cornet de glace
uhn kore-nay duh GLASS

toothbrush
une brosse à dents
ewn bruhss-ah-DAHN

SELFIE SAVED

Lucas thought of a creative way to follow the museum rules. Can you figure out the order in which these scenes occurred?

A.

B.

C.

D.

E.

F.

What is a cow's favorite painting?
Moo-na Lisa

While many museums allow photos to be taken of paintings, the flash on your camera is usually never allowed. Just like exposure to the sun can eventually damage colors on artwork, thousands of camera flashes could damage paintings over time. Keep paintings safe and **TURN OFF YOUR FLASH!**

Leonardo da Vinci painted the *Mona Lisa* in the early 1500s in Florence, Italy. The subject of the painting is a mystery, but many believe Mona Lisa was a Florentine woman named Lisa Gherardini.

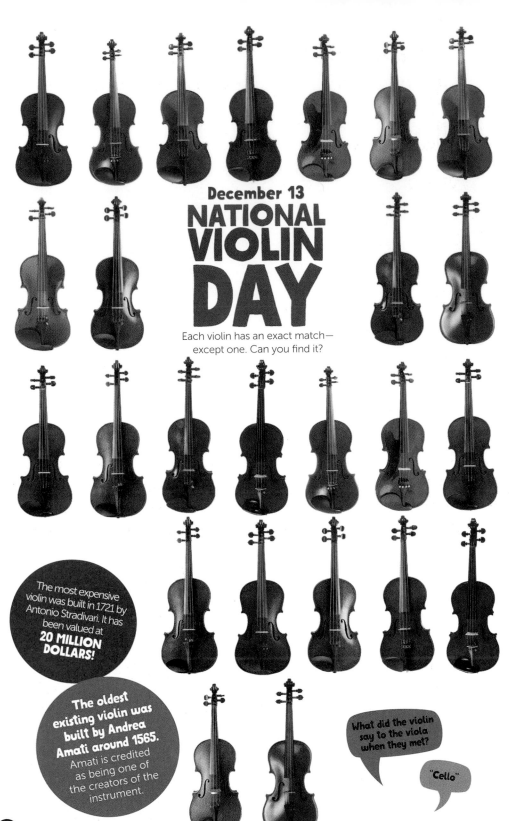

December 13

NATIONAL VIOLIN DAY

Each violin has an exact match—except one. Can you find it?

The most expensive violin was built in 1721 by Antonio Stradivari. It has been valued at **20 MILLION DOLLARS!**

The oldest existing violin was built by Andrea Amati around 1565. Amati is credited as being one of the creators of the instrument.

What did the violin say to the viola when they met?

"Cello"

NATIONAL SHORT STORY DAY

Use one of these story starters to write a story. Or write your own story inspired by the pictures.

IN A LURCH

Chris and Andy were riding the Ferris wheel at the fair. They were having a great time until, suddenly, the ride stopped with a lurch. . . .

CATCHING THE BUS

"I can't be late today, no matter what," Caitlin told herself. But no one told the bus driver. As he drove away without Caitlin, she started to panic. What was she going to do now? . . .

WACKY INVENTIONS

Theo was famous for creating wacky inventions—ones that didn't always work. But he knew his newest invention would change everything. What could possibly go wrong? . . .

NATIONAL COOKIE DAY

Can't get enough cookies? National Bake Cookies Day is December 18!

We listed 10 kinds of cookies here. It's up to you to crack the code and fill in the names. Each number stands for a different letter. Once you know one number's letter, you can fill in that letter in all of the words. Grab some milk and get started!

M A C A R O O N
7 10 1 10 11 2 2 8

_ _ _ _ _ _ _ _
6 5 7 2 8 9 10 11

_ _ _ _ _
13 18 12 10 11

_ _ _ _ _ _
19 2 11 16 18 8 5

_ _ _ _ _ _ _ _ _
12 4 8 12 5 11 13 8 10 14

_ _ _ _ _ _ _ _ _
13 15 2 11 16 9 11 5 10 17

_ _ _ _ _ _ _ _ _ _ _ _
2 10 16 7 5 10 6 11 10 4 13 4 8

_ _ _ _ _ _ _ _ _ _ _ _
14 5 10 8 18 16 9 18 16 16 5 11

_ _ _ _ _ _ _ _ _ _ _ _ _
1 15 2 1 2 6 10 16 5 1 15 4 14

_ _ _ _ _ _ _ _ _ _ _ _
13 8 4 1 3 5 11 17 2 2 17 6 5

The average American eats **18,928** cookies in their lifetime.

BONUS

Did you fill in all the names? Use the same code to answer this riddle.

What did the gingerbread man use to trim his fingernails?

_ _ _ _ _ _ _ _ _ _ _ _ _
10 1 2 2 3 4 5 1 18 16 16 5 11

December 11

NATIONAL HAVE A BAGEL DAY

Plain, sesame, or whole wheat? Make your choice, then find the hidden objects in the scene below.

The bagel's hole isn't just for decoration. Having a hole helps the bagel to bake faster and gives more surface area with that delicious bagel crust.

eyeglasses

ruler

piece of popcorn

envelope

spoon

banana

slice of pizza

fishhook

golf club

crescent moon

football

musical note

olive

December 13

NATIONAL COCOA DAY

Try these four twists on hot chocolate. What other mix-ins can you think of?

The earliest known chocolate drink is believed to have been created around **1700 BCE** by the Olmecs, who lived in what is now southern Mexico. However, since sugar wasn't introduced to the Americas yet, the drink was bitter, not sweet.

Kickin' Hot Cocoa
Sprinkle cayenne pepper and cinnamon into a mug of hot cocoa and stir well.

Choco-Peanut-Butter Blend
Mix a tablespoon of creamy peanut butter into hot chocolate until the peanut butter dissolves.

Caramel Chocolate Swirl
Stir a tablespoon of caramel syrup into a cup of hot chocolate.

Hot Chocolate Float
Add a scoop of mint ice cream into a mug of hot chocolate.

HANUKKAH

Every year, in late November or December, Jewish people enjoy an eight-day celebration that began about two thousand years ago. After a victory over the Syrian-Greek army around 165 BCE, the Jews rededicated the Second Temple of Jerusalem. They found only enough oil to keep the Temple lamp lit for one day. Yet the oil burned until a new supply arrived—eight days later! Today, Jewish people remember this miracle by lighting the Hanukkah menorah—one candle for each day. The traditional potato pancakes called *latkes*, usually fried in oil, are a reminder of that miracle, too.

MAKE A MAGNETIC MENORAH

1. Place a sheet of **blue craft foam** on a protected surface. Cover your palms and fingers with **poster paint**. Overlap your thumbs and spread out your fingers, then press both hands onto the craft foam.

2. Wash and dry your hands. Cover your thumb with gold paint. Make nine thumbprints on **yellow craft foam**.

3. Cut out the "menorah" and the "flames." Glue **magnets** to the back.

4. Put the menorah and flames on a refrigerator. "Light" the candles during Hanukkah.

WHOLE LOTTA LATKES

You're making latkes for two dozen (24) people. You already have oil, salt, pepper, and matzo meal. How much will you spend on the three main ingredients if one potato is 89 cents, one dozen eggs is $2.67, and an onion is 99 cents?

POTATO LATKE RECIPE
(serves 6)
5 large potatoes
3 eggs
1 onion

December 26–January 1
KWANZAA

Kwanzaa is a holiday that was created by Dr. Maulana Karenga in 1966. It celebrates family, community, and culture. The holiday stems from the African tradition of giving thanks for the first fruits of the harvest (*Kwanzaa* means "first fruits" in Swahili).

There are seven principles celebrated during this holiday: **unity, self-determination, collective work and responsibility, cooperative economics, purpose, creativity,** and **faith.** A candle is lit each day on a kinara. Each candle represents one of these principles.

"Heri za Kwanzaa!" means "Happy Kwanzaa!"

Celebrate Kwanzaa by displaying—then eating!— this tasty treat to represent *mazao* ("crops" in Swahili).

Wash your hands before you begin.

Makes 12 cornucopias.

1. Peel two small **bananas**, a **mango**, two **pears**, and two **kiwis**. Wash one cup of **berries**.

2. With an adult's help, cut the fruit into small pieces. (Throw away the pear cores and the mango seed.)

3. Gently combine the fruit in a bowl. Then spoon the mixture into **waffle cones**.

4. Arrange the cones on a large plate or serving tray.

5. When it's time to eat them, you can top each cornucopia with a sprinkle of **coconut flakes** or a drizzle of **honey** or **chocolate sauce**. Enjoy!

MAZAO, one of the symbols of Kwanzaa, represents the harvest and the hard work that went into producing it.

Celebrities who have celebrated Kwanzaa include Oprah, Maya Angelou, and Angelina Jolie.

CHRISTMAS

The Christmas holiday celebrates the birth of Jesus Christ. People decorate Christmas trees with lights and ornaments, do good deeds for others, and give gifts to friends and family.

JINGLE-BELL ORNAMENTS

Make these ornaments to hang on your own tree or to give as a gift.

1. Twist one end of a **fuzzy stick** into a loop. Twist a **jingle bell** onto the other end.

2. Use **colored paper** and **stickers** to create a Nativity scene, a Christmas tree, or a bell. **Tape** the chenille stick to the back. Add a **yarn** bow.

A TREE FULL OF TREATS

Help the mouse find a clear path to the cheese at the top of the tree!

TRICKY TREES

Each of these trees has the numbers 1 through 6 running along the sides. And, in each triangle, each side adds up to the number in the middle. Can you place the numbers in each triangle so that everything adds up correctly? Each of the numbers 1 through 6 is only used once in a triangle.

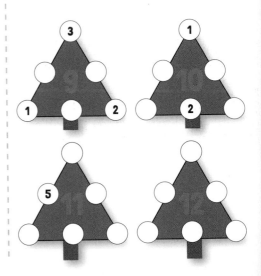

FIXING SANTA'S SLEIGH

While the elves fix up Santa's sleigh, find the eight objects hidden in Santa's workshop.

fried egg

canoe

slice of bread

baseball bat

comb

bell

button

heart

WORLD WILDLIFE CONSERVATION DAY

December 4

This holiday exists to bring awareness to the many wonderful species of wildlife that need our help. Here are a few ideas of how you can help animals in need, not just on this day, but every day.

RECYCLE

Humans make a lot of garbage. Being careless with our garbage is hard on the environment—and some of our favorite animals. Recycling can help control the amount of waste we pile up. Recycling can also protect animal habitats. In fact, the Minnesota Zoo asks that its visitors recycle their phones. The mineral coltan that is used to make phones is mined from lowland gorilla habitats. Recycling phones helps save the gorillas!

STEP-BY-STEP DRAWING

Follow the steps to draw a panda.

1.
2.
3.
4.
5.

There are only **1,800 GIANT PANDAS** living in the wild.

BE SUSTAINABLE

Switching to using metal or other reusable straws can be a huge help. Plastic straws end up in the ocean and hurt animals like sea turtles. If more of us can use reusable straws, then fewer straws will end up as garbage.

Reusable straws are made from metal or glass, and biodegradable straws are made from paper or bamboo.

TAKE CARE WITH GARBAGE

Remember to always throw garbage away in the proper place to keep it out of animal habitats. And make sure things like plastic soda rings are cut so animals, like this seagull, don't trap their heads inside.

INTERNATIONAL MOUNTAIN DAY

This day encourages us to take care of our mountains. Earth's peaks are home to 15% of the world's population. What's more, they provide about half of the world with its drinking water. Join this hiker as she appreciates the beauty of the mountains.

Can you find the 13 objects hiding in the scene?

HOW DO PEAKS PROVIDE DRINKING WATER? Rain and melted snow run down mountains. This water eventually flows to the streams and rivers that supply people's drinking water.

baseball bat

cowboy boot

fish

fork

comb

frog

hat

wedge of orange

needle

paintbrush

slice of pizza

sailboat

watering can

INTERNATIONAL MONKEY DAY

We're not monkeying around—today is the day we celebrate these cute primates. In the puzzle below, fill in the squares so the six letters appear only once in each row, column, and 2 x 3 box. Then read the highlighted squares to find the answer to the riddle.

RIDDLE: What key opens a banana?

Answer:
A _ _ _ _ _ _ _

Letters: **E K M N O Y**

				O	
E			Y		M
K			O	Y	
	E	O			N
O		M			K
			M		

What do you get when you mix a monkey and rainbow paint?

A messy house

Tongue Twister

FIVE FUNKY MONKEYS MUNCHING FIVE FRIED MUNCHIES

273

December 9
NATIONAL LLAMA DAY

We've got lots of love for llamas! Find one trio of identical llamas, four pairs of identical llamas, and one llama with no match in this scene.

BONUS! Say this tongue twister five times fast: Mama Llama's pajama drama.

December 3

NATIONAL MAKE A GIFT DAY

A HANDMADE GIFT MEANS A LOT— AND SO DO COMPLIMENTS!

Add something to your gifts that your friends and family are sure to love: kind words. Wrap your handmade gift in solid-colored paper, and use a marker to write compliments or thank-yous on the paper. You might thank your mom for helping you with your homework. Or let your brother know he's great at telling jokes. A thoughtful note is a valuable gift!

December 20

GO CAROLING DAY

What is your favorite carol to sing? Sing along while you find all 12 hidden objects.

flower

chair

sailboat

coat hanger

hamburger

heart

mitten

candle

watermelon

fork

ice-cream cone

baseball

Take a spin around the globe to see how

December 6
○ ST. NICHOLAS DAY

In Belgium, on December 5, children put out their shoes by the fireplace, along with food and water for St. Nicholas's horse. The next morning, the shoes will be filled with treats like chocolates, cookies, oranges, and toys.

St. Nicholas Day is celebrated in many countries, including the ones listed below. Use the number of letters in each country as a clue to where it might fit in the grid.

AUSTRIA ENGLAND ITALY
BELGIUM FRANCE MEXICO
CANADA GERMANY RUSSIA
CROATIA ICELAND TURKEY

December 12
○ JAMHURI DAY

In Swahili, one of two official languages of Kenya, the word *jamhuri* means "republic." This holiday celebrates Kenya's independence from the United Kingdom on December 12, 1963, as well as Kenya's becoming a republic a year later on December 12, 1964. Kenyans celebrate the holiday with speeches, parades, and feasts to honor the country's culture and heritage.

Kenyan dancers perform a traditional dance during Jamhuri Day celebrations.

THE WORLD

December 24
🔴 NOCHE BUENA

Filipinos celebrate Christmas Eve with a midnight church mass and a traditional feast called Noche Buena, which means "good night" in Spanish. During the Christmas season in the Philippines, beautiful star-shaped lanterns, known as *parols*, light up the night sky and cast a soft glow on streets and homes. The stars remind Christians of the star of Bethlehem, which they believe guided three wise men to the baby Jesus.

Make a Philippine Parol

1. As shown in the diagram, fold a piece of **cardstock** in half. Mark the center of the side opposite the fold. Draw lines from the center to each lower corner. Cut out the triangle, and unfold it to form a diamond. Repeat with four more pieces of cardstock. **Tape** the diamonds together to form a star.

2. For a tassel, cut twenty 10-inch pieces of **yarn**. Fold ten of them in half and tie them together at the fold. Tie another piece of yarn below that. Trim the ends of the tassel. Repeat with the other ten pieces of yarn.

3. Punch a hole in the top point of the star and the two lower points. Tie the tassels to the lower holes. Tie a piece of yarn in the top hole for a hanger.

4. Decorate the star with **glitter glue**.

December 26
🔴 BOXING DAY

Most of the 53 countries in the Commonwealth—nearly all of which are former territories of the British Empire—celebrate Boxing Day. This holiday is spent with family and friends. People often shop or watch sports, and eat leftover Christmas food.

Deondre, Jada, Ashlyn, and Luke are wrapping presents. Follow the ribbons to figure out who's wrapping each gift.

JANUARY

I celebrated the **start of 2023** by _____

_____

_____

For **National Puzzle Day** on **January 29**, I tried

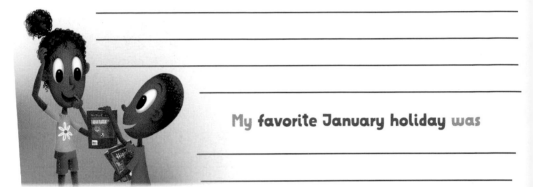

_____

_____

_____

My **favorite January holiday** was

_____

FEBRUARY

On **February 2, 2023,**
the groundhog
☐ **DID** ☐ **DID NOT**
see his shadow.

I made **valentines** for

_____

_____

_____

_____

My **favorite February holiday** was

_____

_____

MARCH

For National Let's Laugh Day
on March 19, these things
made me laugh:

_____

_____

_____

_____

_____

My favorite March holiday was

_____

_____

March 26 was Make Up Your Own Holiday Day.
The holiday I created was _____

_____

_____

This is how you celebrate it: _____

_____

_____

_____

_____

_____

_____

_____

_____

APRIL

On April Fools' Day, I was surprised by _____

_____

_____

_____

I celebrated Earth Day by _____

_____

_____

_____

My favorite April holiday was

_____

_____

MAY

I spent time with
my family in May by

_____

_____

_____

_____

Here is something new I tried in May:

_____

_____

_____

_____

My favorite May holiday was

_____

_____

JUNE

I celebrated the first day of summer by

_____

_____

_____

_____

_____

My favorite June holiday was

_____

_____

_____

I took photos this month to celebrate events like Nature Photography Day on June 15. Here is my favorite photo from June:

PASTE YOUR FAVORITE PHOTO HERE!

JULY

I celebrated Independence Day by

_____
_____
_____

I played these sports or games in July:

_____
_____
_____

My favorite July holiday was

_____
_____

AUGUST

For National Book Lovers' Day on August 9, I read _____
_____
_____
_____

I read _____ books in 2023!

Here are some foods I ate outside in August:

_____
_____
_____
_____

My favorite August holiday was

_____

SEPTEMBER

2023 MEMORIES

I spent time with my friends this month by

_____

_____

_____

_____

_____

_____

My favorite
September holiday was

_____

_____

_____

September 12 is the National Day of Encouragement.
Here are some things that make me feel encouraged:

_____

_____

_____

_____

_____

_____

_____

_____

_____

OCTOBER

For National Do Something Nice Day on October 5, I _____

_____

_____

_____

For Halloween, my costume was

_____

_____

My favorite October holiday was

_____

NOVEMBER

On International Tongue Twister Day on November 12, my favorite tongue twister was

_____

_____

_____

I celebrated Thanksgiving by

_____

_____

_____

My favorite November holiday was

_____

DECEMBER

For Pretend to Be a Time Traveler
Day on December 8, I would travel to

_____
_____
_____
_____

My favorite December
holiday was

_____
_____
_____

I sang or played these songs in December:

_____
_____
_____

_____
_____
_____
_____
_____
_____
_____

2023 MEMORIES

2023 MEMORIES

I learned these three things about myself in 2023:

1. _____
_____
_____
_____

2. _____
_____
_____
_____

3. _____
_____
_____
_____

My favorite part of 2023 was

_____
_____
_____
_____
_____
_____

I tried these three new things in 2023:

1. _____
_____
_____

2. _____
_____
_____

3. _____
_____
_____

My hope for next year is _____
_____
_____
_____

JANUARY

PAGE 7: TANGLED LEASHES

PAGE 7: WHAT'S YOUR DOG IQ?
1. A; 2. A; 3. B; 4. B; 5. A

PAGE 10: HARLEM GLOBETROTTERS DAY

PAGE 11: WINTER X GAMES

PAGE 12: NATIONAL SCIENCE FICTION DAY
Isaac Asimov coined the term *ROBOTICS* in his
1941 short story "Liar!"

PAGE 13: NATIONAL THESAURUS DAY

PAGE 15: NATIONAL POPCORN DAY

PAGE 17: LUNAR NEW YEAR

PAGE 19: PASS THE LUCK, PLEASE!
1. UNITED STATES   4. SPAIN
2. GREECE   5. JAPAN
3. ITALY

PAGE 21: AWESOME BLOSSOM

PAGE 21: FUNNY FLORA

What plant loves math?
A SUM-FLOWER

What do you call a tree robber?
A LEAF THIEF

What did the big flower say to the little flower?
"HI, BUD."

What flower does everyone have?
TULIPS

PAGE 22: NATIONAL TRIVIA DAY
1. A; 2. A; 3. B; 4. A

PAGE 22: NATIONAL HAT DAY

PAGE 23: NATIONAL PUZZLE DAY

PAGE 24: SAINT KNUT'S DAY (SWEDEN)
julstjärna = Christmas star
julklappsstrumpa = Christmas stocking
julgranskula = Christmas ornament
julgransbelysning = Christmas tree lights

PAGE 25: SAINT DEVOTA'S DAY
1. C; 2. H; 3. F; 4. A; 5. G; 6. D; 7. B; 8. E

FEBRUARY

PAGE 30: NATIONAL LIBRARY LOVERS' MONTH

PAGE 30: AUTHOR AUTHOR!
1. D; 2. E; 3. C; 4. F; 5. A; 6. B; 7. I; 8. J; 9. G; 10. H

PAGE 30: SPELL CHECK
WHERE THE WILD THINGS ARE
THE PHANTOM TOLLBOOTH
HAROLD AND THE PURPLE CRAYON
GREEN EGGS AND HAM
GOODNIGHT MOON
HARRIET THE SPY
WINNIE-THE-POOH

PAGE 31: CHILDREN'S DENTAL HEALTH MONTH

PAGE 31: RIDDLE SUDOKU

C	O	S	N	W	R
W	R	N	S	O	C
S	W	O	C	R	N
N	C	R	W	S	O
O	S	C	R	N	W
R	N	W	O	C	S

Why do kings and queens
go to the dentist?
TO GET *CROWNS*

PAGE 32: FEBRUARY 12, 1963

PAGE 33: TOY-STORE TEASER

LION: $6.00
FROG: $3.00
TEDDY BEAR: $5.00
PENGUIN: $8.00

PAGE 34: NATIONAL GIRLS & WOMEN IN
SPORTS DAY

1. B; 2. C; 3. A; 4. A; 5. C; 6. B; 7. B; 8. A;
9. C; 10. A

ALEX FINISHES FIRST!

PAGE 35: SUPER BOWL LVII

What do football champions put their cereal in?
SUPER BOWLS

PAGE 35: SUPER BOWL SUPER STATS
1. C; 2. A; 3. B; 4. A

PAGE 36: OPERA DAY

BOLSHOI THEATRE: RUSSIA
LA SCALA: ITALY
METROPOLITAN OPERA HOUSE: UNITED STATES
NHÀ HÁT LỚN HÀ NỘI: VIETNAM
PALAIS GARNIER: FRANCE
SYDNEY OPERA HOUSE: AUSTRALIA
TEATRO COLÓN: ARGENTINA
WIENER STAATSOPER: AUSTRIA

PAGE 37: GET OUT YOUR GUITAR DAY

PAGE 37: NAME THAT GUITAR

WILLIE NELSON: TRIGGER
B.B. KING: LUCILLE
ERIC CLAPTON: BLACKIE
EDDIE VAN HALEN: FRANKENSTRAT
BRIAN MAY: RED SPECIAL

PAGE 38: NATIONAL FROZEN YOGURT DAY
HERE ARE ANSWERS WE SPOTTED. YOU MAY HAVE FOUND OTHERS.

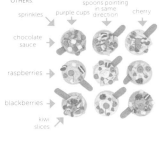

PAGE 39: CHILI DAY

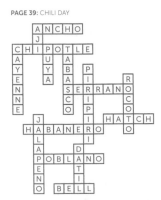

PAGE 40: GROUNDHOG DAY

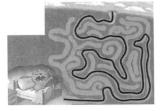

PAGE 41: VALENTINE'S DAY

PAGE 42: WASHINGTON'S BIRTHDAY

HOOVER: HOOVER DAM
KENNEDY: KENNEDY SPACE CENTER
(THEODORE) ROOSEVELT: TEDDY BEAR
LINCOLN: LINCOLN MEMORIAL
JEFFERSON: JEFFERSON MEMORIAL
WASHINGTON: WASHINGTON MONUMENT

They served in this order: Washington (1st president), Jefferson (3rd), Lincoln (16th), T. Roosevelt (26th), Hoover (31st), and Kennedy (35th).

PAGE 43: PANCAKE DAY

What kind of exercises do pancakes do?
JUMPING FLAPJACKS

Who flies through the air covered with maple syrup?
PETER PANCAKE

How is a baseball team like a pancake?
THEY BOTH NEED A GOOD BATTER

What do cow boys put on their pancakes?
MAPLE STIRRUP

PAGE 44: WEATHER STUMPER

PAGE 45: NATIONAL PERIODIC TABLE DAY
BaCoN
BaNaNa
CaNdY
AmErICa
MoUSe
HeLiCoPtEr
FUN

PAGE 47: NATIONAL LOVE YOUR PET DAY
The mischievous pet is the dog.

PAGE 49: NAVAM FULL MOON
POYA DAY (SRI LANKA)

MARCH

PAGE 52: WOMEN'S HISTORY MONTH
1. Marie Curie
2. Amelia Earhart
3. Maria Tallchief
4. Valentina Tereshkova
5. Junko Tabei
6. Sandra Day O'Connor
7. Aretha Franklin
8. Mo'ne Davis
9. Kamala Harris

PAGE 53: NATIONAL UMBRELLA MONTH

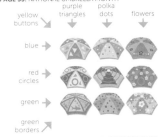

American slang term for *umbrella*: BUMBERSHOOT

PAGE 53: NATIONAL MUSIC IN OUR SCHOOLS MONTH

PAGE 54: NATIONAL NOODLE MONTH
T; F; T; T; F, T; F; T

PAGE 56: MARCH 5, 1963

PAGE 57: MARCH 26, 1953

PAGES 58–59: MARCH MADNESS

PAGE 58: BASKETBALL OR BASEBALL?
1. BASKETBALL
2. BASKETBALL
3. BASEBALL
4. BASKETBALL
5. BASEBALL
6. BASKETBALL
7. BASEBALL
8. BASKETBALL

PAGE 59: WORLD BASEBALL CLASSIC
1. UNITED STATES
2. PUERTO RICO
3. JAPAN
4. NETHERLANDS

PAGE 60: READ ACROSS AMERICA DAY

PAGE 61: TOP ACT
1. *BEAUTY AND THE BEAST*
2. *THE ADDAMS FAMILY*
3. *THE LITTLE MERMAID*
4. *INTO THE WOODS*
8. *LITTLE SHOP OF HORRORS*
9. *THE WIZARD OF OZ*

PAGE 62: NATIONAL PI DAY

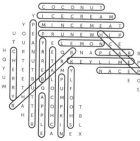

PAGE 66: LEPRECHAUN SHENANIGANS

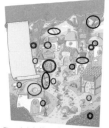

The red-circled leprechaun is the mischief-maker. He took a guitar and hid it above Under the Rainbow Restaurant.

PAGE 68: WORLD WILDLIFE DAY

PAGE 69: EARTH HOUR
CHINA, 1:30 a.m.; UKRAINE, 7:30 p.m.; NEPAL, 11:15 p.m.; MALI, 5:30 p.m.

PAGE 70: INTERNATIONAL MERMAID DAY

PAGE 71: TAKE A WALK IN THE PARK DAY
1. E; 2. C; 3. B; 4. F; 5. A; 6. D

PAGE 72:
INDEPENDENCE DAY (GHANA)

PAGE 73: HOLI (INDIA)

APRIL

PAGE 76: NATIONAL KITE MONTH

PAGE 77: NATIONAL HUMOR MONTH

PAGE 77: LOOK BOTH WAYS!

1. H; 2. G; 3. C; 4. J; 5. A; 6. I; 7. B; 8. F; 9. D; 10. E

PAGE 79: POSTAGE PAW-BLEMS
THIS PACKAGE WILL COST THE MOST TO SHIP.

BONUS: YES, PURRNELOPE HAS ENOUGH MONEY TO SEND ALL FOUR PACKAGES.

PAGE 79: 24 TO THE DOOR

9 + 12	2 x 11	15 + 9	17 + 7
7 + 15	35 – 11	8 x 3	25 - 2
3 x 4	6 x 4	20 + 3	18 + 7
18 + 6	40 - 16	5 x 7	33 - 10

PAGE 79: SUM FUN!
1. 7
2. 8
3. 29
4. 64
5. 7
6. 3,600
7. 10

The world's largest box of chocolates weighed 3,725 pounds.

PAGE 80: SEE IT, SAY IT
1. EGGS OVER EASY
2. SICK IN BED
3. HORSING AROUND
4. SETTLE DOWN
5. DON'T COUNT YOUR CHICKENS BEFORE THEY HATCH
6. TWO RUNNERS ON BASE
7. WIDE AWAKE
8. MINUTE BY MINUTE
9. YELLOW JACKET

PAGE 81: APRIL 21, 753 BCE

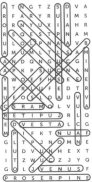

Gods and their mythological responsibility:
1. K; 2. D; 3. O; 4. E; 5. A; 6. R; 7. U; 8. J; 9. N;
10. I; 11. H; 12. M; 13. B; 14. V; 15. C; 16. Q;
17. G; 18. P; 19. S; 20. L; 21. F; 22. T

PAGE 82: PLAY BALL!
1. CODY
2. HECTOR
3. CLAUDIA
4. SETH
5. JACOB
6. ARIEL
7. TROY
8. LINDSEY
9. LAURA

PAGE 82: HOME RUN!

PAGE 83: WORLD TABLE TENNIS DAY

PAGE 83: THE BOSTON MARATHON

PAGE 84: SHELF SHUFFLE

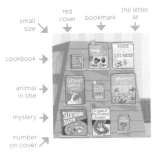

PAGE 84: BOOK SMART
1. ANNE OF GREEN GABLES
2. CHARLOTTE'S WEB
3. A WRINKLE IN TIME
4. DIARY OF A WIMPY KID
5. THE LION, THE WITCH AND THE WARDROBE
6. HARRY POTTER AND THE SORCERER'S STONE
7. CHARLIE AND THE CHOCOLATE FACTORY
8. THE ADVENTURES OF CAPTAIN UNDERPANTS
9. WHERE THE SIDEWALK ENDS
10. IF YOU GIVE A MOUSE A COOKIE

PAGE 84: JUST WING IT

PAGE 86: BOBBIE'S BURRITOS
The order should be F, C, E, A, B, D.

PAGE 87: NATIONAL JELLY BEAN DAY

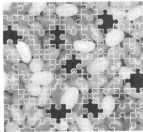

PAGE 90: EASTER SUNDAY

PAGE 91: EID AL-FITR
A fanous is a LANTERN

PAGE 92: ZOOKEEPER'S BYE-BYE
1. CROCODILE
2. BABOON
3. BUFFALO
4. SHEEP
5. GECKO
6. BUTTERFLY
7. KANGAROO
8. POLAR BEAR
9. CHIMPANZEE
10. RATTLESNAKE

PAGE 93: TREEMONTON TOWERS

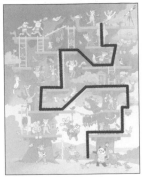

PAGE 94: NATIONAL UNICORN DAY

PAGE 95: TAKE OUR DAUGHTERS AND SONS TO WORK DAY

THE ARTIST HASN'T ARRIVED YET.

PAGE 96: DO YOU KNOW THAT DRAGON? (ENGLAND)

1. F; 2. C; 3. E; 4. A; 5. D; 6. H; 7. B; 8. G.

PAGE 97: FLY IT HIGH (SIERRA LEONE)

MAY

PAGE 100: ASIAN/PACIFIC AMERICAN HERITAGE MONTH

1. Chloe Kim
2. Maya Lin
3. George Takei
4. Michelle Kwan
5. Jose Antonio Vargas
6. Duke Kahanamoku
7. Patsy Mink
8. Kalpana Chawla

PAGE 101: STUCK IN THE STRAWBERRIES

PAGE 102: DRUM MATCH
1. E; 2. C; 3. B; 4. G; 5. A; 6. F; 7. D

PAGE 103: NATIONAL PET MONTH

PAGE 104: LAUNDRY DAY

PAGE 104: A MESSY MAZE

PAGE 105: MAY 29, 1953

PAGE 106: KENTUCKY DERBY

PAGE 110: EAT WHAT YOU WANT DAY

1. APPLE	6. COOKIE
2. POTATO	7. EGGS
3. PEAS	8. BEANS
4. CUCUMBER	9. FISH
5. MILK	10. CHEESE

PAGE 111: NATIONAL HAMBURGER DAY

What did Mr. and Mrs. Hamburger name their daughter? *PATTY*

How do you make a hamburger laugh? *PICKLE IT!*

What kind of dance does a hamburger go to? *A MEATBALL*

PAGE 112: CINCO DE MAYO
1. D; 2. A; 3. F; 4. B; 5. E; 6. C

PAGE 113: MOM MATCH

PAGE 114: JUMBLED FLOWERS
LILY
TULIP
LILAC
DAFFODIL

PAGE 114: FLOWER OR NOT
BLUEBELL
SNAPDRAGON
CHRYSANTHEMUM
RHODODENDRON
GLADIOLUS
CLEMATIS
HYDRANGEA
FOXGLOVE

PAGE 114: COUNT THE CODE
What did the dog do after he swallowed a firefly? *HE BARKED WITH DELIGHT!*

PAGE 114: HIDDEN FLOWERS

As Te**rry** says, vanilla is better than chocolate.

A superhe**ro se**ldom fails.

Ms. Gor**da is y**our new teacher.

This fi**r is** taller than it was last year.

On the **porch, I d**on't get sunburned.

PAGE 115: SEARCHING FOR STARS

PAGE 116: SPACE DAY
STAR, MOON, and *MARS* can be found in *astronomy.*

1. A; 2. C; 3. B; 4. C; 5. A; 6. B

PAGE 118: NO SOCKS DAY

PAGE 118: NATIONAL FROG JUMPING DAY
JORDAN: POLLIE, THIRD PLACE
SKYLER: HOPPY, FIRST PLACE
RILEY: TAD, SECOND PLACE

PAGE 119: INTERNATIONAL MUSEUM DAY

121: VICTORY DAY (RUSSIA)

JUNE

PAGE 124: TRUE OR FALSE?

T; T; T; F; F

PAGE 125: AFRICAN AMERICAN MUSIC APPRECIATION MONTH

1. BANJO	6. CLARINET
2. TROMBONE	7. PIANO
3. TUBA	8. DRUMS
4. SAXOPHONE	9. BASS
5. TRUMPET	10. GUITAR

Why do farmers play soft jazz for their corn? IT'S EASY *ON THE EARS.*

PAGE 126: NATIONAL FRESH FRUIT AND VEGETABLE MONTH

1. In the showroom, a **car rot**ated on a platform.
2. Maya looked **up each** book Liam recommended.
3. The dog's bark **aler**ted the cat.
4. "I'm getting a new bicycle Mon**day**," said Darnell.
5. Adrianna gets **up ear**ly every morning.
6. I bought a tea**pot a**t Oscar's sale.
7. Pete and his mom baked his tea**cher ry**e bread.
8. That clown **can spin a chair** on his hand.

PAGE 127: FISHING FOR HIDDEN WORDS

PAGE 129: JUNE 16, 1963

PAGE 130: INTERNATIONAL DAY OF YOGA

PAGE 131: NATIONAL HOCKEY LEAGUE STANLEY CUP FINAL

1. B; **2.** A; **3.** C; **4.** B; **5.** A

PAGE 132: NATURE PHOTOGRAPHY DAY

PAGE 133: WORLD MUSIC DAY

What do brass instruments wear in the ocean?
TUBA GEAR

PAGE 134: NATIONAL DOUGHNUT DAY

PAGE 135: NATIONAL HERBS AND SPICES DAY

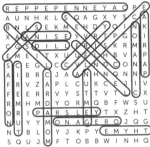

PAGE 139: FIRST DAY OF SUMMER

Best deal: buy the green sunglasses and get a pair of sandals free for a total cost of $20.00.

PAGE 140: World Reef Day
1. A; 2. B; 3. B; 4. A; 5. A; 6. B; 7. B; 8. A; 9. B

PAGE 140: DIVE IN!
Here are the words we found. You may have found others.

age	ferret	raft
barge	fire	rib
bear	free	tear
bite	gate	terrier
brag	gear	tiara
ear	grab	tiger
fair	great	tire
fee	greet	tree

PAGE 143: NATIONAL SUNGLASSES DAY

PAGE 144: DIA DOS NAMORADOS (BRAZIL)

JULY

PAGE 148: ICE CREAM MONTH

1. VANILLA
2. CHOCOLATE
3. COOKIES AND CREAM
4. MINT CHOCOLATE CHIP
5. CHOCOLATE CHIP COOKIE DOUGH
6. BUTTER PECAN
7. COOKIE DOUGH
8. STRAWBERRY
9. MOOSE TRACKS
10. NEAPOLITAN

PAGE 149: NATIONAL BERRY MONTH

PAGE 150: JUMBLED ANIMALS
ZEBRA
CAMEL
PANDA
CHEETAH
POLAR BEAR

PAGE 150: GUESS WHO?
JAGUAR, ELEPHANT, PEACOCK

PAGE 150: LAND OR SEA?

LAND: *KOMODO DRAGON, ALPACA, CHINCHILLA, BONGO*

SEA: *BRITTLESTAR, MANATEE, STINGRAY, BARRACUDA*

PAGE 150: PENGUIN POSES

PAGE 151: PLASTIC FREE JULY

1. paperback
2. paperweight
3. dishcloth
4. tablecloth
5. eyeglass
6. hourglass

PAGE 152: JULY 7, 1928

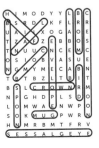

PAGE 153: JULY 10, 1913

PAGE 154: TOUR DE FRANCE

PAGE 155: FIFA WOMEN'S WORLD CUP

PAGE 155: SOCCER TO 'EM

1. B; **2.** B; **3.** B; **4.** A; **5.** B; **6.** A; **7.** B

PAGE 157: NATIONAL MERRY-GO-ROUND DAY

PAGE 160: INDEPENDENCE DAY
Vermont was not one of the 13 original colonies.

PAGE 164: WORLD EMOJI DAY

PAGE 165: NATIONAL WATERPARK DAY

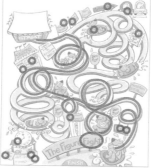

We found *PEAR*, *KARATE*, and *PARKA* in *WATERPARK*.

PAGE 166: LA FÊTE NATIONALE (FRANCE)

PAGE 167: INDEPENDENCE DAY (LIBERIA)

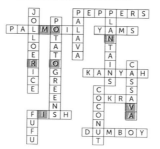

Liberia's capital city is *MONROVIA*.

AUGUST

PAGE 170: NATIONAL CRAYON COLLECTION MONTH

PAGE 170: FAMILY FUN MONTH

HIKE
MOVIES
GAME NIGHT
BAKE
BARBECUE
CAMP
BONFIRE
FISH
BIKE
CRAFT

PAGE 172: DINO-MITE RIDE

PAGE 174: 2023 SUMMER UNIVERSIADE

PAGE 175: 2023 SAILING WORLD CHAMPIONSHIPS

PAGE 176: NATIONAL CLOWN WEEK!

red shoes   bow tie   collar   tears

polka dots →

hats →

orange hair →

square nose →

PAGE 176: CIRCUS LINGO
1. F; **2.** H; **3.** A; **4.** E; **5.** G; **6.** D; **7.** B; **8.** C

PAGE 177: NATIONAL TELL-A-JOKE DAY

Why was the dog excited to go to school?
The class was having a SMELLING BEE.

Why did the dog study before class?
In case the teacher gave a PUP QUIZ

BONUS: There are 71 bones.

PAGE 178: CAMPFIRE DAY AND NIGHT

I'm squishy and sweet and airy and light.
I'm brown when I'm roasted. Inside, I'm still white.
Need s'more hints? This might do the trick:
I'll be at the campfire stuck on your stick.
MARSHMALLOWS

PAGE 179: EAT OUTSIDE DAY

We found these things that rhyme with grill and eat: windowsill, spill, daffodil, quill, windmill, anthill, duck bill, pepper mill, gill, sheet, tweet, feet, cleat, meat, parakeet, dog treat, beet, sweet, wheat, seat, street. You may have found others.

PAGE 180: NATIONAL WATERMELON DAY

PAGE 182: HURRICANE SEASON

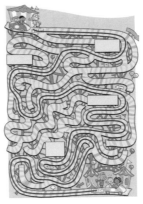

PAGE 184: NATIONAL ROLLER COASTER DAY

PAGE 185: NATIONAL BEACH DAY

The scenes occurred in the following order:
B, A, F, H, D, C, G, E

PAGE 186: ROYAL EDINBURGH MILITARY TATTOO

SEPTEMBER

PAGE 190: NATIONAL HISPANIC HERITAGE MONTH

1. Octaviano Ambrosio Larrazolo
2. Roberto Clemente
3. Rita Moreno
4. Franklin Chang-Diaz
5. Dr. Antonia Novello
6. Dolores Huerta
7. Carlos Santana
8. Sonia Sotomayor

PAGE 191: NATIONAL CHICKEN MONTH

PAGE 192: BETTER BREAKFAST MONTH

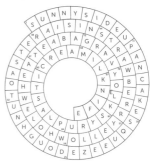

PAGE 193: HAPPY HEALTHY CAT MONTH

PAGE 193: PET-SITTER EDUCATION MONTH

Lucy eats liver.
Bailey eats beef.
Luna eats tuna.
Peanut eats chicken.

PAGE 194: SEPTEMBER 5, 1698

PAGE 194: ANCIENT BEARD TRENDS

1. D; **2.** E; **3.** B; **4.** A; **5.** C

PAGE 195: SEPTEMBER 20, 1973

PAGE 196: RUGBY WORLD CUP

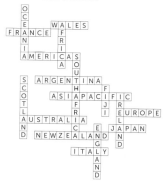

PAGE 197: U.S. BOWLING LEAGUE DAY

PAGE 199: INTERNATIONAL COUNTRY MUSIC DAY

PAGE 201: INTERNATIONAL CHOCOLATE DAY

1. 400
2. 90
3. 5
4. 50 MILLION
5. 1.5 MILLION
6. 40
7. 35

PAGE 202: LABOR DAY

A "SHEAR" PLEASURE. **(HAIRDRESSER)**

I'M DRAWN TO IT. **(ARTIST)**

IT'S A PIECE OF CAKE! **(BAKER)**

OUT OF THIS WORLD! **(ASTRONAUT)**

I GET A KICK OUT OF IT! **(SOCCER PLAYER)**

MOVING RIGHT ALONG. **(TRAFFIC OFFICER)**

AN APPLE A DAY COULDN'T KEEP ME AWAY! **(DOCTOR)**

PAGE 203: NATIONAL GRANDPARENTS DAY

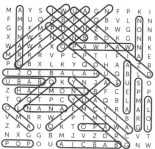

PAGE 205: FIRST DAY OF FALL

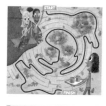

PAGE 207: NATIONAL ELEPHANT APPRECIATION DAY

Why do elephants have trunks?

BECAUSE THEY LOVE TRAVELING

PAGE 208: NATIONAL SKYSCRAPER DAY

1. A; 2. C; 3. B; 4. B; 5. C; 6. A

PAGE 208: NATIONAL AMPERSAND DAY

1. JELLY; 2. LIGHTNING; 3. SOCKS; 4. EGGS; 5. ROLL; 6. THE BEAST; 7. CHEESE; 8. CRAFTS; 9. PEPPER

PAGE 209: INTERNATIONAL SUDOKU DAY

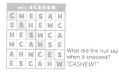

What did the nut say when it sneezed?
"CASHEW!"

PAGE 209: INTERNATIONAL TALK LIKE A PIRATE DAY

What kind of socks does a pirate wear?
ARRR-*GYLE*

PAGE 210: ENKUTATASH (ETHIOPIA)

PAGE 211: FIESTAS PATRIAS (CHILE)

GUITAR
HARP
PIANO
ACCORDION
TAMBOURINE

OCTOBER

PAGE 214: EAT BETTER, EAT TOGETHER MONTH

PAGE 216: GLOBAL DIVERSITY
AWARENESS MONTH

1. CHINA
2. ICELAND
3. JAPAN
4. NORWAY
5. GREECE

PAGE 218: ALBUQUERQUE INTERNATIONAL
BALLOON FIESTA

PAGE 219: OCTOBER 29, 1998

PAGE 220: RECORD SETTERS

5,714 STRIKEOUTS: NOLAN RYAN
4,256 HITS: PETE ROSE
511 WINS: CY YOUNG
1,406 STOLEN BASES: RICKEY HENDERSON
14 WORLD SERIES APPEARANCES: YOGI BERRA

PAGE 221: IF AT FIRST . . .

What do you get when you cross a monster and
a baseball game? *A DOUBLEHEADER*

PAGE 223: DICTIONARY DAY

1. TOY
2. ANT
3. CORN
4. DIRT
5. RAIN
6. TRAIN
7. CARTON

PAGE 223: NATIONAL COLOR DAY

1. RED
2. BLUE
3. BROWN
4. YELLOW
5. GREEN
6. PURPLE
7. ORANGE
8. BLACK

PAGE 225: WORLD PASTA DAY

PAGE 225: PASTA PAIRING
1. F; 2. G; 3. B; 4. H; 5. E; 6. A; 7. C; 8. D

PAGE 228: INTERNATIONAL RACCOON
APPRECIATION DAY

Here are the differences we found:

PAGE 228: WORLD OCTOPUS DAY

PAGE 229: INTERNATIONAL SLOTH DAY
It is 6:00 P.M.

PAGE 230: NATIONAL HAIR DAY

PAGE 231: ADA LOVELACE DAY

Ada created a poster about Hedy Lamarr.

Charles made a scale model about Katherine
Johnson.

Marie wrote a book report about Dorothy Hodgkin.

Eli made a diorama about Edith Clarke.

PAGE 231: NATIONAL MAGIC DAY

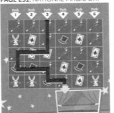

PAGE 233: REPUBLIC DAY (TURKEY)

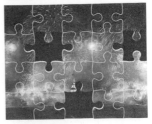

NOVEMBER

PAGE 236: NATIONAL NATIVE AMERICAN
HERITAGE MONTH

PAGE 237: NATIONAL MODEL RAILROAD MONTH

What do you call a locomotive that sneezes?
AH-CHOO-CHOO TRAIN

PAGE 240: NOVEMBER 1, 1848

PAGE 242: NATIONAL TAKE A HIKE DAY

1. Emma planned the route.
2. We stopped to sketch **at** the bridge.
3. Two squirrels **came ra**cing along a log!
4. The whole crew **ate** raisins for energy.
5. We came u**pon chop**ped trees near
a beaver dam.
6. Our pace had to slow **at ch**allenging,
rocky parts of the trail.

There are 10 squirrels in the scene.

PAGE 242: COMPASS CODE

Where's the best place to eat while hiking?
WHERE THERE'S *A FORK IN THE ROAD*

PAGE 243: NATIONAL SQUARE DANCE DAY

PAGE 246: SAXOPHONE DAY

What kind of music do they play at Stonehenge? *HARD ROCK*

How can your hair make music? *WITH A HEADBAND*

Who leads the bird band? *THE CON-DUCK-TOR*

How do you make a bandstand? *TAKE AWAY THEIR CHAIRS.*

PAGE 246: STEP TO THE MUSIC

Tim and Rachel took the same number of steps. Caitlin took the fewest steps.

PAGE 249: TURKEY TROT

PAGE 249: MAKE A MATCH

PAGE 249: FAVORITE FOODS

1. PIE
2. STUFFING
3. GRAVY
4. SWEET POTATOES
5. HAM
6. MASHED POTATOES
7. MAC AND CHEESE
8. GREEN BEAN CASSEROLE
9. CORN BREAD
10. TURKEY

PAGE 251: WORLD RADIOGRAPHY DAY

Xavier ate too many *DOUGHNUTS!*

PAGE 251: BONE UP

The ULNA, RADIUS, and HUMERUS are located in your arm.

PAGE 252: NATIONAL BUTTON DAY

PAGE 253: NATIONAL CAMP DAY

PAGE 254: DÍA DE LOS MUERTOS (MEXICO)

PAGE 255: SAINT MARTIN'S DAY (GERMANY)

DECEMBER

PAGE 259: NATIONAL ROOT VEGETABLE MONTH

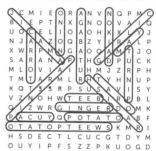

PAGE 259: HIDDEN VEGGIES

1. Please t**ry a m**arshmallow
2. That **bee** t**ri**ed to sting me!
3. I bought a t**eapot** at **O**scar's sale.
4. "He'll **return**," **I** promised.
5. San**dra dishes** out the best pie in town.
6. In the showroom, a **car rot**ated on a platform.
7. Mr. Cas**par snips** hedges into shapes.

PAGE 260: LEARN A FOREIGN LANGUAGE MONTH

1. SPANISH
2. JAPANESE
3. GERMAN
4. RUSSIAN
5. FRENCH
6. ITALIAN
7. SWAHILI
8. CHINESE

PAGE 261: READ A NEW BOOK MONTH

PAGE 262: DECEMBER 5, 1848

PAGE 263: DECEMBER 12, 1913

PAGE 263: SELFIE SAVED

The correct order is F, E, A, D, B, C.

PAGE 264: NATIONAL VIOLIN DAY

PAGE 266: NATIONAL COOKIE DAY

MACAROON

LEMON BAR

SUGAR

FORTUNE

GINGERSNAP

SHORTBREAD

OATMEAL RAISIN

PEANUT BUTTER

CHOCOLATE CHIP

SNICKERDOODLE

What did the gingerbread man use to trim his fingernails?
A COOKIE CUTTER

PAGE 267: NATIONAL HAVE A BAGEL DAY

PAGE 268: WHOLE LOTTA LATKES
$24.43

PAGE 270: A TREE FULL OF TREATS

PAGE 270: TRICKY TREES

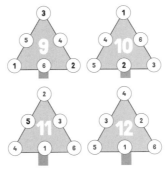

PAGE 271: FIXING SANTA'S SLEIGH

PAGE 273: INTERNATIONAL MOUNTAIN DAY

PAGE 273: INTERNATIONAL MONKEY DAY

What key opens a banana?
A MONKEY

PAGE 274: NATIONAL LLAMA DAY

PAGE 275: GO CAROLING DAY

PAGE 276: ST. NICHOLAS DAY (BELGIUM)

PAGE 277: BOXING DAY
(COMMONWEALTH COUNTRIES)

Abbreviations: GI: Getty Images; SS: Shutterstock.com; WC: Wikimedia Commons iStock/FotoMaximum (200); iStock/Getty Images Plus/Duncan_Andison (55); iStock/Getty Images Plus/monkeybusinessimages (224); iStock/Getty Images Plus/sveta_zarzamora (224); iStock/Getty Images Plus/voltan1 (224); iStock/heywoody (20); iStock/johnandersonphoto (229); ivanastar/GI (2, 33); ivstiv/GI (256); Jaan Künnap/WC (52); jack0m/GI (25, 49, 72, 75, 96, 120, 145, 167, 186, 211, 233, 255, 276); James Keyser/GI (28); jamesbenet/GI (257); Jane_Kelly/GI (24, 25, 48, 49, 72, 73, 96, 97, 120, 121, 144, 145, 166, 167, 186, 187, 210, 211, 232, 233, 254, 255, 276, 277); Janine Lamontagne/GI (151); Janoj/GI (43, 69); janrysavy/GI (256); Jason Clark©/Southcreek Global/Zuma/Alamy Stock Photo (52); JC Olivera/GI (100); jelisua88/SS (FC); jenifoto/GI (159); Jenniveve84/GI (43); jgroup/GI (61); Jim Filipski, Guy Cali Associates, Inc. (8, 9, 14, 18, 29, 55, 67, 74, 85, 87, 88, 204, 244, 245, 257, 258, BC); JimVallee/GI (132); jirkaejc/GI (122); John Ferguson/WC (190); JohnGollop/GI (99); JPC-PROD/GI (99); jsolie/GI (203); Juanmonino/GI (94, 122); Jui-Chi Chan/GI (232); Juj Winn/GI (176); JuliaKa/GI (91); Jupiterimages Corporation (48, 98, 114, 150); JurgaR/GI (120); k_samurkas/GI (75, 220); kanyakits/GI (211); kapulya/Getty (273); karandaev/GI (39, 107); Kathy Hutchins/SS (100); Kativ/GI (272); Kazuharu Harada/GI (257); KenCanning/GI (206); keport/GI (30); khai9000/GI (31); kiboka/GI (5); Kirkikis/GI (125); KoBoZaa/GI (106); koya79/GI (176); Krasimir Kanchev/GI (272); KrimKate/GI (122); Kritchanut/GI (88); krysteq/GI (51); ksushsh/GI (99); Kuzmik_A/GI (111); kyoshino/GI (151, 201); Lady-Photo/GI (121); LauriPatterson/GI (15, 51); LdF/GI (FC, 26); leekris/GI (137); lev radin/SS (28); Library of Congress, Prints and Photographs Division: LC-USZC4-3812 (108); Library of Congress, Prints and Photographs Division: LC-DIG-ds-11820 (28); Library of Congress, Prints and Photographs Division: LC-DIG-ggbain-07682 (52); Library of Congress, Prints and Photographs Division: LC-DIG-ggbain-33189 (220); Library of Congress, Prints and Photographs Division: LC-DIG-hec-40747 (52); Library of Congress, Prints and Photographs Division: LC-DIG-ppbd- 00603 (28); Library of Congress, Prints and Photographs Division: LC-DIG-ppmsca-12373 (190); Library of Congress, Prints and Photographs Division: LC-USZ62-33530 (202); Library of Congress, Prints and Photographs Division: LC-USZ62-86846 (52); Library of Congress, Prints and Photographs Division: LC-USZC2-3565 (166); LindasPhotography/GI (19); linearcurves/GI (156); Litvalifa/GI (27); Louis Requena/Stringer/GI (190); LysenkoAlexander/GI (82); ma_rish/GI (17); Madam Walker Family Archives/A'Lelia Bundles (28); Magone/GI (224); MahirAtes/GI (63, 252); Makidotvn/GI (216); malerapaso/GI (39, 127, 252); MariuszBlach/iStock/Getty Images Plus (189); MARKA/Alamy Stock Photo (52); Massed Pipes & Drums ©The Royal Edinburgh Military Tattoo (186); MediaProduction/GI (207); Merinka/GI (276); meunierd/SS (131); Michael Burrell/GI (82, 88); mikheewnik/GI (98, 188, 212); mil-nik/GI (11); milanfoto/GI (137); mipan/GI (272); Mirrorpix/GI (52); MLENNY/ISTOCK (150); Momento Design/GI (50); Montgomery County Archives (28); monticelllo/iStock (147); Moussa81/GI (99, 199); mphillips007/GI (43, 99, 208, 249); mtphoto19/GI (5); mustafagull/GI (256); mustafaU/GI (167); NASA (28, 100, 129, 141, 190); NASA, ESA, STScl, J. Hester and P. Scowen (Arizona State University) (173); Nastco/GI (134); Natalie Ruffing/GI (93); Nataliia Pyzhova/GI (IFC); National Archives and Records Administration (28); Nenov/GI (60); neopicture/GI (257); Nerthuz/GI (168); NickolayV/GI (72); nikkytok/GI (134); nitimongkolchai/iStock (23); nizha2/GI (22); NOAA National Environmental Satellite, Data, and Information Service (NESDIS) (182, 183); nuiiko/GI (264); nycshooter/GI (82); Olena Kychygina/GI (188); olhakozachenko/GI (195); omersukrugoksu/GI (264); OxanaNigmatulina/GI (189); p_saranya/GI (134); PAKATIP CHAWLEESAEN/GI (205); pamela_d_mcadams/GI (43, 122, 135, 146); Panacea-Doll/GI (97, 260); Panya_/GI (102); Paperkites/GI (113, 123); Passakorn_14/GI (147); Patiwit/GI (212); PaulMaguire/GI (266); Pavlo_K/GI (180, 195); peangdao/GI (189);

PeopleImages/GI (238); PeterAustin/GI (75); PeterHermesFurian/GI (110, 135); PetlinDmitry/GI (244), phallhanit_r/GI (76); Photoevent/GI (135); photokdk/GI (244); photomaru/GI (86, 159); PhotoObjects.net/GI (223); Photos.com/GI (28); pidjoe/GI (125); pjohnson1/GI (50); pkruger/GI (69); Plateresca/GI (39); Ploychan/GI (74); popovaphoto/GI (137); powerofforever/GI (131); princessdlaf/GI (168); Pro2sound/GI (125); public domain (26, 52); R9_RoNaLdO/GI (34); R_Koopmans/GI (147); RamonCarretero/GI (162); Rawpixel/GI (144); rbiedermann/GI (146); Red Herring Design (247); RHD (117); RickLordPhotography/GI (125); RM80/GI (122); RnDmS/SS (145); Robert Laberge/GI (100); RobsonPL/GI (43); Rozaliya/GI (2); s_bukley/SS (28); Samohin/GI (IFC, 2); sarkao/GI (187); sarra22/GI (125); Science Museum Group/WC (230); scisettialfio/GI (3); seb_ra/GI (143); Selektor/GI (26); Serega/GI (166); serezniy/GI (5); SerrNovik/GI (63); setory/GI (74); sezer ozger/GI (232); ShaneMyersPhoto/GI (272); shorenated/GI (69); Silvrshootr/GI (169); sinanmuhit/GI (233); Sjo/GI (264); skodonnell/GI (IFC, 59, 257); Smart/GI (212); smartstock/GI (137); spacezerocom/SS (47); somchaisom/GI (264); Songsak Paname/GI (102); Sonsedska/GI (123); Sovfoto/GI (52); ssucsy/GI (159); Steve Northup/GI (100); Stockbyte/GI (264); stockcam/GI (195); studio22comua/GI (47); studiocasper/GI (19, 39, 77, 213); subjug/GI (121, 195); SunChan/GI (212, 235, 256); surangaw/GI (49); Susanna Blavarg/GI (74); Suzifoo/GI (63, 123); t_kimura/GI (45, 123, 195); Tabitazn/GI (91); tanuha2001/GI (103); Taphouse_Studios/GI (74); tarasov_vl/GI (2); tbralnina/GI (192); Tetiana Lazunova/GI (74); Thomas Northcut/GI (62); Thorsten Spoerlein/GI (92); tifonimages/GI (102); Tim Mosenfelder/GI (190); tobiasfrei/GI (70); tongwongboot/GI (181); ToscaWhi/GI (122); Tsekhmister/GI (3); U.S. Army photo by Sergeant First Class Colin Masterson (276); unalozmen/GI (15); United States Congress/WC (100); United States State Department/WC (100); Unknown/WC (100); User5387422_776/GI (97); Vac1/GI (84); Valengilda/GI (36); vector/GI (111); VeenaMari/GI (61); VIDOK/Getty Images (213); VIDOK/GI (188, 234); vikif/GI (135); VikiVector/GI (69); _Vilor/GI (daffodil), shining_pictures (rabbit), GlobalP (robin), michelangelus (spring), Chereliss (sun), Tetiana Rostopira (peas) (64); Visit Roemvanitch/GI (103); Voren1/GI (58); Vstock LLC/GI (125); VvoeVale/GI (50, 168); Watcha/GI (123); Waynesburg Special Events Commission (163); WerksMedia/GI (71); wildpixel/GI (75); WSM radio/WC (199); wynnter/GI (13); xbrchx/Getty (175); xxmmxx/GI (201); XXMMXX/iStock (15); YinYang/GI (224); yogesh_more/GI (187); Zakharova_Natalia/GI (149); zkruger/GI (19); zoom-zoom/GI (51); Zoonar RF/GI (146); Zoya2222/GI (169).

Illustration Credits: Sebastian Abboud (67); Barroux (213); Constanza Basaluzzo (189, 234); Susan Batori (163); Galia Bernstein (21); Chris Biggin (265); Iryna Bodnaruk (70, BC); Helena Bogosian (259); Scott Burroughs (58-59, 98, 231); John Chad (32); Hayelin Choi (239); Anna Chernyshova (268); Dave Clegg (92, 253, 261); Josh Cleland (71, 79, 110, 133, 169, 177, 209, BC); Garry Colby (34); Daryll Collins (83, 221); David Coulson (15, 27, 74, 98, 123, 153, 168, 188, 241); Russ Cox (33); Jeff Crowther (12); Jef Czekaj (108); Mike Dammer (67, 146, 168, 212, 234, 235, 251); Tim Davis (17, 263); Mike DeSantis (192, 215); Jack Desrocher (116, 126, 223, BC); Chuck Dillon (56, 105); Liz Goulet Dubois (256); Avram Dumitrescu (9); Joey Ellis (44, 273); Valerio Fabbretti (42); Carolina Farias (106); Ruth J. Flanigan (86); Luke Flowers (31, 242); Travis Foster (128); Guy Francis (265); Keith Frawley (256, 261); Anna Garcia (228); Anna Garcia (228); Patrick Girouard (214); Ethel Gold (247); Bill Golliher (175); Barry Gott (238); Melanie Grandgirard (249); Dean Gray (2); Peter Grosshouser (246); Jennifer Harney (251); Christopher Hart (108); Jannie Ho (191, 271); Denise Holmes (224); Laura Huliska-Beith (275); Jessika von Innerebner (229); Kelly Kennedy (6, 13, 51, 53, 57, 60, 116, 146, 147, 165, 168, 169, 184, 188, 208, 209, 212, 273); Sue King (168); Steve Kirk (92); Dave Klug (7, 37, 104, 154, 199, 256);

Genevieve Kote (143); Vanja Kragulj (51); Ken Krug (273); Hilli Kushnir (113); Gary LaCoste (20, 88, 147, 168); Christina Larkins (65); Violet Lemay (200); Pat Lewis (84, 139, 171); Ron Lieser (240); Loufane (50); Mike Lowry (55); Tammie Lyon (189); Steve Mack (7, 26); Buff McCallister (247); Rob McClurkan (21, 43); Katie McDee (146, 234); Valentina Mendicino (274); Susan Miller (247); Paul Montgomery (117); Julissa Mora (27, 157); Mike Moran (25, 41, 77, 82, 95, 142, 147, 149, 188, 202, 213, 235, 237, 249); Mitch Mortimer (54, 124, 151, 228); Dan Moynihan (108); Wally Neibart (78); Neil Numberman (14, 31, 35, 66, 108, 146, 172, 197); Jim Paillot (111, 149, 168, 176, 188, 189, 194, 223); R. Michael Palan (262); Debbie Palen (178); Gina Perry (109); Mike Petrik (265); Tamara Petrosino (90); Dave Phillips (12); Colleen Pidel (26, 50, 51, 74, 123, 137); Rich Powell (10, 15, 30, 124, 162, 179, 194, 261, 263); Robert L. Prince (163); Kevin Rechin (51, 108, 118, 149, 153, 171, 247); Pauline Reeves (185); Andrew Roberts (161, 226-227); Natascha Rosenberg (27); Jane Sanders (2, 26, 27, 75, 98, 234, 256, 257); Amy Schimler-Safford (234); Joe Seidita (16, 173); Rob Sepanak (81); Erica Sirotich (193); Steve Skelton (103); Jackie Stafford (127, 152, 165, 193); Jim Steck (114); BeeJee Tolpa (239); Tracy Walker (89); Chuck Whelon (93, 140); Brian White (22, 94, 207, 225); Pete Whitehead (12, 14, 152); George Wildman (219); Liz M. Williams (224); Xiao Xin (235); James Yamasaki (107); Ron Zalme (90, 119, 272); Kevin Zimmer (IFC, 3, 4, 30, 36, 40, 47, 56, 62, 63, 69, 79, 95, 101, 104, 112, 115, 119, 138, 142, 144, 155, 170, 180, 185, 195, 201, 203, 205, 222, 246, 248, 258, 267, 270, 275, 277, IBC); Jennifer Zivoin (254).

Contributing Writers: Carmen Morais, Annie Rodriguez, Curtis Slepian, Cheryl Solimini.

For information about permission to reprint selections from this book,
please contact permissions@highlights.com.

While every effort has been made to ensure the information in this book is true and correct
at the date of publication, things may change after the time of publication, which may impact
the accuracy. Although the publisher cannot accept any legal responsibility for any errors or
omissions that may be made, please write to us with any concerns at eds@highlights.com.

Published by Highlights Press
815 Church Street
Honesdale, Pennsylvania 18431
ISBN: 978-1-64472-681-5

Manufactured in Jefferson City, MO, USA
Mfg. 03/2022

First edition
Visit our website at highlights.com.
10 9 8 7 6 5 4 3 2 1